Responsibility of Higher Education Systems

# Higher Education: Linking Research, Policy and Practice

*Series Editor*

Bruno Broucker (*KU Leuven, Belgium*)

*Editorial Board*

Ton Kallenberg (*Leiden University, the Netherlands*)
Rosalind Pritchard (*Ulster University, UK*)

VOLUME 1

The titles published in this series are listed at *brill.com/eair*

# Responsibility of Higher Education Systems

*What? How? Why?*

*Edited by*

Bruno Broucker, Victor M. H. Borden, Ton Kallenberg and
Clare Milsom

BRILL
SENSE

LEIDEN | BOSTON

All chapters in this book have undergone peer review.

Library of Congress Cataloging-in-Publication Data

Names: Broucker, Bruno, editor. | Borden, Victor Mark Halfleigh, 1957-
 editor. | Kallenberg, Ton, 1960- editor. | Milsom, Clare, editor.
Title: Responsibility of higher education systems : What? How? Why? /
 edited by Bruno Broucker, Victor M. H. Borden, Ton Kallenberg and Clare
 Milsom.
Description: Leiden ; Boston : Brill | Sense, 2020. | Series: Higher
 education: linking research, policy and practice, 2666-7789 ; volume 1 |
 Includes bibliographical references.
Identifiers: LCCN 2020023484 (print) | LCCN 2020023485 (ebook) | ISBN
 9789004436534 (Paperback : acid-free paper) | ISBN 9789004436541
 (Hardback : acid-free paper) | ISBN 9789004436558 (eBook)
Subjects: LCSH: Education, Higher--Aims and objectives. | Education,
 Higher--Social aspects. | Educational leadership.
Classification: LCC LB2322.2 .R47 2020  (print) | LCC LB2322.2  (ebook) |
 DDC 378--dc23
LC record available at https://lccn.loc.gov/2020023484
LC ebook record available at https://lccn.loc.gov/2020023485

Typeface for the Latin, Greek, and Cyrillic scripts: "Brill". See and download: brill.com/brill-typeface.

ISSN 2666-7789
ISBN 978-90-04-43653-4 (paperback)
ISBN 978-90-04-43654-1 (hardback)
ISBN 978-90-04-43655-8 (e-book)

Copyright 2020 by Koninklijke Brill NV, Leiden, The Netherlands.
Koninklijke Brill NV incorporates the imprints Brill, Brill Hes & De Graaf, Brill Nijhoff, Brill Rodopi,
Brill Sense, Hotei Publishing, mentis Verlag, Verlag Ferdinand Schöningh and Wilhelm Fink Verlag.
All rights reserved. No part of this publication may be reproduced, translated, stored in a retrieval system,
or transmitted in any form or by any means, electronic, mechanical, photocopying, recording or otherwise,
without prior written permission from the publisher.
Authorization to photocopy items for internal or personal use is granted by Koninklijke Brill NV provided
that the appropriate fees are paid directly to The Copyright Clearance Center, 222 Rosewood Drive, Suite
910, Danvers, MA 01923, USA. Fees are subject to change.

This book is printed on acid-free paper and produced in a sustainable manner.

# Contents

List of Figures and Tables   VII
Notes on Contributors   IX

Introduction   1
> *Ton Kallenberg, Victor M. H. Borden, Bruno Broucker and*
> *Clare Milsom*

### PART 1
## *Higher Education's Students and Staff*

1   Towards 'Relevant & Effective' Teaching-Learning Processes in Indian
Higher Education   13
> *Wafa Singh*

2   Expanding Inquiry on Intercultural Wonderment to Optimize Study
Abroad Learning Contexts   33
> *Lisa M. Davidson and Mark E. Engberg*

3   The Long-Term Career Consequences of College Undermatching   51
> *Marjolein Muskens, Gregory C. Wolniak and Lex Borghans*

4   Between Trust and Strategic Behavior of Academic (Middle) Leaders in
Higher Education: The Levels of Strategy   74
> *Ton Kallenberg*

5   Politicians and Bureaucrats in a Humboldt Type System: The Case of
Italy   93
> *Alfredo Marra and Roberto Moscati*

### PART 2
## *Higher Education Systems: (Responsible?) Practices and Policies*

6   University Mergers in Austria: Experiences and Future Scenarios for
Organizational Development in Higher Education   111
> *Attila Pausits*

# CONTENTS

7    What Does It Mean to Be a Responsible 21st Century South African University?   127
     *Denyse Webbstock*

8    The Central Government in Higher Education: Defining Areas of Responsibility between State Ministry and Governmental Agencies in Austria and Norway   141
     *Philipp Friedrich*

9    External Accountability in Ethiopian Public Higher Education   161
     *Solomon Gebreyohans Gebru*

10    Finnish-Russian Double Degree Programs: When Partners' Responsibilities Become a Challenge for Internationalization   185
     *Svetlana Shenderova*

## PART 3
## *Higher Education Impact*

11    High-Impact Practices, Degree Completion, and Academic Quality: A Study of Student Participation in Practices That Promote Success   207
     *Kathi A. Ketcheson*

12    The Productivity of Leading Global Universities: Empirical Insights and Implications for Higher Education   224
     *Jiale Yang, Chuanyi Wang, Lu Liu, Gwilym Croucher, Kenneth Moore and Hamish Coates*

13    Third Mission at Austrian Universities of Applied Sciences and the Translational Role of Hybrid Middle Managers   250
     *Martina Gaisch and Daniela Nömeyer*

14    Lessons Learned and Future Directions   270
     *Bruno Broucker, Victor M. H. Borden, Clare Milsom and Ton Kallenberg*

# Figures and Tables

### Figures

3.1 Standardized differences before and after matching. 60

3.2 Net monthly earnings separated by undermatching, first-generation status and age. 65

4.1 Strategic roles of academic leaders. 79

4.2 Levels of strategy. 81

4.3 Framework. 82

8.1 Autonomy-capacity arrangements for HE agencies in relation to ministry (2nd function). 148

8.2 Ministry-agency relationship in Austria and Norway by the end of 2017. 155

11.1 Retention rates for first-time, full-time enrolled freshmen and transfer students (Source: Portland State University Student Information System). 213

11.2 Six-year graduation rates first-time, full-time enrolled freshmen and transfer students (Source: Portland State University Student Information System). 213

11.3 Course mapping: Participation in HIPS by students graduating in six years or fewer. 220

12.1 Aggregate TI total factor productivity estimates. 235

12.2 Aggregate TI single factor productivity estimates. 236

12.3 Education and research productivity change estimates sorted by total factor productivity rank. 237

12.4 Aggregate DEA estimates. 240

12.5 University DEA productivity estimates. 244

13.1 Departments where TM activities are most likely to be found. 261

### Tables

2.1 Theoretical dimensions of development related to intercultural wonderment. 40

3.1 Logistic regression estimates of individual propensities to undermatch. 59

3.2 Results of PSM. 59

3.3 Descriptive statistics among study variables (original sample). 61

3.4 Estimated relationship between college undermatching and outcomes in adulthood. 62

3.5 Estimated relationship between college undermatching and outcomes in adulthood, by students' first-generation status. 63

3.6 Estimated interaction effects between undermatching and age, in general and by students' first-generation status. 64

| | |
|---|---|
| 4.1 | Means of trust, strategic roles and levels of strategy. 84 |
| 8.1 | Autonomy-capacity arrangements for bureaucratic organizations (1st function). 147 |
| 8.2 | Overview empirical material. 150 |
| 8.3 | Austria. 153 |
| 8.4 | Norway. 154 |
| 8.5 | Summary of main differences between cases. 156 |
| 9.1 | Sub-types of external accountability. 166 |
| 9.2 | Types of accountability relationships. 167 |
| 9.3 | External accountability relationships (based on interview results). 173 |
| 10.1 | Finnish universities: Reasons to cooperate. 190 |
| 10.2 | Russian universities: Reasons to cooperate. 192 |
| 11.1 | Portland State new undergraduates, fall term 2018. 212 |
| 11.2 | NSSE high-impact practices. 215 |
| 11.3 | Portland State University courses mapped to HIPS. 216 |
| 11.4 | Example courses assigned to HIPS. 216 |
| 11.5 | Freshman NSSE responses and enrollment in HIPS (N = 179). 218 |
| 11.6 | Senior NSSE responses and enrollment in HIPS (N = 912). 219 |
| 11.7 | Program and department survey: HIPS in the curriculum. 221 |
| 12.1 | List of sampled countries and universities. 228 |
| 12.2 | Potential indicators for modelling productivity of higher education. 229 |
| 12.3 | Parameters, indicators and data selected for this research. 230 |
| 12.4 | Descriptive statistics for selected indicators. 234 |
| 12.5 | University TI education, research, TFP and SFP estimates. 238 |
| 12.6 | University DEA total, education and research estimates. 242 |

# Notes on Contributors

*Victor M. H. Borden*
(PhD) is Professor of Higher Education at Indiana University Bloomington, where he also directs the Carnegie Classification of Institutions of Higher Education. Previously, he directed the institutional research operations of four higher education institutions. Dr. Borden's general area of scholarship is on the assessment of higher education institutional and program performance. Dr. Borden has published over 150 research articles and book chapters, delivered over 275 workshops, seminars, keynote, peer-reviewed and invited presentations, internationally. Dr. Borden was a Fulbright Specialist in South Africa and is a Past President of the Association for Institutional Research.

*Lex Borghans*
is professor of labor economics and social policy at the School of Business and Economics at Maastricht University. His research focusses on the economics of education, the measurement of skills and non-cognitive skills and the economics of personality traits.

*Bruno Broucker*
(PhD) is guest professor at the KU Leuven Public Governance Institute (Belgium), higher education expert at the (HE) Institute of Tropical Medicine, and member of the executive committee of the European Higher Education Society (EAIR). He has published on higher education policy and governance, higher education reform and the Bologna Process in journals such as *Higher Education Policy, Studies in Higher Education, Higher Education Research & Development* and the *European Educational Research Journal.* He is lead editor of the book *Higher Education System Reform: An international Comparison after twenty years of Bologna* (Brill Sense, 2019) and Editor-in-Chief of the book series *Higher Education: Linking Research, Policy and Practice.*

*Hamish Coates*
is a Tenured Professor at Tsinghua University's Institute of Education, Director of the Higher Education Research Division, and Deputy Director of the Tsinghua University Global Research Centre for the Assessment of College and Student Development. He was Professor of Higher Education at the University of Melbourne, Founding Director of Higher Education Research at the Australian Council for Educational Research, and Program Director at the LH Martin Institute for Tertiary Leadership and Management. He concentrates on improving the quality and productivity of higher education.

### Gwilym Croucher

is a research academic in the Melbourne Centre for the Study of Higher Education, as well as Program Director at the LH Martin Institute at the University of Melbourne. A higher education researcher, he was a 2017–2018 Fulbright Scholar and has been a Chief Investigator on Australian Research Council and Office for Learning and Teaching funded projects.

### Lisa M. Davidson

serves as the Senior Assessment Associate in the Searle Center for Advancing Learning and Teaching at Northwestern University in Evanston, Illinois (USA). In this role, she provides expertise related to assessment, evaluation, and research related to learning, development, and teaching within university contexts. Dr. Davidson earned her PhD in higher education from Loyola University Chicago (USA). Her research and practice center culturally relevant assessment and evaluation. In particular, Dr. Davidson's research focuses on inclusively theorizing and measuring outcomes and impact related to intercultural exchange and international education.

### Mark E. Engberg

(PhD) is a Professor of Higher Education and Associate Dean at the Morgridge College of Education at the University of Denver. He received his master's degree in Counseling Psychology from Northwestern University and doctoral degree in Higher Education from the University of Michigan. His research examines access and opportunity in American Higher Education, the educational benefits of diversity, and the development of global learning among college students.

### Philipp Friedrich

is a PhD candidate at the Department of Education, University of Oslo, Norway. He holds a bachelor degree in political science from the University of Vienna, Austria, and a master degree in Higher Education Studies from the University of Oslo. In his current dissertation project, he examines the role of state ministries and governmental agencies in higher education. Philipp is member of the German network for early higher education researchers (HOFONA) and was a visiting student researcher at SCANCOR, Stanford University in 2018. One of his dissertation articles was awarded the Best Paper Prize at the EAIR conference 2019 in Leiden.

### Martina Gaisch

(PhD) is professor of English, intercultural competence and diversity management at the University of Applied Sciences Upper Austria, Austria. She completed her doctoral studies in philosophy at the University of Vienna. As an applied linguist working at a school of informatics her research focuses on the interface of educational sociology, higher education research and sociolinguistics. She has profound insights into seven different universities throughout Austria, Germany, France and the UK where she lived, studied and conducted research.

### *Solomon Gebreyohans Gebru*

is an assistant professor of political science and strategic studies at Mekelle University, Ethiopia. He has two master degrees (in governance and development, University of Antwerp, Belgium and in governance and regional integration, Yaoundé University-II, Cameroon) and a Bachelor degree in political science and international relations, Addis Ababa University, Ethiopia. He participated in several local and international research projects and has published several articles. He is currently undertaking his PhD research on higher education governance in Ethiopia, under the Global Minds Scholarship, at the KU Leuven, Belgium.

### *Ton Kallenberg*

(1960) studied pedagogical sciences (didactics with as specialization organization & policy) at Leiden University, and defended his PhD thesis at Tilburg University. He fulfilled several functions on educational management at Leiden University, Erasmus University Rotterdam and the Open University. He has been linked as Professor at the School of Education at Leiden University of Applied Sciences. Currently he is Director Education and Student Affairs at the faculty Humanities of Leiden University. His research and publications are focusing on (academic) leadership in education; policy and organization in education; on didactics in higher education and on teacher education programs.

### *Kathi A. Ketcheson*

(PhD) is a research professor and director of institutional research and planning at Portland State University. Dr. Ketcheson has over 35 years of experience in higher education and has served as director since 1998. She holds a bachelor's degree in history from the University of Washington, and an MPA (Public Administration) and PhD in Urban Studies from Portland State. She has published and presented widely, specializing in accreditation and assessment. She serves on numerous committees and leadership groups at Portland State and is active nationally in the Association for Institutional Research and other higher education associations.

## Lu Liu

is a postdoctoral researcher at Tsinghua University. He has completed his PhD in 2018 at the Nanjing Agricultural University. He holds a Bachelor of Commerce and Master of Management from Victoria University Wellington and Massey University in New Zealand. Dr. Liu's doctoral study concentrated on world-class university governance mechanisms. He has participated in national research projects and published numerous papers.

## Alfredo Marra

is Associate Professor of Administrative Law at the University of Milano-Bicocca. Department of Law. His research interests concern public law, generally conceived, and specifically administrative judicial proceedings, market's regulation, public organization and higher education. He contributed to the creation and is still directing the University Observatory (www.osservatoriouniversita.unimib.it) which deals with the census and analysis of the legal transformations affecting the Italian University.

## Clare Milsom

is Professor of Academic Practice and Academic Registrar at Liverpool John Moore University. She is a National Teaching Fellow, an elected member of the EAIR (European Higher Education Society) executive committee and a QAA Reviewer. A palaeontologist by background Clare has worked in higher education for almost 30 years. She is known for her work on the evaluation of survey qualitative data and the second year experience of students at university.

## Kenneth Moore

completed his doctoral degree at the University of Melbourne. He is a data scientist and education expert. He has worked on and led projects in several countries including the United States, Australia, Indonesia and China. He has consulted for small-and-medium enterprises (SMEs), education institutions and not-for-profit organizations. Ken excels in program evaluation, strategy development, workshop facilitation and organizational performance assessment.

## Roberto Moscati

is Former Professor of Sociology of Education, at University of Milano-Bicocca, Department of Sociology and Social Research. His main research interests are comparative analysis of higher education systems; education policy; teaching and learning activities; student life, education and development; civic culture and national identity. He is a member of the Internal Evaluation Unit at IULM University, Milano, Italy; the Quality Assurance structure and at University of

NOTES ON CONTRIBUTORS

Milano-Bicocca, Italy; the Editorial Board of "Tertiary Education and Management"; the Scientific Council of the Portuguese "Assessment and Accreditation Agency" (A3ES)-Lisbon and the Scientific Council of "Italian Centre for Research on Universities & Higher Education Systems"-UNIRES, Bologna University.

### Marjolein Muskens

(PhD) is senior researcher at ResearchNed, a private research institute for social-scientific research and policy advise. She is also appointed as researcher at the school of Business and Economics at Maastricht University. Marjolein holds a masters' degree in behavioural science, and a PhD degree in economics. Her major research interests include developmental pathways related to socioeconomic status, opportunities for low-income students in education, and their experiences in educational settings. She works on the cutting edge of scientific research and policy research, and is involved in international research networks such as the EAIR and AERA.

### Daniela Nömeyer

studied social and cultural anthropology at the University of Vienna. She is currently head of department for quality management at the University of Applied Sciences Upper Austria and a lecturer for quality management. Her research focuses on the interactions between universities and society and the strategic development and impact measurement of the "Third Mission".

### Attila Pausits

is associate professor for educational management and lifelong learning and head of the Centre for Educational Management and Higher Education Development at Danube University Krems. He is the academic director of the Erasmus Mundus Joint Master Program "Research and Innovation in Higher Education, MSc". Dr. Pausits is Chairman of the European Higher Education Society (EAIR) and spokesman of the Austrian Higher Education Researchers Network as well as Editor of the e-journal *Working Papers in Higher Education Studies.*

### Svetlana Shenderova

is a researcher of EDUneighbours study of Finnish-Russian double degree implementation, hosted by Tampere University, Finland, and funded by the Kone Foundation. She has worked for 30 years in research, administration, consulting and expertise in the fields of higher education policies, internationalization, university governance and degree program management focusing on transaction costs of EU-Russian internationalization. She has worked in academia as an associate professor being involved in teaching, research and consulting projects in nine Russian universities. Svetlana holds a DEconSc (St. Petersburg State University of Economics and Finance, 2012) and PhD in Political Economy (St. Petersburg State University, 1997).

### Wafa Singh

is senior consultant-researcher based in India. Presently, she is associated with Ammachi Labs, a research center based at Amrita University, in Kerala, India. Her core areas of expertise include participatory/community-based research, community engagement and social responsibility in higher education. Previously, she has served as the India Coordinator of the UNESCO Chair in Community Based Research & Social Responsibility in Higher Education. She also has several research papers and book chapters to her name, including the book *Knowledge & Engagement: Building Capacities for the Next Generation of Community Based Researchers* (co-editor; PRIA/University of Victoria, 2016).

### Chuanyi Wang

is an Associate Professor at the Institute of Education, Tsinghua University. His research fields include graduate education and assessment of higher education. His co-authored book *Research on Graduate Education Structure Adjustment in China* (Economic Science Press, 2015) was awarded the first prize for the National Excellent Educational Science Research Achievements. He is the Deputy Secretary General of Academic Committee of Chinese Society of Academic Degrees and Graduate Education.

### Denyse Webbstock

(PhD) has been Senior Director: Institutional Planning, Evaluation and Monitoring at the University of Johannesburg since 2019, previously Director of Monitoring and Evaluation of the Council on Higher Education (CHE) in Pretoria where she was responsible for the CHE's publications, including *Higher Education Reviewed: Two Decades of Democracy* (CHE, 2016), *Reflections of South African University Leaders, 1981–2014* (CHE, 2016), a number of issues of the CHE's scholarly journal *Kagisano* and of publications including *Briefly-Speaking, VitalStats* and the *Higher Education Monitor*. She has a PhD in Policy Studies from the University of KwaZulu-Natal, and a Postgraduate Diploma in International Relations from the University of Amsterdam.

### Gregory C. Wolniak

is Associate Professor of Higher Education at the University of Georgia. His research interrogates how college students' socioeconomic trajectories are affected by their experiences in college, educational choices, institutional environments, and the degree to which learning and developmental gains made during college translate to post-college outcomes. His work has been published in a variety of outlets, including journal articles, policy reports, and books, with featured pieces in media outlets such as *The Atlantic, The Chronicle of Higher Education*, and *Inside Higher Education*. He co-authored *How College Affects Students: 21st Century Evidence that Higher Education Works* (Wiley/Jossey-Bass, 2016).

### *Jiale Yang*

is pursuing her doctoral degree at the Institute of Education, Tsinghua University. She gained her bachelor's degree in economics and master's degree in economics and management of education. Her research interests include economics of education, educational policy and graduate education. She has participated in several national research projects and has published numerous papers.

# Introduction

*Ton Kallenberg, Victor M. H. Borden, Bruno Broucker and Clare Milsom*

### Abstract

The EAIR-conference 2019 brought together scholars, practitioners and policymakers in higher education to discuss the issue of responsibility of Higher Education. The book sets out this theme and discusses responsibility in a number of key areas for higher education: governance and management, teaching and learning, quality, research, social responsibility, internationalization, institutional research and continuing professional development. A selected number of papers presented at the conference are part of this book. Herewith this volume presents a stimulating and careful set of analysis about the multiple and complex responsibilities of Higher Education Institutions.

### Keywords

responsibility – higher education systems – higher education policy – EAIR

## 1 The Theme of 'Responsibility in Higher Education'

In more recent decades, there have been worldwide pressures to increase accessibility to higher education as well as the transfer and application of knowledge to the service of society's immediate needs (Schinkel, 2015). This demonstrates the responsibility of higher education systems and higher education institutions on two distinct levels. First on the individual level, where education represents an important access door to the labor market, and second on the societal level where HE institutions contribute to the public good. The fuel that keeps the engine of HE running is the research she conducts to produce knowledge and contribute to science. A primary task of the state has therefore resulted into keeping the accessibility of HE as high as possible, while developing at the same time cost-effective HE systems that channel increasingly diverse students appropriately to an increasingly diverse array of providers, including traditional universities and the growing array of new forms of provision.

© KONINKLIJKE BRILL NV, LEIDEN, 2020 | DOI: 10.1163/9789004436558_001

The general responsibility of higher education institutions however goes beyond developing knowledge, and educating future generations (Antonelli, Patrucco, & Rossi, 2011; Huber, 2016). HEIS contribute to innovation and to the solution of complex and wicked problems, provide advice to organizations, policymakers and individuals, and contribute to society on the economic, social, political, ecological and other challenges she is confronted with. Although, 'responsibility' is a frequently used and commonly understood concept, its complexity becomes evident when it is discussed within the context that stroke the world while this book was being compiled. At the same moment the editors of this book were writing the introductory chapter the world was confronted with the Covid-19 epidemic, which resulted in a situation of national lockdowns, a drop in international traffic, and a general slowing down of all public life. While shops were closed, companies tried to survive the economic consequences of the lockdown, and HEIS shifted completely from face-to-face education to online education and contributed significantly to the development of vaccines against this unknown and rapidly spreading infectious disease. There is no doubt HE will remain crucial in the rebuilding of the post-covid-19 world as many challenges at different levels will have increased worldwide. What is then the responsibility of HE? How can we frame this concept? Should it be reframed? What do higher education institutions take responsibility for? Will universities now maybe become even more responsible for society, students and staff, than in the past? How can responsible research and teaching now be designed, under the hypotheses that coronaviruses can occur yearly and international students will be confronted with difficulties in travelling or mass face-to-face education becomes less evident? How can global challenges be faced by responsible universities? What is responsible research, and whereto should research funding go primarily? How can governance help higher education institutes to be responsible and take over responsibility? Moreover, what does this all mean for the organization and administration levels? Above all, the question arises as to how responsibility can be assumed and how the universities deal with the associated manifold requirements, challenges and missions.

This book includes a number of chapters dedicated to responsibility in Higher Education, in its broad sense. It is a compilation of papers presented at the 41st EAIR (the European Higher Education Society) annual forum in 2019. The conference brought together scholars, policymakers and practitioners in the field of higher education to share their research and perspectives on the changing nature of responsibility in the higher education sector. This book aims to contribute not only to the understanding the responsibilities of universities and the challenges posed to the production and circulation of knowledge, it also raises questions regarding the role of higher education in society, discusses the current status of higher education in a number of areas, and reflects on its future. The respective authors of the chapters also represent a large diversity: scholars, policymakers and practitioners have all contributed to this volume, and based their chapter on research, on evidence informed policy, on personal experience and quite often on a mixture. This elevates the richness of the book and its relevance for a large audience. The 41st Annual EAIR forum thoroughly debated the complexity of responsibility by focusing on a number of themes and questions.

## 1.1      *Responsible Governance and Management*

What happens when universities apply the neoliberal model in its extreme? How can the idea of academic freedom be reconciled with the economic demand for higher education institutions (HEIs) to be financially viable; to climb the league tables; to construct courses that are useful to employers; to produce beneficial research? What if standards slip, academics become out-of-touch, students grow complacent or management is brutal? The idea of responsibility in governance and management of HEIs touches every aspect of university functioning, pointing up tensions that inhere within institutions. One person's 'freedom' can become another person's servitude. How can universities best exercise public responsibility towards their host 'body politic'? And, in what ways might they show lack of public responsibility, or even become irresponsible? HEIs are also expected to be responsive to the needs of all their stakeholders including students, staff, society and future generations. Furthermore, social responsibility is becoming a matter of 'standards' to large organizations, either public or private. HEIs are major economic and social actors, they are often a major employer and an economic engine within their region, and social responsibility standards apply to them as well. Whether it's awareness about diversity issues or their environmental footprint, leadership and management of HEIs ought to reflect this role as well as high academic and societal ambitions.

## 1.2      *Responsibility for Quality*

What does it mean to have trust in, being accountable for, and taking responsibility for the quality of higher education? There is great pressure from governments and society on public institutions to be permanently accountable and transparent. At the same time, institutions in the public sector are being pushed to act more like private, proprietary businesses, including models of operation that protect assets and seek competitive advantage over institutions that compete for clients and resources. However, even though institutions, including higher education institutions, are in general prepared to give account, the constant pressure is often perceived as a major bureaucratic and administrative burden. There is also an increasing need for professionals working within higher education institutions to be able to focus more on future quality improvement rather than on accounting for the past. The bureaucracy entailed in the latter, for example, risks distracting practitioners and policy makers from the core tasks of education and research. All this takes place in a context in which all universities are expected to do more and perform better with the same (or, in some cases, decreasing) resources. Within this complex range of influences, higher education must shape its quality management in a responsive and proactive way.

## 1.3 *Responsible Teaching and Learning*

What do we teach, how do we teach, and who do we teach? How does this impact our students now and in their future working lives, social relations, and civic engagement? The responsibilities of higher education are seen differently across countries and by different stakeholders, yet the Council of Europe (2007) formulated a broad consensus on the key aspects involved: personal development, sustainable employment, and active citizenship. The EU Reference Framework (2018) specifies eight key competences that HEIs are expected to deliver to meet the qualifications framework: literacy, multilingual skills, STEM and digital competences, as well as personal, meta-learning and social competences, citizenship, entrepreneurship, and cultural awareness and expression. All this may be seen as 21st century formulations of 19th century ideals of Bildung, albeit with significant differences, if not in content, then in context.

## 1.4 *Responsible Research*

What types of research will be supported by the institutions and be external funders, including the government? How will demands for providing support to commercial applications affect the public availability of research findings? How do we support essential areas of research that are not as closely related to current pressing societal and industrial issues? Current changes in modern societies directly and indirectly influence research networks, processes and systems. Globalization and new communication technologies among other factors, have led to critical reflections on research dissemination and the nature of research. Scholars, as well as society, demand more open access in the publication of research, transparency of ethics, use of larger data sets, and innovative ways to collaborate internationally. Research is not anymore the sole province of scholars at universities – there is a vital claim for concrete advantages and contributions to solve complex problems. Researchers are

INTRODUCTION

called upon to take up their responsibilities in knowledge infrastructures and in the knowledge society. The changing nature of academic work, knowledge, and knowledge development within certain 'helix'-constellations are central to the changing role of higher education institutions in our society. A deep understanding of the responsibility of research, researchers and their institutions is therefore, vital to understanding higher education at large.

## 1.5  *Social Responsibility*

What is social responsibility of HEIs? Are they accountable for the future success of their students? Do they have any responsibility for how the results of research are used within the public and private sectors? Are they responsible for the living circumstances of their local communities? Social responsibility is guided by the pursuit of excellence in teaching, training, research and institutional performance. It builds on the relevance of services offered by higher education institutions to the perceived priority needs of their respective societies; the quest for balance between short-term pertinence and service and long-range quality, between basic and applied research and between professional training and general education. Over the last three decades, research transfer, contract research, serving societal demands and employability, as well as the adequate qualification and professional development of young academics have evolved into core functions of HEIs. The institutions determine objectives and institution-wide consensus on subject-related, personal or professional competences that respond to societal demands. Due to changes in governance paradigms (new public management), HEIs have also moved from supply to demand driven organizational forms. This also includes more competitiveness among institutes whilst increasing responsiveness has also undermined cooperation and coordination at a system level.

In addition to these key questions regarding the responsibilities of HEIs and the higher education sector more broadly, the EAIR conference, and therefore this book as well, examines issues related to the role of institutional research, the impact of internationalization, and the critical importance of continuing professional development for higher education's vitality in the coming years. *Institutional research* helps higher education institutes to more clearly define these responsibilities and also to check that they meet their objectives in this respect. Collecting and analyzing data can provide useful information for policy decisions, on teaching and learning, research, and public service, and also on profiling and positioning the institutions themselves. *Internationalization* is a relatively new and broad concept for the higher education sector. Over the last 30 years European programs for research and education, in particular the ERASMUS program, the Marie Curie Fellowships, but also the Bologna process, have fostered a broader and more strategic approach to internationalization across the EU and provide examples for parallel strategies in other parts of the world. Common goals and objectives of internationalization strategies have been and are still the competition for talented students and scholars; mobility; an increased importance of international reputation, visibility and competitiveness; as well as economic gains. *Continuing professional development* (CPD) is a requirement for all professionals in the current fast-changing world and a key attitude in keeping them interested and interesting. CPD refers to the process of tracking and documenting the skills, knowledge and experience gained in formal and informal study and work processes as well as featuring systematic, on-going and self-directed learning. These processes vary from structured continuing education programs to non-structured, self-directed methods of development. In the specific arena of Higher Education, CPD encompasses all those activities that help faculty members to improve their capacity to become more effective teachers and to carry out other parts of their multifaceted roles, such as conducting research, contributing to administrative activities, writing publishable materials, and collaborating with community partners. The quality of non-academic staff is an equally important factor in the quality of Higher Education. HEI program that pay attention to the CPD of professional and technical service teams are of increasing importance. The experiences and the effects of these programs are also potentially highly influential in improving the student experience.

HEIs provide education, original research outputs and interact as an institution within society. Thus, HEIs for centuries have played a crucial role in fostering environments where innovation prospers. However, this influential position obviously comes with great responsibility.

As stated above, the chapters in this volume constitute a selection of some of the best papers presented at the 41st 2019 EAIR Forum under the broad theme "Responsibility of higher education systems: What? Why? How?" The Forum addressed these topics by convening approaches to the understanding of the interactions between policy drivers, researchers and institutional practices. The Forum attracted more than 300 researchers from around the world that contributed to the discussions based on research in the field of higher education, institutional research and case studies on that theme, as well as policy-based accounts.

The first chapter, by *Singh*, provides insight into new paradigms in Indian Higher Education regarding the pursuit of relevant and effective teaching-learning processes. She describes the context and challenges faced by what is now the second most populous, but likely soon the most populous country in the world. Noting the general antiquated state of teaching and learning within

INTRODUCTION

the country, and the related lack of quality in student learning outcomes, she explores the need to modernize the teaching/learning enterprise, and provides several examples of where and how that is happening within the country, ending with a call for action to amplify and broadly institutionalize these nascent efforts.

*Davidson and Engberg* present the concept of intercultural wonderment as students' underlying curiosity to seek out novel experiences and their willingness and capacity to deal with discomfort while studying abroad. In their opinion it's important to align both educational practice and research related to study abroad.

In the third chapter, *Muskens, Wolniak and Borghans*, investigate the long-term consequences of college undermatching on career and personal well-being. When students attend institutions that are less selective than their academic credentials would permit (i.e., 'undermatching'), this may reinforce social and economic inequality, especially for first generation students. Yet little is known about its long-term, post-college consequences for careers. Results show that undermatching is negatively related to wages during adulthood, and show negative relationships between undermatching and satisfaction with aspects of one's job that increase with age. It also appears that these relations are most pronounced among first-generation students. The authors highlight the significant implications for the understanding about the consequences of undermatching in relation to outcomes later in life, and for the formulation of policies for promoting long-term career success and social mobility aimed at first-generation students.

*Kallenberg* investigates the relationship between trust, strategic behavior of academic (middle) leaders, and their aspiration to achieve personal, organizational or societal strategic levels regarding the organizational strategy. The findings of this Dutch research show a strong relationship between relational based and organizational based trust and the strategic roles academic leaders fulfill during strategic processes on the university. Because academic leaders play a crucial role in the difference between successful and unsuccessful strategies of the university, this is a strong appeal to equip their position with sufficient degrees of autonomy in order to prevent them from pursuing too many personal levels of strategy.

In Chapter 5, *Moscati and Marra* discuss the rapid increase of administrative activities in the Italian higher education system as well as in its individual university with relevant consequences on the level of bureaucratization of the academic life.

*Pausits* explores in detail issues and prospects related to within- and cross-sector mergers in the Austrian context. Pausits traces the evolving impetus and objectives for European higher education institution mergers over the past 50 years, noting the shift from higher education system restructuring and economies of scale, to global competition and the pursuit of improved rankings. He then uses within- and cross-sector scenarios of Austrian HEI mergers to examine opportunities and constraints of these institutional changes.

*Webbstock* explores three themes of the South African debate with respect to responsibility. These themes include (a) the dichotomy of the global versus the local in defining university identity and purpose; (b) the binary necessities to widen access, and to ensure sustainability; and (c) the responsible curriculum. She concludes that the South African position requires hard policy choices to be made in order to achieve an appropriate balance and consistent set of principles.

In the eighth chapter, *Friedrich* compares Austria and Norway in their description of how areas of responsibilities are defined. Through the presentation of an analytical framework Friedrich describes the changes in HE bureaucracy that resulted from sectoral reform. He identifies differences in authority and autonomy and the capacity for future development. This approach provides insights into the operation of transformational change processes within higher education.

*Gebru* investigates the orientation, types and mechanisms of external accountability in Ethiopian public higher education. After providing a thoughtful and thorough discussion of the concept of accountability, he reports the results of a study that employs both document analysis and interviews among principles and agents to examine the current status of accountability in the Ethiopian higher education sector. He concludes that the external system of accountability in Ethiopia lacks predictable effective consequences (political, academic, legal and financial) and demands the attention of various stakeholders.

In Chapter 10, *Shenderova* discusses how the division of responsibilities influences the implementation of master's double degrees from the example of Finnish-Russian partnerships studied in 2017–2020. Her research concentrates on cases of the internal allocation of responsibilities in double degrees within each partner university, including the role of central/faculty and administrative/academic departments. In addition, the author investigates how Finnish and Russian universities allocate responsibilities for double degrees between one another. The chapter demonstrates the role of transaction costs challenging double degree implementation and university internationalization.

*Ketcheson* explores the relationship between High-Impact Practices and graduation outcomes at an urban university in the US. Her results indicate that student self-reports may be different from their actual exposure to these

INTRODUCTION

practices, and she suggest a method for identifying high-impact practices in the curriculum, combining enrollment data with qualitative data gathered from faculty. She confirms the importance of collaboration between the AQC and the institutional research department in addressing questions of quality and teaching and learning effectiveness.

*Yang, Wang, Liu, Croucher, Moore and Oates* analyze the productivity of a sample of leading universities to tease out implications for higher education policy and practice. According to them value of higher education might be gained by reaching outside the system in order to innovate to truly global universities. It depends on the courage of academic leaders to strive for 'world class' research and possibly 'world class education'.

The final chapter, by *Gaisch and Nömeyer*, looks at third mission activities as an integral part of universities of applied sciences (UAS) in Austria and sheds light on the perceived role of these institutions of higher learning as to their responsibility in terms of regional engagement, innovation and knowledge transfer in their local areas. They draw parallels between the German UAS sector where transfer centers are broadly established at the sectoral level and the Austrian higher education landscape, where three regionally dispersed knowledge transfer centers were set up with the aim to start-up finance projects along the lines of knowledge and technology transfer. They identified the translational role of hybrid middle managers as a crucial ingredient in successful third-stream activities. It was stated that although it may be beneficial to have a scientific background in terms of credibility and standing in the relevant community, it might not be enough to be a good researcher.

Overall, we believe this volume presents a stimulating and careful set of analysis about the multiple and complex responsibilities of Higher Education Institutions. We hope that this volume will contribute to encourage higher education researchers to pursue further those relevant research themes within various national and institutional contexts.

### References

Antonelli, C., Patrucco, P. P., & Rossi, F. (2011). The economics of knowledge interaction and the changing role of universities. In F. Gallouj & F. Djellal (Eds.), *The handbook of innovation and services: A multi-disciplinary perspective*. Edward Elgar.

Calhoun, C. (2006). The university and the public good. *Thesis Eleven, 84*, 7–43.

Huber, B. (2016). The role of universities in society. Challenges ahead. In N. C. Liu et al. (Eds.), *Matching visibility and performance* (pp. 91–99). Sense Publishers.

Schinkel, W. (2015). Wat zijn de publieke taken van de universiteit? *Beleid en Maatschappij, 42*(1), 51–54.

# PART 1

## *Higher Education's Students and Staff*

∵

CHAPTER 1

# Towards 'Relevant & Effective' Teaching-Learning Processes in Indian Higher Education

*Wafa Singh*

### Abstract

Considering the challenging times we are living in; the importance of Higher Education Institutions (HEIs) today (as the producers and disseminators of knowledge) is more than it ever was in human history. However, their contribution will be driven by how 'relevant & effective' its Teaching-Learning (T-L) processes are, which are rightly said to be at the 'heart' of HEIs. In this context, India presents a very interesting narrative. Faced with challenges and opportunities both; Indian HEIs have been traversing along this journey towards 'relevant & effective' T-L processes, slowly but surely. This chapter explores this journey of Indian HEIs, as it presents a nuanced analysis of its problems and potential, alike.

### Keywords

relevant – effective – Teaching-Learning (T-L) – Higher Education – India

## 1 Introduction

India is a unique country, presenting an exclusive blend of challenges and opportunities. It is also increasingly becoming an active player in shaping the global development agenda, and this trend is expected to gain further traction in the coming decades. However, this will depend on how India grows as a nation, overcoming its challenges and converting them into opportunities, both of which are present in abundance.

India has one of the youngest populations in the world and the window of demographic dividend opportunity is available for five decades from 2005–2006 to 2055–2056, longer than any other country in the world (Press Information Bureau (PIB), 2019a). This contemporary reality is a huge opportunity for

© KONINKLIJKE BRILL NV, LEIDEN, 2020 | DOI: 10.1163/9789004436558_002

India and will undoubtedly have significant implications in driving economic growth with the increase in the working population. However, here is where the challenge also lies. India at the moment is facing a lack of skilled graduates and an increase in unemployment across the country. This aspect can easily change the benefit of demographic dividends into a bane. Coupled with a complex development discourse (India being ranked 129th out of 189 countries on the Human Development Index 2019, as reported by the United Nations Development Program (UNDP), and 147 out of the 157 countries, according to the Commitment to reducing inequality (CRI) index released by OXFAM in 2018) this poses a serious challenge.

In light of these realities, 'critical societal institutions' will have an important role to play in the times to come. Higher Education Institutions (HEIS) will be one of them, for mainly two reasons. *First*, India's demographic reality and an increasing pool of young student population and *secondly*, the latter's role as a public good with unique social responsibilities in producing knowledge for societal development and sustainability. Considering that Indian HEIS are one of the most resourced institutions (physical infrastructure; digital/financial/intellectual capacity; and youthful abundance) (Tandon, 2017a), it may appear at the outset that the future looks good. However, this aspect has hidden clauses. The Higher Education (HE) sector in India today, is replete with an equal proportion of challenges; the most critical one relating to its Teaching-Learning (T-L) processes.

The system is beset by issues of low-quality T-L in many of its institutions, such as the growing divergence between curricula and contemporary societal/market demands, traditional pedagogies and educational models, and rigid disciplinary boundaries. These limitations negatively impact the learning outcomes of the emerging new graduates who will form the backbone of the working population in the future. With the rapidly changing skills requirements and the new graduates demonstrating skill deficits, it is evident that Indian HE is struggling to keep up to this rapidly changing and dynamic context. However, being a land of equal opportunities, our HEIS in recent times have begun to step up their game and there have been efforts at transforming the TL processes, aided by positive reinforcement coming from HE policy makers.

Therefore, this chapter attempts to explore this aspect of Indian HE in more detail. While it begins by giving an overview of Indian HE and its present positioning, it moves on to examining its TL processes in particular, laying out its challenges threadbare while also accounting for the opportunities. Doing so, the chapter proposes a call for action for transforming TL processes, and also illustrates what is practically being done. Lastly, it concludes with weaving the threads of emerging lessons and charting a pathway for the future.

## 2    Indian Higher Education (HE): An Overview

The Indian HE system commanded awe and respect in the ancient world (Kumar, 2017, p. xxv). Its history can be traced back to the existence of *Takshashila University* (the world's first university) and *Nalanda University* (the world's first residential university), which were revered for their quality of knowledge generation and spirit of learning (Singh & Tandon, 2015). Today, the Indian HE sector is the third largest in the world; next only to United States & China (Press Information Bureau (PIB), 2019; Sheikh, 2017; Sarin & Dholakia, 2016), and is at the initial phases of massification (Sharma, 2019). This statement is justified by these statistics: the number of Universities in India stands at 993, with 39931 colleges and 10725 stand-alone institutions (Ministry of Human Resource Development (MHRD), 2019a). Student enrolment stands at 37.4 million; while the Gross Enrolment Ratio (GER) stands at 26.3% (MHRD, 2019a, p. ii). Further, the MHRD has set a target of achieving 32% GER by 2022. Going by the current growth rates, this target is likely to be met in the next couple of years (Ravi, Gupta, & Nagaraj, 2019).

With respect to governance and management of Indian HE; MHRD is the nodal ministry responsible for the overall development of HE in India. Under MHRD, come various regulatory bodies, which regulate Higher Education Institutions (HEIS) at different levels. While the University Grants Commission (UGC) acts as the over-arching regulatory body. Other regulatory bodies such as Medical Council of India (MCI), All India Council for Technical Education (AICTE) and the Bar Council India (BCI), among others, manage different professional courses run by colleges and Universities (Centre for Civil Society, 2015). Additionally, the National Board of Accreditation (NBA) (established by AICTE) and National Assessment and Accreditation Council (NAAC) (established by UGC) are primarily responsible for assessment and accreditation of HEIS.

## 3    Indian Higher Education vis-à-vis Contemporary Realities

The capacity and scale of the Indian HE sector is assurance enough that this sector will be a key determinant in charting India's growth story over the next few decades. Notwithstanding this reality, the sector is currently facing some of the biggest challenges. Two most important and critical ones are unskilled and jobless graduate and structural-functional issues.

### 3.1 Unskilled and Jobless Graduates

In India, we stand at a crucial and interesting juncture today. As we are witnessing demographic dividends, the *Economic Survey Report* (2019) notes that this process will peak around 2041, when the share of working-age (20–59 years) population is expected to hit 59%. While this appears to be an opportunity, the challenge associated with it is the widening skills gaps in young graduates. This has resulted in a pool of unemployable graduates in the country. A recent report by an employability assessment company, *Aspiring Minds*, states that over 80% of Indian engineers are unemployable for any job in the knowledge economy (Aggarwal, Nithyanand, & Sharma, 2019).

The India Skills Report (2019–2020) on the other hand, does report that the percentage of employable graduates has increased over the past 5 years (47% as compared to 33% in 2014) (Wheebox, 2019). Despite this reality, the fact that more than half our youthful population still comes under the unemployable category is a matter of collective concern and has attracted the attention of academics and policy makers in recent times. The authors of the India Skills report too, acknowledge the fact that we have a long way to go and there is an urgent need to bridge the employability gap by focusing on the learning outcomes of students.

This reality poses serious accountability questions on our HEIs, considering their responsibility to nurture skilled youth, who can contribute to the nation's development, using their knowledge and skills. Their job is made more challenging considering the diverse backgrounds and profiles of present-day students.

### 3.2 Structural-Functional Issues in Indian HE

Indian HE also faces significant challenges from within, such as a cramped institutional vision and systemic rigidity leading to lack of innovation and positive change. Kumar (2017) argues that Indian HEIs have not yet fully absorbed the contemporary global realities of knowledge creation and their relevance for social transformation, and as a result continue to function under cramped vision. As a result, mediocrity has been institutionalized, leading to a complete lack of creativity and innovation.

Excessive systemic rigidity worsens the problem by leaving little or no space for positive transformations. The aspect which is impacted the most by such rigidity is academic discourse, in particular about Teaching-Learning (T-L) processes. Despite advances in teaching aids and infrastructure, T-L processes in Indian HE do not paint a very promising picture, and the major reasons behind this have been identified as the prevalence of outdated curricula, absence of relevant courses (linked to societal realities) and the continuation of traditional pedagogies (MHRD, 2019a; Nadar, 2018; FICCI, 2017; Sharma & Sharma, 2015; Singh, 2011; Chahal, 2015).

Considering that TL processes are one of the most important constituents of an academic framework, these challenges are a point of serious concern. The gaps in the TL process also almost directly result in the 'non-achievement' of effective learning outcomes, thereby resulting in widening the skill gap in students and fresh graduates. This then naturally impacts their employability prospects. Analyzing this in the global context, the situation appears to be even more worrisome. At the global level, (as per the Global Skills Index 2019), India lags behind its peers with respect to future job skills: ranked 44th out of 60 countries in the technology domain; 50th in business skills and 51st in data science (Coursera, 2019). This report also attributes this 'lag' to India's growing number of under-skilled workers, "... a result of poor-quality HE combined with a very young population" (p. 30).

With this background, this chapter will essentially focus on studying and analyzing the T-L processes in Indian HE.

## 4 Teaching-Learning (T-L) Processes in Indian HE

T-L processes are at the heart of any educational institution. The way teaching is imparted and learning outcomes are derived, determines how useful, relevant or valuable an educational system is. However, despite this universally known reality, our country is still reflecting on what to teach, how to teach and whom to teach (Parikh, 2017). Ideally, what to teach gets determined by the socio-cultural context and the needs of the era, decade, century and millennium; how to teach gets determined by the values and philosophies of the institution, the faculty and teachers, and also by the assumptions of learning in the T-L process; and, whom to teach gets determined by the generation of the times and the educational policies of the government (Parikh, 2017).

As teaching enables learning of the students (Tandon, 2017b); it is natural that the questions on what/how/whom to teach will have huge implications on the learning outcomes of students, thus impacting the TL processes. For instance, effective learning begins with a curriculum that is engaging and relevant – pedagogical practices determine the learning experiences that are provided to students thus directly influencing learning outcomes – while the diversity in teaching determines the high quality of learning (MHRD, 2019, p. 239). With this background, it is useful to analyze the situation in the Indian context, from the lens of contemporary problematics and potential opportunities.

### 4.1 *Contemporary Problematics*

Academic literature and several reports have time and again flagged the deficiencies in the T-L process in Indian HE, which in turn negatively impacts the structural and functional ethos of the latter. Parikh (2017) argues that the students today have lost interest in the whole process of learning due to the way the HEIs in general and universities in particular conduct themselves. In order to understand the reasons behind the students being weaned away from contemporary T-L processes, it is important to study the exact nature of 'conduct' of the T-L processes at HEIs that is driving this change. Further exploration of this aspect in the Indian context interestingly leads us to the initial questions posed by Parikh (2017) on what is being taught, how it is being taught and whom it is being taught.

### 4.1.1 Prevalence of Outdated Curriculum (Driving the Aspect of 'What Is Being Taught/Learnt')

This has been a challenge of Indian HE for some time now. Several reports have continued to raise this issue. For instance, a British Council Report (2014) entitled *Understanding India*, outlined the challenges of outdated and rigid curricula. The draft National Education Policy (2019) also opines that curricula remains narrow, rigid and archaic and have not responded to modern advances in disciplinary knowledge or in educational practice. Ravi et al. (2019, p. 14), also mentioned the "... limited scope for innovation in terms of curriculum in traditional degrees as the syllabus is prescribed by the affiliating university". Another report published by IBM Institute for Business Value (2017, p. 8) says that "approximately 59% of Indian educators agree to the fact that the curricula used by Indian HEIs are outdated and irrelevant". To make matters worse, each discipline has a rigidly defined framework of what can be taught and curriculum and course outlines are approved only when they follow rigid, specified disciplinary requirements (Tandon & Pandey, 2019).

### 4.1.2 Continuation of Traditional Pedagogical Techniques

Another significant challenge with respect to T-L processes in Indian HE has been that the continuation of traditional pedagogical techniques (input oriented; lecture based approaches rather than student centered; output based rather than outcome based; template driven rather than enquiry driven) have resulted in rote learning (British Council, 2014). This has given students little opportunity to develop a range of transversal skills, including critical thinking, analytical reasoning, problem solving and collaborative working, critical for the 21st century job market, thereby widening the skill gap. In the foreword to Kumar's (2017) book, *The Future of Indian Universities,* Virander Chaun shares that "our pedagogical practices have not evolved to match developments in educational theory and advances in other human and social sciences". Kumar adds, in the book's preface, "... while we may be doing reasonably well in delivering styled traditional educational contents, the dominant pedagogical practices are increasingly seen as inadequate for practical coping in everyday life and in professional practice". Therefore, while the complexities of the world put huge demands on our youth to acquire practical, conceptual and cultural skills, it is imperative for our HEIs to follow pedagogical designs that facilitate this aspect.

### 4.1.3 Absence of Diversified, Flexible and Interdisciplinary Learning Opportunities for New Age/Non-Traditional Learners

The draft National Education Policy (2019b) acknowledges the fact that India's HE has developed rigid boundaries of disciplines and fields, along with a narrow view of what constitutes education and who are the takers of this education. This system has as a result, produced thousands of students with identical education rather than true individuals exercising their own creativity and developing their own interests (MHRD, 2019).This aspect has important implications considering the surge of 'non-traditional' students (first generation learners; part-time students/workers, have at least one dependent, etc.), who have new and varying aspirations and demands with respect to learning outcomes (FICCI, 2018). Further, access to diverse and regulation-free T-L opportunities by mid-career professionals, early career faculty or even research scholars remains a rare proposition in India. Some of the core values that this group of learners expects from TL process of today is that it be flexible, diversified and also offer interdisciplinary learning opportunities. However, these are exact changes Indian HEIs have been unable to bring about.

While flexibility and diversity in TL processes is critical to cater to this new generation of learners; equally important is the aspect of inter-disciplinarity. Very few HEIs in India offer space and opportunities for interdisciplinary learning, partly due to the rigidly defined disciplinary boundaries and partly due to constrained vision. As a result, the aspect of cross learning between disciplines and peer learning among students from different backgrounds is completely missed, which is so critical to develop students as thorough professionals.

### 4.2 *Potential Opportunities*

Having a fair understanding of the problematics of the T-L processes in Indian HE, it is also important to discuss the opportunities at hand. In the context of T-L process in Indian HE, these opportunities are being offered by two major non-academic sectors: policy & civil society.

### 4.2.1 Opportunities in HE Policy

The Indian HE system in recent times has been slowly but surely making positive strides towards making T-L processes in higher education more 'relevant and effective'. This has been possible by some promising initiatives by Indian HE policy regulators in the last few years, who have attempted to address the challenges and make space for positive changes. For instance, UGC in the year 2014 launched a Scheme on *Establishing Centers for Fostering Social Responsibility and Community Engagement* in Indian Universities (Singh & Tandon, 2014). Specifically, it emphasized the "... promotion of practical learning and problem-solving competencies among students and introduction of experiential learning in curricular and co-curricular programs" (p. 117).

In 2016, MHRD launched a plan on establishing 'World Class Institutions' (WCIS). The plan specifically articulates that such institutions should offer inter-disciplinary courses, in addition to regular courses, especially as related to emerging technology and the development needs of the country.

NAAC has also been placing particular importance on innovative T-L processes in HEIs, for improving the overall quality of HE. Recently, it revised its Quality Indicator Framework (QIF) for assessment of Universities. QIF attributes the highest weights to scores for accreditation to *curricular aspects and T-L framework combined*, while the second highest weight is attributed to research, innovations and extensions (NAAC, 2019).

In 2018, MHRD launched *Unnat Bharat Abhiyaan* (UBA) 2.0 (a flagship program of the government of India) with a vision to induce transformational change in rural development by leveraging knowledge institutions to build architecture of an inclusive India (PIB, 2018). Among the focal points of UBA 2.0 is the introduction of curricular reforms, accompanied by introduction of new pedagogies in order to ensure that the T-L processes in Indian HEIs are conducted in a responsible and effective manner. In line with UBA 2.0, the UGC (in February 2019), drafted a *National Curriculum Framework and Guidelines for Fostering Social Responsibility and Community Engagement in Higher Education Institutions in India.* These guidelines place an added emphasis on T-L process and outlines the practice of adapting existing courses to fit into contemporary social realities and designing new courses that are locally useful and globally relevant (UGC, 2019).

UGC (in the year 2019) also introduced the *Learning Outcomes Based Curriculum Framework* for undergraduate education, as an important point of reference for designing effective T-L strategies. Further, as a direct outcome of the *Skill India Mission*, the Indian government has particularly focused on the development of 21st century skills (such as critical thinking, problem solving, etc.) by providing skills-based education under the National Skill Qualification Framework (NSQF) in colleges and Universities through its scheme of community colleges, degree programs and Deen Dayal Upadhyay Centres for Knowledge Acquisition and Upgradation of Skilled Human Abilities and Livelihood (DDU KAUSHAL Kendras) (PIB, 2019b). Additionally, in an attempt to introduce more contemporary & relevant courses, AICTE has decided that no new conventional discipline will be allowed as of academic year 2020–2021 (PIB, 2019b).

Lastly, the draft National Educational Policy (2019) assures that

> ... curriculum and pedagogy in higher education will move away from rote learning of facts and mechanical procedures, and will help young people prepare to contribute both as active citizens of a democracy and as successful professionals in any field. (p. 242)

### 4.2.2 Opportunities in Civil Society

Interestingly, Indian civil society has begun to offer innovative alternatives to TL processes. By collaborating with HEIS, the sector has recently begun to share its experiential knowledge base with students in an attempt to improve their learning outcomes while also making teaching a more engaged and effective process. Although this is only happening in pockets at the moment, it is surely worth mentioning. One Civil Society Organization (CSO) whose effort stands out in this domain is Participatory Research in Asia (PRIA). Based in Delhi, PRIA has undertaken several initiatives to bridge the divide between the world of practice and the world of theory so that the T-L process for students can be made more relevant and effective. It has collaborated with many HEIS across India and mentored students in developing practical real-life skills, while working with communities in real time. Doing so, it has supported student internships, partnered in community-based research projects and also developed courses. These courses are essentially meant to enhance the professional skills of learners and their content is prepared jointly by practitioners having field expertise and teachers/researchers possessing theoretical knowledge (PRIA, 2014).

PRIA is also home to the UNESCO Chair in Community Based Research & Social Responsibility in Higher Education, and has played an important role in steering its latest initiative, Knowledge for Change (K4C) globally and particularly in India. K4C is an international partnered training initiative between HEIS & CSOS for co-creation of knowledge through collective action by academics & community groups working together in various training hubs around the world for addressing the United Nations Sustainable Development Goals (UN SDGS). The ultimate objective of K4C is to train students in Community Based Participatory Research (CBPR). The most unique aspect of K4C which can have huge implications on the TL processes in HEIS is the pedagogical principles it follows, which especially focus on experiential learning, development of skills like critical thinking, reflection, and analytical reasoning, and adopting innovative methods of learning and doing. Doing so, it aims to enhance the knowledge of the students, building their skills and competencies and also raising awareness on contemporary issues.

Looking at this in light of the challenges of TL processes described above, it can easily be said that K4C can prove to be transformative for TL processes in the years ahead. One such example of transformation led by K4C is visible at Pandit Ravi Shankar Shukla University (PRSU) in Raipur. This is elaborated in the next section.

## 5  'Relevant and Effective' T-L Processes in Indian HEIS: A Call for Action

Incentivized by the new HE policy moves, and energized by the momentum provided by civil society (even though incremental at the moment), several HEIS in India have begun to align themselves and their TL processes to the new paradigm of change. In the bargain, the high accreditation scores by NAAC and monetary support from MHRD/UGC (under various schemes) comes as collateral benefits for the HEIS. This development has also been impacted by reports from reputed national think tanks like the Federation of Indian Chambers of Commerce and Industry (FICCI). For instance, the FICCI & EY Report (2015) advocated for the revision/update of curricula and introduction of blended learning, flipped classrooms, and experiential learning. Recent reports by FICCI (endorsed by MHRD) also proposed: a shift to a more learner centric TL ecosystem from the traditional instructor/subject centric TL processes; incorporation of innovative pedagogies; and adoption of flexibility in TL opportunities (FICCI, 2017, 2018). Other credible reports (IBM IBV, 2017; Ravi et al., 2019) have also advocated for the need to update the curriculum (in line with contemporary requirements), incorporation of new age pedagogies for development of 21st century skills (useful for the job market).

Apart from this, several recent developments in the global academic arena have also influenced this transformation. The two most important ones have been the United Nation's emphasis on the role of HEIs in sustainable development (Francois, 2017; UN, 2015) and the global call on HEIs to act responsibly and cater to local needs and global demands (GUNi, 2017).

All of the above have influenced and impacted Indian HEIs in a multitude of ways. In the context of this chapter, we are especially interested in how these have played a role in transforming the T-L practices. Collating the discussions and arguments put forth in this chapter, it can be said that what is needed today is a *new age call for action* for making TL processes relevant and effective in Indian HE today. This call for action seeks to address not only the contemporary problems, but also attempts to answer key questions like what to teach, how to teach and whom to teach. Accordingly, this call for action constitutes three basic pointers.

1. *Answering the 'what to teach' question:* Developing curricula and courses that are 'new age' and 'engaged' with contemporary social realities.

Dynamic revision of curricula and introduction of new courses are essential to further learning objectives of the students and to make them future-ready. Unless the curricula and courses at hand relate and respond to its immediate reality at the local and national level, and the students have a real appraisal of their context (social, cultural, environmental, etc.), the basic purpose of education is defeated. The importance of having the right curricula and courses has direct implications not only on the learning outcomes of the students, but also their employment prospects. Students trained in solely traditional courses are increasingly finding it difficult to secure jobs in the competitive and demanding job market, which prefers candidates having studied the subject matter that is most needed for 21st century jobs.

2. *Answering the 'how to teach' question:* Incorporating learner centric pedagogies that promote experiential/applied learning and can help students to develop 21st century skills for employability.

The importance of new approaches to learning that is experiential and applied and can help students develop critical 21st century skills is paramount. The universities of the future will have to discover new TL models and frameworks, built on multiple mediums of instructions and learning for the generation of new and socially relevant knowledge. Multi-modal pedagogies (in addition to classroom and laboratories) such as blended learning models and flipped classroom must be considered. Also, a fine balance between classroom and practice in real-life settings must be achieved. This is important because 'learning by doing' is the key to developing critical skills, and unless this practical approach to learning is incorporated in TL processes, achieving the desired objective will be difficult.

3. *Answering the 'whom to teach' question:* Offering diversified, flexible and interdisciplinary TL opportunities to cater to the needs and aspirations of 'non-traditional' and 'new age learners', and for creation of a broader education ecosystem, for enhancing TL outcomes.

There can be little debate on the fact that our TL processes need to be more diversified and flexible, and also open to interdisciplinary learning, new ideas and innovation. This can be made possible only if the education ecosystem is broadened to create spaces for new TL models. To do so, it is essential to blur the boundaries between academic disciplines and facilitate TL models where students from different disciplines can come together to study, work and learn. Another modality can be to foster partnerships and collaborations with other academic institutions (opportunities for knowledge exchange, peer and cross learnings) and non-academic actors like the government, for policy support to revamp TL processes; industry, which can provide ideas for curricular innovation and skill development, in line with the latest requirements of the job market; and CSOs, who can help complement theoretical understanding with experiential learning.

## 6 Islands of Excellence: HEIs Leading the Way

In light of the above discussion on challenges, opportunities and recommendations, it is also important to see what is practical, realistic and what is currently being done. Some promises emerge here. In recent times, there have emerged islands of excellence, in the form of HEIs that have put in practice some values/aspects of innovative TL processes (as described in the previous section) in order to make it more 'relevant and effective'. The upcoming section accounts for a few such illustrative examples of HEIs who have attempted align their TL processes with the new age call for action as described above.

### 6.1 *Revised Curriculum & New Courses*

Exclusive innovations have emerged in Indian HEIs that have attempted to revise curricula to suit contemporary contexts (macro perspective), while also introducing new courses that cater to local realities and demands (micro perspective). An example of the former is *the Indian Institute of Forest Management (IIFM)*, located in the city of Bhopal, in the state of Madhya Pradesh. In a novel initiative, IIFM has expanded the curriculum of the Master's course in Forest Management to introduce the aspect of Sustainable Development Goals (SDGs). The course on Development Management has been expanded to include an understanding of SDGs in the framework of adaptive management. Foundational teaching of the SDGs is thus linked to development management, thereby preparing students to use adaptive techniques in the context of achieving the SDGs (Tandon & Pandey, 2019). Given the professional nature of this course, addition of this aspect to the curriculum has straight gains in terms of making the students better equipped not only theoretically, but also helps them develop skills which would aid their employment prospects in the future, as forestry and natural resource management professionals.

Further, few HEIs in India have begun to design and introduce new courses at undergraduate and graduate levels in response to various local challenges. Pandit Ravi Shankar Shukla University (PRSU), situated in Raipur in the state of Chhattisgarh has been leading the way in this regard. The *Centre for Women's Studies* at PRSU has taken a step forward in this direction and has introduced a *Certificate Course on Community Based Participatory Research* (CBPR) in 2018, in partnership with the State Planning Commission (SPC) of Chhattisgarh and PRIA (CWS, PRSU, 2019). The learning objectives of the course include understanding and practicing theories and strategies of CBPR, with a focus on widening access opportunities for indigenous women (a major constituent of the population of Chhattisgarh, severely lagging on development parameters). Interestingly, PRSU leads the Raipur hub under the K4C India program, and the introduction of this new course is the direct result of UNESCO Chair's K4C initiative, led by PRIA. The pedagogy of the course is built on the broad pedagogical principles of the K4C program focusing on balancing classroom theory with field practice, development of new age skills like critical thinking and reflection and adoption of multiple modes of learning and enquiry.

### 6.2    *Learner Centric Pedagogies, Focusing on Experiential and Applied Learning*

Some Indian HEIs have begun to adopt new, experiential and applied approaches to learning, focusing on the development of 21st century skills such as critical thinking, problem solving, introspective reflection and analytical reasoning. Amrita Vishwa Vidyapeetham, based in Kollam in the state of Kerala has been doing just this. The university has been unique in constantly encouraging students to look beyond campuses and classrooms into the society. Worth mentioning here is Amrita's *Live-in-Labs* program, which exclusively focuses on social engagement by students/faculty with an objective to use classroom knowledge for furthering development outcomes, especially in rural India. The program aims to expose youth to problems faced by rural communities in India. Through experiential learning opportunities, participants put theory into practice by generating innovative solutions, thereby developing critical and collaborative problem-solving abilities (Amrita University, n.d.).

Further, Bhagat Phool Singh Mahila Vishwavidyalaya (BPSMV), located in Sonepat in the state of Haryana, has been one of the very few universities which have institutionalized transformed T-L practices through a formally operational structure known as the *Centre for Society University Interface & Research (CSUIR)*. The centre, by way of offering courses such as *integrated energy resource management, microfinance practices and women, folk medicine and co-operative management*, trains students on their local societal realities and builds their capacities to work on local issues (Singh & Tandon, 2014, p. 118). The pedagogy is structured around a fine balance of classroom learning and its practical application in the field. CSUIR in essence, aims at creating a liaison between the university and the society. The underlying idea behind its conception is twofold. First, the university believes that education is a process that requires practical exposure for learners beyond their conventional syllabus and classroom teaching, as education is not comprehensive unless coupled with practical application (Singh & Tandon, 2015). The second idea is that the life of villagers is difficult and there is a lot that the university students can do to make it easier, cleaner and more hygienic by developing small technologies for their day-to-day use (Singh & Tandon, 2015).

### 6.3 *Diversified, Flexible and Interdisciplinary TL Opportunities for Non-Traditional and New Age Learners*

The challenge of academic rigidities and disciplinary boundaries is undoubtedly a major one in Indian academia. While we still have a long way to go, there have emerged some HEIs that have attempted to move beyond boundaries in offering holistic and interdisciplinary learning opportunities to students, scholars and practitioners alike. An institution leading this change from the front has been the Indian Institute of Management, Udaipur (IIM-U). IIM-U partners with the School of Public Policy at Duke University, USA to bring together a mixed cohort of scholars and practitioners from varied disciplines and backgrounds (sciences, humanities, public policy etc.), annually for a course on development management aimed at building capacities of future development leaders (IIM-U, 2019).

These students (from Duke University, USA; Uppsala University, Sweden & Indian HEIs) and professionals (mid-career development professionals from India) are at various stages of their careers and placed at different points on the learning curve. The course is organized in a way that includes a fine mix of classroom learning, hands-on practicum and field research. The participants are put in different groups, and the same group has to work together through the entire duration of the program. This includes conducting a full-fledged field-based research project in the rural villages of Rajasthan, which weaves in the knowledge and understanding of different disciplines like social sciences, statistics, natural resource management, public policy, and business. The mix of cultures and knowledge perspectives among the students also opens the gates of lateral learning amongst the group members. There is so much to learn from each other's experiences, and the author can vouch for it as she herself completed the program that was conducted from June 14 to July 27, 2019.

In addition to the above HEIS, India is also witnessing the emergence of 'new actors' who are providing innovative T-L opportunities that are relatively flexible, cost-effective and tailored to meet the requirements of new age professionals and scholars. A leading example in this regard is the *Course on Rural Community Engagement*, jointly offered by the Mahatma Gandhi National Council for Rural Education (MGNCRE) (an institution under the MHRD) and PRIA International Academy (PIA) (education wing of PRIA), with a two-fold vision: firstly, to build capacities of scholars and professionals in rural community engagement; and secondly, to institutionalize rural community engagement as a field of study in Indian HEIS' (PRIA, n.d.). This course constitutes three components: online learning; face to face interaction; and a mandatory field work component. The idea behind this structure is to not only develop the learner's professional competencies, but also build soft skills and communication skills.

Therefore, opportunities for overcoming the challenges are many and varied. What is needed is to seize the momentum and scale up the positive experiments in T-L processes, in order to inch towards the desired transformation.

## 7    Takeaway Lessons for the Future

Higher education in the future will have two key purposes: firstly, providing solution to societal challenges; and secondly, preparing the youth in a manner that they can engage with life and living processes and their own identity. To achieve this futuristic perspective, there is an urgent need to focus on developing institutional processes, pedagogical systems and social bases that make educational processes and learning outcomes relevant, effective and meaningful for new age students. Among all such processes, the most important is the T-L processes in HE, as they are the key to learning and knowledge and play an important role in helping HE achieve its purpose. In the Indian context, this becomes even more important considering the times we are living in, where we are faced with both social challenges and a surging youth population. The aforementioned account on analyzing TL processes in Indian HE has some important messages for its transformation. It will be useful to weave them together, so that the chapter can be given a meaningful closure.

Universities need to focus on enhancing knowledge, raising skills and building core competencies of students. There is no question of prioritizing one over the others. To achieve this objective; revision of curricula and introduction of 'new-age' courses (IIFM & PRSU), taking into account multiple perspectives (contemporary social reality, market demands, student's aspirations); incorporating pedagogies focusing on the development of skills and competencies of students (Amrita Vishwa Vidyapeetham & BPSMV); and offering diversified, flexible and interdisciplinary learning opportunities (IIM-U) will be crucial.

To achieve the above, it is important to open up the education ecosystem, to make space for partnerships and collaborations with other universities (as in the case of IIM-U), CSOs (example of PRIA), government (as in the case of PRSU, collaborating with SPC, and the collaboration between MGNCRE & PIA), and industry. This will offer unique opportunities for innovation in TL processes, which will be important for not only adding value to the process and impacting learning outcomes, but will be relevant and meaningful considering the demands of the 21st century.

Finally, all the above ideas and strategies for transforming T-L processes will hold no value if the same is not institutionalized within a university. Scattered or individual attempts at transformation are often unsustainable in the long run, as they are often led by an individual or groups of individuals, who may not succeed in scaling up the efforts. Institutionalization of T-L processes (as in the case of BPSMV) ensures that the changes sought are accepted across university departments and faculties lines.

As the concept of social responsibility of HE gathers steam in academic discourses, transforming TL processes will play an important role in increasing the social responsibility quotient of HEIs. Making students aware of their social realities and responsibilities through socially relevant courses and experience-based learning in real-time (an aspect which has been reiterated by UGC) will ensure that the 21st century learners not only acquire critical skills and competencies, but also emerge as socially responsible and aware citizens.

Finally, policy support for any change or new idea is an important determinant of the fate of the latter. The absence of well-directed policies leads to continuation of the status quo with little space for accommodating any new practice. Policy endorsements on the other hand, can ensure the enforcement of new ideas and changes within the framework in a systemic and organized manner. The Indian case is a good example in this regard. Here, the endorsements from higher education regulators provided the necessary push for adoption of new T-L processes. This has been one of the main drivers behind the new experiments in T-L that we are witnessing today.

Therefore, one thing is a given; old ways of thinking and doing will no longer serve the purpose. The time has come to think and act innovatively, in order to ensure that T-L processes are made 'relevant and effective', and they continue to be a value proposition in HEIs. A step forward in this direction can be adopting a fresh approach to T-L processes – one which is more contextually relevant, engaged and learner-centric.

### Acknowledgement

The author would like to thank Dr Rajesh Tandon and Dr Budd Hall, Co-Chairs, UNESCO Chair in Community Based Research & Social Responsibility in Higher Education, for being the inspiration behind putting this chapter together.

### References

Aggarwal, V., Nithyanand, S., & Sharma, M. (2019). *National employability report (Engineers): Annual report 2019*. Retrieved February 14, 2020, from https://www.aspiringminds.com/research-reports/national-employability-report-for-engineers-2019/#

Amrita University. (n.d.). *About live-in-labs program*. Retrieved February 21, 2020, from https://www.amrita.edu/international/live-in-labs/about

British Council. (2014). *Understanding India: The future of higher education and opportunities for international cooperation*. Retrieved February 15, 2020, from https://www.britishcouncil.org/sites/default/files/understanding_india_report.pdf

Centre for Civil Society. (2015). *Regulatory structure of higher education in India*. Retrieved February 14, 2020, from https://ccs.in/sites/default/files/research/research-regulatory-structure-of-higher-education-in-india.pdf

Centre for Women's Studies (CWS), Pandit Ravi Shankar Shukla University (PRSU). (2019). *Certificate Course in Community Based Participatory Research (CBPR) 2018–2019*. Retrieved February 21, 2020, from http://www.prsu.ac.in/Admin_1/Upload_Data/Courses/590.pdf

Chahal, M. (2015). Higher education in India. *International Journal of Business Quantitative Economics and Applied Management Research, 1*(11), 67–74.

Coursera. (2019). *Global skills index 2019*. Retrieved February 16, 2020, from https://pages.coursera-for-business.org/rs/748-MIV-116/images/global-skills-index.pdf?utm_medium=coursera&utm_source=small-org&utm_campaign=website&utm_content=gsi-small-org-ty-middle-download-gsi

Economic Survey. (2019). *India's demography at 2020: Planning public good provision for the 21st century*. Retrieved February 14, 2020, from https://www.indiabudget.gov.in/budget2019-20/economicsurvey/doc/vol1chapter/echap07_vol1.pdf

FICCI. (2015). *State-focused roadmap to India's "Vision 2030"*. Retrieved February 21, 2020, from http://ficci.in/spdocument/20657/FICCI-EY-Report-2015%20.pdf

FICCI (2017). Social Outreach in Higher Education. Retrieved December 18, 2019 from http://unescochair-cbrsr.org/pdf/resource/Social_Outreach_in_Higher_Education.pdf

FICCI (2018). University of the Future: Bringing Education 4.0 to life. Retrieved February 17, 2020, from http://ficci.in/spdocument/23043/higher-education-ficci-Report.pdf

Francois, E. J. (2017). Preparing global citizenry: Implications for the curriculum. In GUNi (Ed.), *Towards a socially responsible university: Balancing the global with the local (Higher Education in the World 6)* (pp. 194–208). Retrieved from http://unescochair-cbrsr.org/pdf/resource/GUNI_6th_report.pdf

GUNi. (Ed.). (2017). *Towards a socially responsible university: Balancing the global and the local*. Retrieved December 18, 2019, from http://unescochair-cbrsr.org/pdf/resource/GUNI_6th_report.pdf

IBM Institute for Business Value. (2017). *Upskilling India: Building India's talent base to compete in the global economy*. Retrieved February 15, 2020, from https://www.ibm.com/downloads/cas/RMJXDJWX

Indian Institute of Management-Udaipur (IIM-U). (2019). *Summer school for future leaders in development*. Retrieved February 21, 2020, from https://www.iimu.ac.in/media/news/summer-school-for-future-leaders-in-development

Kumar, C. R. (Ed.). (2017). *The future of Indian universities*. Oxford University Press.

MHRD. (2016). *Policy on establishment of world class institutions*. Retrieved December 18, 2019, from https://mhrd.gov.in/sites/upload_files/mhrd/files/Public%20Consultation%20Document.pdf

MHRD. (2019a). *All India survey on higher education 2018–219*. Retrieved February 14, 2020, from https://mhrd.gov.in/sites/upload_files/mhrd/files/statistics-new/AISHE%20Final%20Report%202018-19.pdf

MHRD. (2019b). *Draft national education policy 2019*. Retrieved February 15, 2020, from https://mhrd.gov.in/sites/upload_files/mhrd/files/Draft_NEP_2019_EN_Revised.pdf

Nadar, R. N. (2018). *Contemporary issues & challenges in the Indian education system*. Retrieved February 14, 2020, from http://www.iosrjournals.org/iosr-jbm/papers/Conf.ADMIFMS1808-2018/Volume-1/13.%2086-91.pdf

National Assessment & Accreditation Board (NAAC). (2019). *Criteria and weightages*. Retrieved February 21, 2020, from http://naac.gov.in/index.php/assessment-accreditation#process

TOWARDS 'RELEVANT & EFFECTIVE' TEACHING-LEARNING PROCESSES 31

OXFAM. (2018). *The commitment to reducing inequality index 2018*. Retrieved February 17, 2020, from https://oxfamilibrary.openrepository.com/bitstream/handle/10546/620553/rr-commitment-reducing-inequality-index-2018-091018-en.pdf

Parikh, I. J. (2017). The future of Indian Universities: Voices for within beckoning for the future. In C. R. Kumar (Ed.), *The future of Indian universities* (pp. 54–68). Oxford University Press.

PIB. (2018). *Unnat Bharat Abhiyaan 2.0*. Retrieved February 21, 2020, from https://pib.gov.in/newsite/PrintRelease.aspx?relid=181909

PIB. (2019a). *India needs a world class higher education system: Vice President*. Retrieved February 14, 2020, from https://pib.gov.in/newsite/PrintRelease.aspx?relid=189828

PIB. (2019b). *Government of India has taken several steps for skill development in Higher Education: HRD minister*. Retrieved February 20, 2020, from https://pib.gov.in/newsite/PrintRelease.aspx?relid=191727

PRIA. (2014). *PRIA's engagements with Higher Education Institutions (HEIs)*. Retrieved February 15, 2020, from http://unescochair-cbrsr.org/unesco/pdf/resource/PRIA_Engagement_with_Higher_Educational_Institutions.pdf

Ravi, S., Gupta, N., & Nagaraj, P. (2019). *Reviving higher education in India*. Retrieved February 14, 2020, from https://www.brookings.edu/wp-content/uploads/2019/11/Reviving-Higher-Education-in-India-email-1.pdf

Sarin, S., & Dholakia, N. (2016). Higher education in India at a crossroads: The imperative for transcending stagnation and embracing innovation. In R. V. Turcan, J. E. Reilly, & L. Bugaian (Eds.), *(Re)discovering university autonomy*. Palgrave Macmillan.

Sharma, S., & Sharma, P. (2015). Indian higher education system: Challenges & suggestions. *Electronic Journal for Inclusive Education, 3*(4).

Sharma, Y. (2019). *India in 'initial' stages of higher education massification-report*. Retrieved February 14, 2020, from https://www.universityworldnews.com/post.php?story=20191128104421724

Sheikh, Y. A. (2017). Higher education in India: Challenges & opportunities. *Journal of Education and Practice, 8*(1), 39–42.

Singh, J. D. (2011). Higher education in India: Issues, challenges & suggestions. In S. P. Singh & K. L. Dengwal (Eds.), *Higher education* (pp. 93–103). Lambert Academic Publishing.

Singh, W., & Tandon, R. (2015). India: New hopes and fresh beginnings. In B. Hall, R. Tandon, & C. Tremblay (Eds.), *Strengthening community university research partnerships: Global perspectives* (pp. 113–128). PRIA/University of Victoria.

Tandon, R. (2017a). *Making the commitment: Contribution of higher education to SDGs*. Retrieved February 21, 2020, from http://unescochair-cbrsr.org/pdf/resource/Making%20the%20Commitment_SDGs-Sep_2017_final.pdf

Tandon, R. (2017b). *Education for public good*. Retrieved December 18, 2019, from http://unescochair-cbrsr.org/pdf/resource/Convocation_Address_at_RGUKT_May_2017.pdf

Tandon, R., & Pandey, P. (2019). Disciplines, professions and Sustainable Development Goals (SDGs): Challenges in higher education in India. In GUNi (Ed.), *Implementing the 2030 agenda in higher education institutions: Challenges and responses* (pp. 47–53). GUNi.

United Nations (UN). (2015). *Transforming our world: The 2030 agenda for sustainable development.* Retrieved February 21, 2020, from
https://sustainabledevelopment.un.org/post2015/transformingourworld

United Nations Development Program. (2019). *Human development report 2019.* Retrieved February 17, 2020, from http://hdr.undp.org/sites/default/files/hdr2019.pdf

University Grants Commission (UGC). (2019). *National curricular framework and guidelines for fostering social responsibility and community engagement in higher education institutions in India.* Retrieved February 21, 2020, from
https://www.ugc.ac.in/pdfnews/6202338_Public-Notice-Fostering052019.pdf

Wheebox. (2019). *India skills report 2019.* Retrieved February 14, 2020, from
https://www.aicte-india.org/sites/default/files/India%20Skill%20Report-2019.pdf

CHAPTER 2

# Expanding Inquiry on Intercultural Wonderment to Optimize Study Abroad Learning Contexts

*Lisa M. Davidson and Mark E. Engberg*

### Abstract

This chapter presents an emerging concept within the context of higher education study abroad, *intercultural wonderment*. This concept is understood as students' underlying curiosity to seek out novel experiences and their willingness and capacity to deal with discomfort while studying abroad. We review findings related to intercultural wonderment from earlier research efforts with which we have been involved. In particular, we discuss some of the applications and limitations of this earlier work. We present our current thinking about inquiry on intercultural wonderment as it relates to informing both educational practice and research related to study abroad. The chapter concludes by explaining research with which we are presently involved and implications for optimizing teaching, learning, assessment, and research in study abroad contexts.

### Keywords

intercultural wonderment – intercultural competencies – study abroad

## 1 The Need to Optimize Learning within Study Abroad

The benefits of studying abroad are extensively documented in higher education literature, particularly the ways in which these experiences expand students' understanding of global issues and foster a variety of other intercultural competencies (Engberg, 2013; Vande Berg, Paige, & Lou, 2012). However, also discussed are concerns related to study abroad contexts, including academic and financial barriers, lack of faculty and staff support, and the overall level of exposure to and immersion in host countries (Bell, 2016; Twombly, Salisbury, Tumanut, & Klute, 2012; Vande Berg et al., 2012). Too often, indicators of

© KONINKLIJKE BRILL NV, LEIDEN, 2020 | DOI: 10.1163/9789004436558_003

effective study abroad programs are relegated to reporting programmatic outputs, such as the numbers of educational programs offered and student participants (Engle & Engle, 2003). There is comparatively less effort expended on evaluating participants' learning and development and any longer-term impact (McLeod et al., 2015).

The transformative outcomes of study abroad are so often assumed in this educational context (Engle, 2013). However, actualizing such an impact requires optimizing the design, implementation, and assessment of developmentally appropriate study abroad learning contexts. Truly transformative experiences also require educators to consider the evidence-based intercultural learning opportunities available to students before, during, and after their studies abroad. There are several factors, however, that may hinder optimizing many of these learning contexts.

First, many study abroad contexts lack a robust theory of change that illustrates an evidence-based understanding of the intended growth or change in students' learning as a result of studying abroad and the programmatic aspects that are theoretically influential. This broader imprecision around the educational purposes and processes of study abroad results from and contributes to the lack of empirical research and evaluation that illustrates the impact of study abroad (McLeod et al., 2015). Second, for study abroad programs that articulate program- and course-level learning objectives (i.e., what students should know, value, and be able to do as a result of their study abroad experiences), there is often an assumption that merely studying abroad and immersing oneself in a new country is sufficient in realizing these learning objectives. This type of black box approach is problematic in that it falls short of unpacking how different programmatic aspects of study abroad experiences specifically influence the achievement of different learning objectives. Further, such an approach lacks a more nuanced understanding of how students' developmental readiness influences their proclivities to actively think about and interact with their host country. An optimal approach, therefore, must clearly articulate how study abroad learning objectives influence the developmental readiness of students to enter into novel intercultural contexts. Efforts to optimize study abroad must, therefore, inform course and program design, instructional approaches, the assessment of students' learning and development, and evaluating the effectiveness of this learning context.

As such, we approach this chapter with implications related to how study abroad research and practice domains can optimize students' learning. Some of our earlier work (Engberg & Jourian, 2015; Engberg, Jourian, & Davidson, 2016) has examined a concept we refer to as intercultural wonderment, which we have broadly defined as students' proclivities to engage in transformative experiences while studying abroad. We have examined the ways in which different programmatic features of study abroad programs directly influence these proclivities and indirectly influence a host of global learning outcomes by spurring intercultural wonderment. Our ongoing research focuses on understanding the curricular and co-curricular features of abroad experiences that provide the necessary structures to maximize student learning and development. From a research perspective, our current inquiry attempts to theoretically elaborate on precise dimensions of students' development that influence their engagements in the types of programmatic aspects that the study abroad literature suggests are beneficial. We argue that a black box of sorts exists relative to the domains of intercultural competencies frequently examined. From a practice perspective, our current inquiry stands to inform the learning and developmental outcomes of study abroad programs and other programmatic components including course design, instructional approaches, the assessment of learning, and program evaluation.

Where have we already been? Through two empirical studies – which we review shortly – we have examined the proclivities encapsulated by the intercultural wonderment concept and its role as a critical mediator that stands between the intentional design of different study abroad programmatic elements and the realization of global outcomes that span cognitive, intrapersonal, and interpersonal domains of students' development. Where are we heading? This earlier work, while addressing many of the concerns raised in recent years about the literature base surrounding study abroad, was also subject to a number of limitations that have contributed to our current thinking and conceptualization of intercultural wonderment. We use this chapter to discuss our initial conceptualization of intercultural wonderment, the limitations of this previous work, our current thinking, and future studies that can provide greater clarity and understanding of our conceptualization of intercultural wonderment.

## 2       Background on Intercultural Wonderment

It is important to identify the discovery of the concept of intercultural wonderment, as it provides transparency around its theoretical development and insight into the future work related to its conceptualization. The origin of the concept is steeped in survey research that emanated from the Global Perspective Inventory (GPI; Braskamp, Braskamp, & Engberg, 2013). The GPI is a widely used survey designed to measure college students' development of a global perspective, a construct that includes three developmental domains related to how individuals think (cognitive development), feel (intrapersonal development), and relate (interpersonal development) across cultural differences (Research Institute for Studies in Education, 2017). There are six GPI scales that span these cognitive, intrapersonal, and interpersonal domains of development with two scales per developmental domain. In each developmental domain, one scale is derived from cultural development theories (i.e., Kegan's (1994) concept of self-authorship and King and Baxter Magolda's (2005) concept of intercultural maturity). The other scale is derived from intercultural communication theory (i.e., Chen and Starosta's (1996) triangular model of intercultural communication competence). While the inventory has gone through several iterations since its origination in 2008, the survey is currently offered in three different forms for (i) new entering college students, (ii) general populations of college students, and (iii) students who study abroad.

The concept of intercultural wonderment was initially derived through an exploratory factor analysis of the GPI's study abroad form data (Engberg & Jourian, 2015). That initial exploratory phase uncovered a factor with good reliability that included four items: How often did you intentionally push yourself out of your comfort zone?; How often did you feel immersed in the culture of the host country?; How often did you on your own explore new habits and behaviors while studying abroad?; and How often did you interact with individuals from the host country outside of the classroom? Together, these items spoke to the *"underlying curiosity in individuals to seek out new and different experiences while studying abroad"* and their *"willingness and capacity to deal with discomfort and disequilibrium"* (Engberg & Jourian, 2015, p. 1).

We then theoretically mapped these concepts to the extant literature, focusing on the disequilibrium that occurs when students encounter provocative moments (Pizzolato, 2005); the recalibration of underlying cognitive structures that manifests from exposure to such moments (Piaget, 1985); and the developmental complexity that stems from making meaning out of provocative encounters (Baxter Magolda, 2008; Kegan, 1994). Additional literature attested to the ways in which provocative encounters trigger more active forms of thinking and learning (Gurin, Dey, Hurtado, & Gurin, 2002), and how cultural exchanges augment creativity and attenuate conformity to one's cultural norms and ideas (Cheng, Leung, & Wu, 2011). Finally, the concept of mindful wonderment, which focuses on *"a way to maintain open wonder and curiosity about possibilities for seeing, hearing, and even responding to others from a fresh perspective"* (Lewis, Davis Lenski, Mukhopadhyay, & Cartwright, 2010, p. 83) encapsulated our belief that fostering intercultural wonderment among study abroad students was essential in achieving a host of global learning and developmental outcomes.

EXPANDING INQUIRY ON INTERCULTURAL WONDERMENT

The purpose of our first empirical test of intercultural wonderment was twofold: (i) to understand its influence on a set of developmental outcomes included on the GPI study abroad form and (ii) to understand how different pre-departure and study abroad contextual factors (e.g., the influence of faculty and staff, community-based class assignments, reflective activities, sharing and discussing one's experience with others) influenced intercultural wonderment (Engberg & Jourian, 2015). Findings from this initial study confirmed two important aspects of intercultural wonderment. First, when regressing intercultural wonderment and a number of study abroad contextual factors on the GPI's developmental outcomes, we found that only intercultural wonderment was a consistently strong and significant predictor of the outcomes. Second, when regressing the study abroad contextual factors onto the GPI's intercultural wonderment construct, we found that all of the contextual factors were significant predictors of intercultural wonderment. Thus, this study led us to hypothesize that intercultural wonderment was the "connective tissue between intentionally structured programmatic components of the experience and students' development of a global perspective" (Engberg, Jourian, & Davidson, 2016).

Our next study sought to empirically test our hypothesis that intercultural wonderment mediated different programmatic components of a study abroad experience and a host of global learning and developmental outcomes. Using more rigorous structural equation modeling procedures, we examined our hypothesis across three of the GPI's developmental outcomes: students' knowledge of different cultures (cognitive), their affective reactions to cultural difference (intrapersonal), and their openness and acceptance toward difference (interpersonal; Engberg et al., 2016). The results of this study confirmed the mediating role of intercultural wonderment and demonstrated that the programmatic components only indirectly influenced the GPI's developmental outcomes through the intercultural wonderment construct. This was a critically important and significant finding for several reasons. First, this finding emphasizes that immersion in a new country is a necessary but insufficient condition to spur developmental changes in students. Merely sending students abroad is no guarantee that substantive learning and development will occur. Second, this finding suggests that more efforts are needed to intentionally design curricular and co-curricular experiences that enlarge students' curiosity and proclivities to actively explore aspects of the host country and its people. When these experiences are novel and push students outside of their comfort zones – a hallmark of the intercultural wonderment construct – learning is much more likely to occur. Finally, the results speak to the need to actively measure the impact of different programmatic offerings through the lens of intercultural wonderment. This is particularly important given that many programmatic design features do not directly influence global outcomes.

## 3 Existing Limitations of the Intercultural Wonderment Construct

The theoretical and empirical work related to intercultural wonderment (Engberg et al., 2016; Engberg & Jourian, 2015) marked significant contributions to the study abroad, global learning, and student learning assessment contexts for the aforementioned reasons. However, more recently we have concluded that additional inquiry that expands the theoretical understanding of intercultural wonderment would be beneficial. Specifically, this inquiry should theoretically elaborate on the specific areas of development that are required in order to engage in the types of behaviors understood as intercultural wonderment. In other words, there are implied dimensions of development within the existing intercultural wonderment construct that must be understood more clearly.

More precisely understanding the areas of development that comprise intercultural wonderment stands to inform various programmatic aspects before, during, and after studying abroad. For instance, findings stand to inform the design, content, instruction, and assessment of pre-departure learning opportunities. Before students study away, attributes of their learning opportunities could be intentionally structured to cultivate the dispositions and attitudes that relate to a proclivity to engage in culturally novel experiences and learn about one's self and others. Furthermore, pre-departure assessment approaches stand to be informed by the particular developmental dimensions and processes uncovered. These findings also inform the types of learning opportunities during study abroad – and, of equal importance – opportunities to reflect on existing, changing, and new insights throughout such opportunities. Finally, these findings inform assessing students' learning and development during and after studying abroad. Instrumentation (quantitative or qualitative) could be developed to measure the theoretically distinct areas of development and process-related elements that comprise the expanded intercultural wonderment construct. The discussion that follows provides a more detailed rationale for expanding the dimensions included in the intercultural wonderment construct. We focus the following discussion on our initial understanding of developmental dimensions related to the existing intercultural wonderment construct. We then apply this understanding as context for our current and future inquiry.

EXPANDING INQUIRY ON INTERCULTURAL WONDERMENT

## 4 Understanding Developmental Dimensions

As previously stated, intercultural wonderment's initial conceptualization was theoretically informed by the concepts of mindful wonderment (Lewis et al., 2010), mindfulness (Langer, 1989), cognitive disequilibrium that arises from novel intergroup contact (Gurin et al., 2002), self-authorship and meaning making (Kegan 1994), and intercultural maturity (King & Baxter Magolda, 2005). Engberg and Jourian (2015) applied this theoretical understanding to the study abroad context and understood intercultural wonderment as behaviorally manifested when students in this context (i) intentionally pushed themselves outside of their comfort zones, (ii) immersed themselves in the host country's culture, (iii) explored new habits and behaviors, and (iv) interacted with residents of the host country outside of the classroom. As described, Engberg and Jourian (2015) operationalized intercultural wonderment as a single scale that measured the extent of student engagement in those particular activities while studying abroad.

Theoretically elaborating on the developmental dimensions that underlie intercultural wonderment must begin by aligning the above behavioral manifestations originally described by Engberg and Jourian (2015) with requisite areas of development. In order to engage in those activities, what attitudes, dispositions, and knowledge must be developed? To answer this question, we first draw from the construct's original theoretical bases along with literature in new areas and propose more nuanced ways to understand distinct areas of development. Second, we connect our ongoing qualitative inquiry that aims to build the theory of intercultural wonderment through the narratives of students who have studied abroad. We present the theoretical case first, discussing our initial understanding of potential areas of development to examine. We then present ideas for empirical work in this area and detail the research with which we are currently involved.

Theoretically, we argue there are three major developmental dimensions that should be more deeply investigated as these relate to students' engagement in the behaviors initially described. For reasons outlined below, these three areas are conceptually distinct yet theoretically related in important ways. First, intentionally pushing one's self outside of one's comfort zone necessitates an awareness of disequilibrium. As such, more fully understanding the role and extent of mindfulness (Langer, 1989) in students' various abroad contexts will be critical. Second, as students explore unfamiliar relationships, contexts, and perspectives throughout their time abroad, we argue that curiosity (i.e., a proclivity to seek particular types of information; Young, 2018) drives some of this. We contend that this necessitates a deeper understanding of the different mechanisms that operate to motivate students to seek new information in novel contexts. Finally, Engberg and Jourian's (2015) original concept was partially underpinned by the concepts of cognitive disequilibrium, self-authorship, and intercultural maturity. Students' reconstruction of knowledge is a key outcome related to each of these concepts. As such, we must better understand precisely what is required for students to change

TABLE 2.1   Theoretical dimensions of development related to intercultural wonderment

| Area of development | Theoretical dimensions | Relation to intercultural wonderment |
| --- | --- | --- |
| Mindfulness (Langer, 1989) | – Novelty seeking (remaining open and curious)<br>– Engagement (interacting with novel aspects)<br>– Novelty producing (creating new cognitive categories)<br>– Flexibility (viewing experiences from multiple perspectives) | – Intercultural wonderment implies an *awareness of cognitive contradictions* within novel intercultural contexts. |
| Curiosity (Litman, 2005; Young, 2018) | – Information-seeking desire for different types of information<br>– Desire for new information stimulates interest (i.e., interest-type curiosity) or relieves uncertainty (i.e., deprivation-type curiosity) | – Intercultural wonderment relates to *exploring new relationships, contexts, and perspectives.* Understanding why students seek new information and the types of information they seek during study abroad is critical. |
| Reconstruction of knowledge (Dole & Sinatra, 1989) | – Students' existing knowledge and any motivation to acquire new information<br>– Information that students should integrate into their understanding and the extent that it is perceived as coherent and compelling<br>– Students' cognitive engagement (the effort students expend processing information) | – Understanding *what students already know*, how they know, and their level of commitment to their existing conceptions illuminates critical baseline information about students' development.<br>– Only through *high metacognitive engagement* is conceptual change possible. |

their understanding, focusing on students' awareness of any existing conceptions and the various motivations to consider novel information (Dole & Sinatra, 1998). These three dimensions are summarized here and discussed below.

### 4.1 *Mindfulness*

Langer (1989) initially advanced the construct of mindfulness using a cognitive information-processing framework. This initial conceptualization is particularly salient to study abroad contexts, as Langer's (1989) construct involves four distinct yet related dimensions: (i) novelty seeking (i.e., a proclivity to remain open and curious in one's environment), (ii) engagement (i.e., one's likelihood to interact with and attend to changes in one's environment), (iii) novelty producing (i.e., one's ability to actively create new categories instead of relying on existing knowledge), and (iv) flexibility (i.e., one's ability to view one's experiences from multiple perspectives and adapt one's behavior in response to environmental feedback). Langer's (1989) mindfulness concept arose from her research on mindlessness, which she understood as resulting from "*premature cognitive commitments or the tendency to apply previously formed mindsets to current situations, which lock individuals into a repetitive unelaborated approach to daily life*" (Haigh, Moore, Kashdan, & Fresco, 2011, p. 12).

A critical component of the intercultural wonderment construct is the implied awareness of disequilibrium, that is, intentionally pushing one's self out of one's comfort zone. This component was partially derived from the concept of cognitive disequilibrium, or the discrepancy between novel information and existing knowledge structures that produces confusion because a new experience is jarring and incomprehensible (Piaget, 1985). This stands to be a powerful catalyst for students' development. Study abroad contexts have a high degree of potentially unfamiliar elements, including the geography, transportation, language, and cultural customs. Such unfamiliarity provides opportunities for the disruption and discrepancy (i.e., disequilibrium) that stimulate cognitive growth (Gurin et al., 2002). Langer (1989) argued that these novel opportunities can spur mindful thinking because individuals in unfamiliar contexts have limited meaning-making scripts with which to consider their experiences. To achieve cognitive development, individuals must first be aware (i.e., mindful) of any cognitive contradictions. This type of mindful thinking requires students to engage metacognitively, question information previously taken for granted or assumed, and identify alternative perceptions (Langer & Moldoveanu, 2000). Such awareness, critical as it is, often precipitates a host of potential affective states, including uncertainty, instability, and anxiety (Gurin et al., 2002).

Knowing the extent to which students push themselves beyond what is comfortable is definitely useful in understanding students' engagement in opportunities that stand to promote their cognitive development. However, understanding students' cognitive and affective experiences with discomfort, especially when encountering new places and people, stands to inform teaching and learning strategies. For example, how do students understand which aspects of their encounters are most unfamiliar? How, if at all, does unfamiliarity relate to their discomfort? To what extent do they consider what (or who) about any given encounter caused them to feel uncomfortable? What do students do if they realize they are uncomfortable? How do they feel when they first encounter something new? What do they take away from the experience, how does that differ from their initial understanding, and what most influences what they took away? Understanding students' abilities to be aware of what they perceive and feel and how these processes influence them stands to inform educational opportunities designed to cultivate these important skills and dispositions.

### 4.2 *Curiosity*

Theoretically part of the construct of mindfulness (Langer, 1989), the concept of curiosity in part explains students' underlying motivation to interact with various aspects of their study abroad contexts. In fact, Langer (1989) originally explained that the novelty-seeking dimension of mindfulness influences the engagement dimension. That is, one's open and curious orientation in any given context influences the extent of their interactions. In a study abroad context, Young (2018) argued that given the expected challenges of navigating new contexts, students could be expected to encounter information gaps while studying abroad, where curiosity would undergird the desire to resolve tensions related to that gap. In both of these examples, it is clear that curiosity motivates individuals in particular ways. However, what exactly is curiosity, and why is it important to understand students' experiences of this while they study abroad?

The concept of curiosity can be understood as an information-seeking desire for different types of information. Broadly, curiosity can be understood as one's desire for new information that either stimulates interest (i.e., interest-type curiosity) or relieves uncertainty, for example, deprivation-type curiosity, which stands to relieve any negative affect from feeling deprived of information (Litman, 2005). Importantly, distinctly different underpinnings drive one's proclivity to seek new information. Curiosity can involve seeking four distinct types of information: (i) intellectual knowledge, (ii) sensory stimulation, (iii) adventurous or thrilling experiences, and (iv) interpersonal knowledge (Litman & Pezzo, 2007). Studying abroad offers opportunities for students to seek various types of information. However, seeking interpersonal information is particularly relevant to how many study abroad learning objectives are framed in terms of cross-cultural competencies that are inherently relational. Salient to our inquiry, Litman and Pezzo (2007) argued that curiosity about others' internal life experiences is critical in the development of empathy, emotional intelligence, social comparisons, and relationship building, which are among key intercultural competencies.

Given that the intercultural wonderment concept relates to exploring new relationships, contexts, and perspectives, it seems particularly important to understand why students studying abroad seek new information and the types of information they seek in their intercultural contexts. This is particularly salient because curiosity motivates engagement in one's environment (Langer, 1989). For example, Young (2018) found that while studying abroad, students initially sensed feeling curious in a rather bifurcated way: either through meeting new people (through conversations) or encountering new places (through sensory, introspective questioning). What drove these different experiences seems useful to understand. Do students seek out (or conversely avoid) particular contexts for particular reasons? Are there other person- or context-specific attributes at play? It also seems useful to understand how students have explored new contexts before studying abroad to understand more generally how they approach novel contexts and whether the intercultural nature of study abroad changes this.

### 4.3 Reconstruction of Knowledge

A deeper understanding of how students experience mindfulness and curiosity is critical since these concepts influence students' engagement with cultural differences. These types of engagements are theoretical catalysts for cognitive restructuring and more advanced perceptual processes as they serve to disrupt the automatic, repetitive, mindless thinking so prevalent in everyday life (Haigh et al., 2011). More deeply understanding how students experience mindfulness could illuminate what motivates their engagement and metacognitive outcomes (i.e., how their thinking has changed). Understanding the role of curiosity in students' experiences illuminates the type of information students seek and its role in their engagement. Understanding how students reconstruct knowledge serves to add nuance to understanding students' motivations to develop more complex ways of thinking.

Given educators' interest in their students' acquisition of more complex ways of understanding, they should be aware of what is involved in actualizing this more advanced process of meaning making. Educators must understand aspects related to learners (e.g., understanding their existing knowledge and any motivation to acquire new information), the information we want students to integrate into their understanding (e.g., the extent that it is perceived as coherent and compelling), and the extent of students' cognitive engagement (e.g., the effort students expend processing information; Dole & Sinatra, 1998). In a study abroad context, if educators can understand this complex process in ways that are digestible, they stand to structure their teaching and learning opportunities in ways that set up students to consider themselves and any new information in transformative ways.

Dole and Sinatra's (1998) cognitive reconstruction of knowledge model provides a useful framework to understand the types of information that would be useful to know about students' experiences while studying abroad. We discuss this model in more detail here. According to Dole and Sinatra's (1998) model, educators must first understand students' existing conceptions, including how much is known and the quality of existing knowledge. They outline three qualities of students' existing conceptions that influence their likelihood of conceptual change (i.e., strength, coherence, and commitment). Understanding what students know, how they know, and their level of commitment to their existing conceptions underscores the need to assess students' knowledge and learning before their study abroad experiences, which is often ignored in research contexts (Dole & Sinatra, 1998). Second, educators must understand students' motivation to process any new information presented to them through classroom, co-curricular, and other experiential opportunities. The motivation dimension involves multiple elements that span four broader areas. First, this dimension involves understanding students' levels of dissatisfaction produced by the types of cognitive conflict or dissonance discussed earlier. This happens, for example, when students' existing structures are unable to accommodate new information or when two divergent views are held simultaneously. Second, it involves understanding students' perceived interest in a topic. It is critical to understand whether students have a stake in the outcome, their emotional involvement relative to the information, and their sense of efficacy related to the topic. Third, it involves understanding students' learning contexts, which includes peers and instructors as well as interactions with community members. Fourth, it involves understanding students' underlying need for cognition. For example, some students are challenged by considering many sides of an issue and are intrinsically motivated to engage with information and ideas. It benefits study abroad educators to understand students' motivations to learn new information and attend to these. Finally, Dole and Sinatra (1998) discuss the extent of students' cognitive engagement with information as a critical dimension that influences conceptual change.

EXPANDING INQUIRY ON INTERCULTURAL WONDERMENT

They argue that only through high metacognitive engagement is conceptual change possible.

Critical thinking is a nearly ubiquitous learning objective in study abroad (and other) learning contexts. As such, examining how students experience thinking about their thinking – and the outcome of doing so – in study abroad contexts seems critical. To comprehend how students experience this, we might ask them about new contexts and encounters with new people that were particularly transformative. What were instances that helped students understand something differently than before? Identifying what changed is important, so asking them to compare their understandings before and after these encounters is key. Identifying what motivated these particularly transformative encounters is also important. Asking about motivating factors such as personal relevance or interest, disequilibrium or discomfort, and context variables that influenced the transformative nature of these encounters would be useful.

## 5    Continued Inquiry on Intercultural Wonderment

The aforementioned argument to expand the theorization of intercultural wonderment to include developmental dimensions undergirds our interest in continued inquiry in this area. Here, we share our current and ongoing research plans. Currently, we are conducting intensive student interviews with undergraduates who recently returned from studying abroad to better understand, through their narratives, their proclivity to experience novel situations in their study abroad contexts. Importantly, we are investigating cross-cultural considerations in students' understandings, as some scholars have questioned whether study abroad experiences categorically relate to positive learning and developmental outcomes for all students (e.g., Twombly et al., 2012). As such, we have structured our data-gathering efforts to elicit nuance related to culturally-variable understandings and experiences while abroad.

In our present inquiry, we are using grounded theory methodology, an inductive-deductive approach that allows us to gradually generate theory and concepts from the student data we collect (Charmaz, 2006). Researchers do not begin grounded theory studies with preconceived theoretical frameworks. We are mindful of Blumer's (1969) notion of sensitizing concepts (i.e., initial ideas to pursue, sensitizing one to ask particular types of questions about one's topic). The concepts we discussed above certainly arose from our disciplinary backgrounds and prior research efforts. These concepts provide a theoretical rationale to think more deeply about aspects of intercultural wonderment.

The concepts we discussed served solely as starting points as we drafted the initial interview protocol. In alignment with grounded theory methodology, we are currently refining these conceptual understandings as themes emerge from our student data.

More longer-term, we are interested in two areas of inquiry. First, we hope to utilize the findings from our grounded theory study to develop instrumentation to both indirectly and directly measure the dimensions of development included in the expanded intercultural wonderment construct. We hope to develop and validate a survey to measure students' self-reported development (i.e., indirect measurement) along the distinct dimensions of development that emerge from the grounded theory study. We also hope to develop a rubric that uses the dimensions of development as distinct criteria to evaluate students' work (i.e., direct measurement). These measures stand to contribute much to study abroad and global learning assessment, evaluation, and research contexts. In practice, the measures stand to provide a framework for how these areas might understand their objectives, activities, and impact, and they provide ways to collect evidence that informs a variety of institution-wide and programmatic decisions. In research contexts, these measures stand to contribute in two ways. Their conceptual underpinnings provide a framework to understand and investigate dimensions of students' learning and development. Also, data collected from these instruments can be used to investigate particular dimensions of intercultural wonderment.

Second, extending the initial survey-based efforts, we imagine using Astin's (1991) Input-Environment-Outcomes (I-E-O) framework to measure how students develop intercultural wonderment. The I-E-O framework is widely used in the United States to assess students' learning and development. The model accounts for students' inputs (I), or the knowledge, skills, and attributes they bring with them to college or that they have prior to engaging in particular opportunities like studying abroad. The model also includes environmental (E) aspects related to students' college experiences, such as types of engagement, perceptions of their campus climate, and other environmental attributes. Finally, the model includes learning and developmental outcomes (O), or what students take away from learning opportunities like studying abroad. Astin (1991) underscores the interrelatedness among the framework's three components and explains that the components should not be isolated in framing the assessment of students' learning and development. In I-E-O terms, we imagine using the intercultural wonderment items (outcomes) and developing survey items to also measure inputs and environments to allow for more contextual analyses. This offers scholars opportunities to investigate the development of intercultural wonderment in terms of students' pre-existing attributes before studying abroad and their perceptions of various attributes of their study abroad program contexts.

As study abroad programs continue to expand globally, more efforts are needed to optimize these learning contexts. Specifically, we must carefully consider the ways that study abroad program design, instruction, assessment, and evaluation enhance students' learning and development. Related to this charge, our earlier work revealed two important findings related to intercultural wonderment. First, intercultural wonderment serves as an important catalyst for students' development as they participate in particular programmatic aspects of their study abroad experience. Second, study abroad contextual factors such as faculty and staff, particular assignments, as well as reflective and interactive activities influence the development of intercultural wonderment. Given the significance of intercultural wonderment relative to the development of global learning outcomes, we must acquire a deeper understanding of what, exactly, underlies students' proclivities to challenge themselves and explore novel intercultural contexts while studying abroad. As such, we are presently expanding inquiry on intercultural wonderment, centering these questions: What are the dimensions of development encapsulated by intercultural wonderment? Is intercultural wonderment understood differently based on any characteristics of students or their learning contexts?

This expanded understanding of the developmental dimensions of intercultural wonderment stands to inform both study abroad practice and research. In practice, those charged with designing, delivering, assessing, and evaluating study abroad programs can apply the developmental dimensions of intercultural wonderment to different program- and course-level aspects.

- The developmental dimensions can inform study abroad program- and course-level learning objectives.
- Faculty can identify learning opportunities that cultivate the specific dimensions of students' development encapsulated by intercultural wonderment.
- Faculty can apply the dimensions of intercultural wonderment to their instructional strategies. For instance, they can prioritize assignments or other opportunities for students to reflect on existing, changing, and new understandings of particular aspects related to the course.
- Those responsible for assessing students' learning and development can use the instrumentation we plan to develop to measure (i) students' *baseline* levels of intercultural wonderment to inform course context or to be used for comparative purposes after the course, (ii) learning *during* study abroad to gauge progress toward achieving course learning objectives, and (iii) students' development after studying abroad to understand the extent of

learning objective achievement and/or growth over the study abroad experience.

- Those responsible for evaluating the effectiveness and impact of study abroad programs and curricula can use the expanded intercultural wonderment concept as an evidence-based outcome itself or as a mechanism that theoretically relates to other intended learning, development, or change.
- From a research perspective, the expanded inquiry we describe attempts to fill two critical gaps relative to the domains of intercultural competencies frequently examined in study abroad literature. First, our earlier work suggests that intercultural wonderment can be understood as both a developmental outcome itself and as a critical mediator for the development of other intercultural competencies. Our continued inquiry aims to robustly theorize some of the dimensions of development that influence students' proclivities to engage in particular phenomena related to intercultural competencies. This stands to inform scholars' understandings of areas of development examined in study abroad learning contexts. Second, the instrumentation we seek to develop to measure intercultural wonderment will provide student data for other scholars to investigate various dimensions of students' development related to intercultural wonderment. Considered together, we hope our expanded inquiry encourages both study abroad educators and scholars to deeply consider the pathways to developing students' intercultural competencies and approaches to actualizing and ensuring such development.

### References

Astin, A. W. (1991). *Assessment for excellence: The philosophy and practice of assessment and evaluation in higher education.* American Council on Education.

Baxter Magolda, M. B. (2008). Three elements of self-authorship. *Journal of College Student Development, 48,* 491–508.

Becker, P. H. (1998). Pearls, pith, and provocations: Common pitfalls in grounded theory research. *Qualitative Health Research, 3*(2), 254–260.

Bell, R. (2016). Concerns and expectations of students participating in study abroad programs: Blogging to reveal the dynamic student voice. *Journal of Research in International Education, 15*(3), 196–207.

Blumer, H. (1969). *Symbolic interactionism.* Prentice-Hall.

Braskamp, L. A., Braskamp, D. C., & Engberg, M. E. (2013). *Global Perspective Inventory (GPI) manual.* Global Perspective Institute.

Charmaz, K. (2006). *Constructing grounded theory: A practical guide through qualitative analysis*. Sage Publications.

Chen, G. M., & Starosta, W. J. (1996). Intercultural communication competence: A synthesis. *Annals of the International Communication Association, 19*(1), 353–384.

Cheng, C., Leung, A. K., & Wu, T. (2011). Going beyond the multicultural experience-creativity link: The mediating role of emotions. *Journal of Social Issues, 67*(4), 806–824.

Dole, J. A., & Sinatra, G. M. (1998). Reconceptualizing change in the cognitive construction of knowledge. *Educational Psychologist, 33*(2–3), 109–128.

Engberg, M. E. (2013). The influence of study away experiences on global perspective-taking. *Journal of College Student Development, 54*(5), 466–480.

Engberg, M. E., & Jourian, T. J. (2015). Intercultural wonderment and study abroad. *Frontiers: The Interdisciplinary Journal of Study Abroad, 25*, 1–19.

Engberg, M. E., Jourian, T. J., & Davidson, L. M. (2016). The mediating role of intercultural wonderment: Connecting programmatic components to global outcomes in study abroad. *Higher Education: The International Journal of Higher Education Research, 71*(1), 21–37.

Engle, L. (2013). *What do we know now and where do we go from here? Opening Plenary*. Forum on Education Abroad. Retrieved from https://aucp.fr/wp-content/uploads/2017/01/Keynote-with-slides.pdf

Engle, L., & Engle, J. (2003). Study abroad levels: Toward a classification of program types. *Frontiers: The Interdisciplinary Journal of Study Abroad, 9*(1), 1–20.

Gurin, P., Dey, E. L., Hurtado, S., & Gurin, G. (2002). Diversity and higher education: Theory and impact on educational outcomes. *Harvard Educational Review, 72*(3), 330–366.

Haigh, E. A. P., Moore, M. T., Kashdan, T. B., & Fresco, D. M. (2011). Examination of the factor structure and concurrent validity of the Langer Mindfulness/Mindlessness Scale. *Assessment, 18*(1), 11–26.

Kegan, R. (1994). *In over our heads: The mental demands of modern life*. Harvard University Press.

King, P. M., & Baxter Magolda, M. B. (2005). A developmental model of intercultural maturity. *Journal of College Student Development, 46*(6), 571–592.

Langer, E. J. (1989). *Mindfulness*. De Capo Press.

Langer, E. J., & Moldoveanu, M. (2000). The construct of mindfulness. *Journal of Social Issues, 56*(1), 1–9.

Lewis, R., Davis Lenski, S., Mukhopadhyay, S., & Cartwright, C. T. (2010). Mindful wonderment: Using focus groups to frame social justice. *Journal for Social Action in Counseling and Psychology, 2*(2), 82–105.

Litman, J. A. (2005). Curiosity and the pleasures of learning: Wanting and liking new information. *Cognition and Emotion, 19*, 793–814.

Litman, J. A., & Pezzo, M. V. (2007). Dimensionality of interpersonal curiosity. *Personality and Individual Differences, 43*(6), 1448–1459.

McLeod, M., Carter, V., Nowicki, S., Tottenham, D., Wainwright, P., & Wyner, D. (2015). Evaluating the study abroad experience using the framework of Rotter's Social Learning Theory. *Frontiers: The Interdisciplinary Journal of Study Abroad, 26*, 30–38.

Piaget, J. (1985). *The equilibrium of cognitive structures: The central problem of intellectual development.* University of Chicago Press.

Pizzolato, J. E. (2005). Creating crossroads for self-authorship: Investigating the provocative moment. *Journal of College Student Development, 44*, 797–811.

Research Institute for Studies in Education. (2017). *Global perspective inventory: Theoretical foundations and scale descriptions.* Iowa State University.

Twombly, S. B., Salisbury, M. H., Tumanut, S. D., & Klute, P. (2012). Study abroad in a new global century: Renewing the promise, refining the purpose. *ASHE Higher Education Report, 38*(4).

Vande Berg, M., Paige, R. M., & Lou, K. H. (2012). *Student learning abroad: What our students are learning, what they're not, and what we can do about it.* Stylus Publications.

Wong, E. D. (2015). Beyond "It was great"? Not so fast. *Frontiers: The Interdisciplinary Journal of Study Abroad, 26*, 121–135.

Young, C. D. (2018). *Encountering the emergence of curiosity in a student sojourn experience* (Unpublished doctoral dissertation). Miami University, Oxford, OH.

CHAPTER 3

# The Long-Term Career Consequences of College Undermatching

*Marjolein Muskens, Gregory C. Wolniak and Lex Borghans*

### Abstract

When students attend institutions that are less selective than their academic credentials would permit (i.e., "undermatching"), this may reinforce social and economic inequality, especially for first generation students. Yet little is known about its long-term, post-college consequences for careers. Drawing on longitudinal data from Germany (SOEP, $N = 8,336$) and applying propensity score matching techniques, results show that undermatching is negatively related to wages during adulthood, replicating previously published findings in the U.S. Moreover, results show negative relationships between undermatching and satisfaction with aspects of one's job that increase with age. It also appears that these relations are most pronounced among first-generation students. In sum, the findings support perspectives on undermatching that are grounded in notions of academic misalignment and peer effects. These findings have significant implications for our understanding about the consequences of undermatching in relation to outcomes later in life, and for the formulation of policies for promoting long-term career success and social mobility aimed at first-generation students.

### Keywords

undermatching – career outcomes – socioeconomic status – propensity score matching

## 1 Introduction

It is well established that graduating from highly selective colleges and universities is associated with better career opportunities and higher wages compared to graduating from less selective institutions, and there is at least

© KONINKLIJKE BRILL NV, LEIDEN, 2020 | DOI: 10.1163/9789004436558_004

modest evidence to suggest this association is causal (Mayhew, Rockenbach, Bowman, Seifert, & Wolniak, 2016). Because of these career and economic benefits, undermatching (when students attend a less selective college than their credential would permit) has been generally considered an undesirable occurrence in one's educational trajectory (Tiboris, 2014). Undermatching is a particular concern given evidence that students from lower socioeconomic status (SES) backgrounds are more likely to undermatch than students from higher-SES backgrounds, thus reinforcing social and economic inequalities (Bastedo & Jaquette, 2011; Deutschlander, 2017; Hoxby & Avery, 2013; Roksa & Deutschlander, 2018).

However, with the exception of one study to date (Ovink, Kalogrides, Nanney, & Delaney, 2018), very little is known about the direct relationship between undermatching in college and students' experiences beyond college and once in the labour market, and we are aware of no prior study that has examined if a student's socioeconomic status (SES) moderates these relations. The current study aims to fill this knowledge gap by using data from Germany that span more than three decades. Specifically, we focus attention on the added value of higher education in individual's developmental pathways in terms of post-college labour market participation and subjective well-being within the context of work. We specifically aim to replicate some of the finding from a recent study by Ovink et al. (2018), which found, within the U.S. context, that undermatching predicts lower levels of full-time employment and, to a lesser extent, lower wages within the first few years of leaving college. In addition to replicating Ovink et al.'s work in the German context, we add to the literature by investigating satisfaction with work and income in adulthood (outcomes that were not examined by Ovink et al.). We pay particular attention to investigating the moderating role of SES across these relationships.

Myriad personal reasons influence whether or not a student attends an undermatched institution and, therefore, it is important to account for selection bias when examining outcomes associated with undermatching. For obvious reasons, it is not possible to randomly assign students to undermatched and matched groups. Therefore, in order to isolate the effect of undermatching and reduce some of the accompanying bias, we utilized quasi-experimental techniques design to reduce selection bias (Raudenbush & Bryk, 2002) by adjusting for pre-existing differences between groups of interest (e.g., matched and undermatched students). The advantage of this approach centres on removing the confounding influence of differences in outcomes that may be associated with exposure to a "treatment", which may simply reflect pre-existing differences rather than the influence of the treatment (Grunwald & Mayhew, 2008). In this chapter, we aim to minimize the degree to which selection bias confounds the estimated effects of undermatching in college by using propensity score matching (PSM). The goal of PSM is to simulate random assignment (Rosenbaum & Rubin, 1983) and is important for gaining insight into the possible causality of the relationships we study. Importantly, recent critiques emphasize that reduction in endogeneity is not always achieved with PSM (Liu & Borden, 2019). Therefore, it is of utmost importance to test and demonstrate whether the PSM technique actually leads to the reduction of selection bias.

## 2  Prior Evidence and Plausible Mechanisms

Put simply, we lack empirical evidence on the long-term, career implications of undermatching and must therefore draw from multiple frameworks in grounding the present study. While the large majority of prior studies have focused on undermatching as an outcome in and of itself (e.g., Belasco & Trivette, 2015; Hoxby & Avery, 2013), only two published studies that we are aware have extended inquiry beyond initial enrolment in college: Muskens et al.'s (2019) study of subjective experiences during college among students in the Netherlands, and Ovink et al.'s (2018) examination of U.S. students within the first few years of completing college. Muskens et al. found a negative relationship between undermatching and student satisfaction within the Dutch context, where the findings were particularly strong for first-generation students. Particularly germane to the present study, Ovink et al. found a strong negative relationship between undermatching and full-time employment (and earnings, though the association was weaker) within the first few years of completing college, based on a longitudinal sample of U.S. college students.

As mentioned, the bulk of prior research on undermatching has focused on the factors that predict undermatching in college. The resulting evidence indicates that a student's likelihood of undermatching is affected by non-academic factors, including college search activities, attitudes related to campus social life and living at home, and dimensions of social and cultural capital (Belasco & Trivette, 2015; Deutschlander, 2017; Ovink et al., 2018; Roksa & Deutschlander, 2018). These studies and others (e.g., Smith, Pender, & Howell, 2013) have also found that lower-SES students are more likely to undermatch than their higher-SES peers (Bastedo & Jaquette, 2011; Hoxby & Avery, 2013; Ovink et al., 2018; Smith et al., 2013).

We have found no prior study that has examined undermatching in relation to the subjective facets of careers or extended beyond the first few years after college. We have addressed both with this study and have grounded our analyses in terms of three key perspectives that suggest the mechanisms by which undermatching may influence long-term outcomes.

First, the academic misalignment perspective supports the notion that undermatching during college will lead to lower levels of satisfaction in the long run. Fundamentally, by undermatching, students follow a less rigorous or challenging program, impeding their opportunity to reach their full academic potential (Hoxby & Turner, 2013). The misalignment – or lack of fit – between an institution and a student's capacity (Hoxby & Turner, 2013) eventually leads to diminished satisfaction during college (Muskens et al., 2019). A negative association between undermatching and well-being thus supports the academic misalignment hypothesis. The recent study by Muskens et al. (2019) adds evidence in support of this hypothesis with respect to satisfaction with academic and social aspects of college toward students' last year in higher education. It remains unknown if, or to what extent, the negative influence of undermatching on measures of satisfaction extend beyond the college years.

Second, the social misalignment perspective suggests that undermatching may lead to greater satisfaction in the long run. Studies have shown that upward social mobility may accompany stressful experiences among low-SES individuals that ultimately has negative consequences for individual well-being (Jury et al., 2017) and health (Miller, Yu, Chen, & Brody, 2015; Wickrama et al., 2016). For example, low-SES students attending highly selective institutions have been found to experience social exclusion and feelings of mismatch (Jury et al., 2017). The predominant cultural orientation in highly selective institutions is focused on independence, preferring working independently and prioritizing individual goals above others' goals. As lower-SES students may be more likely to focus on interdependence (e.g., working together, prioritizing collective goals above individual goals), a cultural mismatch can occur when low-SES students attend highly selective institutions (Stephens, Townsend, & Dittmann, 2019). However, in less selective institutions, this sort of cultural mismatch is less likely to occur for low-SES students given that students from similar backgrounds comprise a more substantial share of the institution's student population (OECD, 2019). To the extent that attending an undermatched institution circumvents negative experiences in college, it potentially contributes to more positive experiences in college, which may translate to more favorable attitudes towards work once in the labour market.

The third key perspective guiding our study is grounded in human capital theory. Specifically, the concept of peer effects may explain the effect of undermatch on outcomes such as earnings and employment. The concept of peer-effects has been used to examine educational contexts, as defined by peers, in relation to student outcomes (Manski, 1993; Wolniak & Ballerini, 2019), and is premised on the notion that an institution's selectivity is assumed to be an indicator of academic "quality", such that the average behaviors of a group of students influences the behavior of the individual students that comprise a group (Carrell, Fullerton, & West, 2009; Sacerdote, 2001). For example, if students in more selective institutional environments bring greater academic motivation and aptitude, and embrace more rigorous academic demands than students at less selective institutions, then simply following the established institutional and social norms within a selective institution will lead a given student to develop more human capital during college, translating to career or labor market advantage. Therefore, the peer-effect perspective suggests that undermatching would be negatively associated with career outcomes like employment and earnings relative to matching in selective institutions, due to lower average academic profiles of the students' peers.

Though focused on a different set of outcomes – ones that occur over the course of the first year of college – a recent study by Wolniak and Muskens (2019) uncovered positive associations between undermatching and noncognitive development (e.g., academic self-efficacy) during the first year of college among a national sample of college students in the Netherlands; the findings were particularly prominent among first-generation students. The study's findings suggest that, at least in the first year of college and from a developmental perspective, undermatching may not yield universally negative outcomes for all students. Although speculative, the moderating effect of socioeconomic status on the effects of undermatching found by Wolniak and Muskens partially support the social misalignment perspective. In sum, whereas the social misalignment perspective predicts undermatching may have positive consequences in terms of psychological outcomes like satisfaction with one's career, the academic misalignment perspective predicts an opposite (negative) effect of undermatching on psychological outcomes. Furthermore, from the peer effects perspective, undermatching will yield a negative influence on career outcomes like earnings and employment.

## 3    Study Aims

The aim of the current study is to examine the long-term effects of undermatching on career outcomes and personal well-being, and the moderating role of first-generation status. To circumvent difficulties with regard to the estimation of both undermatching and students' eligibility for admissions to selective colleges, we examined data from Germany, where, because of typical features in the German educational system, both undermatching and students' eligibility are relatively easy to determine. Ultimately, we have designed the study to address the following three research questions:

- Research Question 1: *What are the long-term effects of college undermatching on career outcomes, including employment, earnings and satisfaction?*
- Research Question 2: *Do the effects of undermatching differ for individuals who were the first in their family to attend college compared to those who were not? In other words, are the effects of undermatching general for all individuals, or conditional on first-generation status?*
- Research Question 3: *Does the influence of undermatching and first-generation status on career outcomes strengthen, weaken, or remain consistent as more years pass following college graduation?*

## 4 Methods

### 4.1 *Participants and Data*

Data for this study come from the Socio-Economic Panel (SOEP), a large-scale longitudinal study in Germany with more than 20,000 participants sampled since 1984. Subjects participated since 1984, or since their birth, and have been examined longitudinally every year thereafter through questionnaires and interviews, spanning a total of 33 waves (from 1984 to 2017). While older participants may have completed questionnaires across every year from 1984 to 2017, younger participants born after 1984 would have completed questionnaires across fewer years. Every participating subject who entered the study was followed longitudinally over this timespan, and because of variation in participants' generation, we were able to analyze the effect of age on our outcome measures. Importantly, although it is adequate to assume that generations are equally represented across the sample, it is possible that societal changes during the last decades confound the age-effects. In our sample, most respondents (79%) participated at least twice. Our analytic sample ($N$ = 8,336) was comprised of those respondents who completed some form of higher education. From this sample, about 23% were characterized as having undermatched (as defined below). The average age of the respondents during participation ranged from 21 to 94 ($M$ = 41.76, $SD$ = 13.37). Since students' typical graduation age in Germany is 23.9 (OECD, 2019), the average amount

LONG-TERM CAREER CONSEQUENCES OF COLLEGE UNDERMATCHING

of years in the labor market after college in this sample is approximately 18 years.

## 4.2 *Measures*

### 4.2.1 Dependent Variables

We examined four dependent variables. The first dependent variable indicates whether the respondent reported having a fulltime job (1 = yes, 0 = no). Second, we included the amount of money respondents earned per month (self-reported) as a dependent variable. The third dependent variable is satisfaction with work overall, measured with a single item on a 10-point scale (1 = very unsatisfied, to 10 = very satisfied). Finally, we measured satisfaction with job-related income, by way of a single item on a 10-point scale (1 = very unsatisfied, to 10 = very satisfied).

### 4.2.2 Independent Variables

Our primary independent variable was undermatching. In Germany, there are two types of higher education institutions: highly selective and less selective. For highly selective institutions (Universitaet, Technische hochschule), students may apply only if they have attained a diploma in the highest level in high school (Abitur). For less selective institutions, students are eligible to enroll if they receive a diploma from a lower level of secondary education (e.g., Fachhochschulreife) or tertiary education (Fachschule). For these students, a diploma from the highest level of secondary education (i.e. Abitur) is not required. Therefore, respondents are determined as 'matched' if they were eligible for the most selective institutions in higher education and subsequently attended an institution characterized as 'most selective'. Furthermore, respondents were determined as undermatched if they were eligible for the most selective institutions in higher education and subsequently attended a less selective institution. The well-defined and centralized distinction between highly selective and less selective institutions in Germany offers a relatively clear framework to determine academic undermatch and represents what Bastedo and Flaster (2014) have identified as an "ideal situation for studying undermatch" (p. 98).

### 4.2.3 Covariates

Covariates include indicators for age, gender, immigrant status, parental educational attainment (secondary and tertiary), and number of siblings. Our primary indicator of socioeconomic status (SES) was first-generation status (1 = Neither parent had obtained a degree in higher education, 0 = One or both parents had attained a degree in higher education), which we included alongside parents' occupational status, based on the International Socio-Economic Index of occupational status (ISEI). While many prior studies have demonstrated the career and economic effects of one's major field of study in college (Mayhew et al., 2016), we were unable to include major as a covariate due to data limitations; the data lacked a measure for major or major type that was comparable across the years examined.

### 4.3    Propensity Score Matching

In testing the relationship between undermatching and subsequent career outcomes, it is important to recognize that students' choice of institution may be based on a set of systematic, non-random features. In other words, selection effects need to be addressed in examining the long-term influence of undermatching. For example, it is possible that less affluent students are more likely undermatch and face additional barriers related to subsequent work experience or career satisfaction relative to their more affluent peers. In this way, matched and undermatched students would differ on relevant characteristics that spuriously inflate the estimated effects of undermatching when using traditional multivariate techniques. A methodology that addresses this problem is PSM (Thoemmes & Kim, 2011). PSM allows us to statistically generate equivalent treatment and comparison groups (e.g., students who undermatched versus students who matched, respectively), before examining group differences in outcomes. Two comparable groups are created based on several observed precollege covariates (Rosenbaum & Rubin, 1983).

We estimated the propensity to undermatch using a logit model by regressing whether or not a student attended an undermatched institution on each of the covariates mentioned above (see Table 3.1). The resulting estimates were then assigned to each respondent, representing their propensity to undermatch (versus match). We then used a two-to-one nearest-neighbour matching, with a 0.02 caliper level without replacement.

Table 3.2 shows that matching effectively achieved statistical balance across all covariates. Results show that matched and undermatched students initially differ significantly on five out of twelve covariates, which were all accounted for by the PSM adjustments (see Table 3.2). Furthermore, the matching procedure reduced the relative multivariate imbalance (L1) from 0.87 to 0.82, corresponding to an acceptable 10.34% imbalance reduction (Iacus, King, & Porro, 2009). After matching, no covariates exhibited a large imbalance ($|d| > 0.25$). Figure 3.1 displays the overall standardized differences across all covariates before and after matching. In sum, these results indicate that it is acceptable to assume that the PSM procedure did well to account for selection bias related to the observed covariates.

# LONG-TERM CAREER CONSEQUENCES OF COLLEGE UNDERMATCHING

TABLE 3.1    Logistic regression estimates of individual propensities to undermatch

| Variable | Odds ratio | Standard error | p-Value |
|---|---|---|---|
| Female | 1.04 | 0.05 | .483 |
| Age | 0.98** | 0.00 | < .000 |
| Immigrant status | 1.09 | 0.12 | .464 |
| First-generation | 1.10* | 0.05 | .044 |
| Highest level SE father | 0.83* | 0.11 | .042 |
| Highest level SE mother | 0.84 | 0.09 | .095 |
| Highest level HE father | 0.80* | 0.11 | .033 |
| Highest level HE mother | 0.81 | 0.12 | .074 |
| Occupational status parents | 1.00 | 0.00 | .125 |
| Siblings (yes/no) | 1.20* | 0.08 | .026 |
| Number of sisters | 0.99 | 0.04 | .837 |
| Number of brothers | 0.98 | 0.04 | .503 |

\* $p < .05$; \*\* $p < .01$; $N = 8,336$

TABLE 3.2    Results of PSM

| | Unadjusted sample | | | Propensity score-adjusted sample | | |
|---|---|---|---|---|---|---|
| | Matched | Undermatched | t-value | Matched | Undermatched | t-value |
| Female | 0.49 | 0.50 | 1.391 | 0.50 | 0.50 | 0.01 |
| Age | 45.49 | 43.03 | −7.01** | 43.19 | 43.04 | −0.41 |
| Immigrant status | 0.05 | 0.06 | 2.00** | 0.05 | 0.06 | 0.41 |
| First-generation | 0.53 | 0.63 | 5.68** | 0.63 | 0.63 | 0.19 |
| Highest level SE father | 0.35 | 0.25 | −9.02** | 0.25 | 0.25 | −0.46 |
| Highest level SE mother | 0.20 | 0.14 | −7.16** | 0.14 | 0.14 | −0.36 |
| Highest level HE father | 0.32 | 0.21 | −9.61** | 0.21 | 0.21 | −0.07 |
| Highest level HE mother | 0.15 | 0.10 | −6.76*** | 0.10 | 0.10 | 0.06 |
| Occupational status parents | 44.26 | 40.81 | −5.19** | 41.10 | 40.78 | −0.43 |
| Siblings (yes/no) | 0.73 | 0.74 | 1.34 | 0.74 | 0.74 | 0.59 |
| Number of sisters | 0.64 | 0.63 | −0.14 | 0.63 | 0.62 | 0.57 |
| Number of brothers | 0.65 | 0.66 | −0.06 | 0.62 | 0.63 | 0.84 |
| N | 6558 | 1884 | | 3765 | 1883 | |

Note: Results before and after generating balance among undermatched and matched students using PSM.

\*\*$p < .01$; \*\*\* $p < .001$

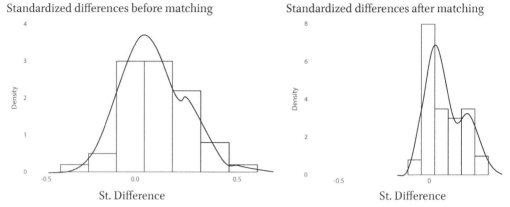
FIGURE 3.1   Standardized differences before and after matching

### 4.4   *Analysis*

In testing the relationship between undermatching and subsequent outcomes, we used multivariate mixed modelling with repeated measures (with SPSS 24) to estimate the effects of undermatching. Either logistic or linear modelling was used depending on the particular outcome measure being estimated. To address Research Question 1 we regressed each outcome variable on undermatching within the full propensity score-adjusted sample. In addition, we segmented the sample according to first-generation and continuing-generation status to examine if the influence of undermatching on career outcomes is conditional on first-generation status. In so doing, we addressed Research Question 2. Finally, we investigated Research Question 3 by examining the interaction effects of age and undermatching to determine if the influence of undermatching changes as more years pass following college. We examined the interaction effects among the full sample and among the samples that were segmented by first-generation status. Descriptive statistics for all variables are presented in Table 3.3.

## 5   Results

### 5.1   *Effects of Undermatching on Career Outcomes*

After balancing the sample across the full set of covariates for the undermatched and matched groups, we estimated long-term, post-college effects of undermatching on four career-related outcomes. For the outcome measure 'Full time employed', due to its binary nature, we estimated a logistic mixed model with repeated measures, with undermatching as the predictor and age as the "within subjects" factor. For each of the other (non-binary) dependent

TABLE 3.3    Descriptive statistics among study variables (original sample)

| | 1 | 2 | 3 | 4 | 5 | 6 | 7 | 8 | 9 | 10 | 11 | 12 | 13 | 14 | 15 | 16 | 17 |
|---|---|---|---|---|---|---|---|---|---|---|---|---|---|---|---|---|---|
| Mean or proportion | 0.23 | 0.58 | 2447 | 7.36 | 7.01 | 0.49 | 44.94 | 0.05 | 0.55 | 0.33 | 0.19 | 0.29 | 0.14 | 43.48 | 0.73 | 0.65 | 0.64 |
| SD | 0.42 | 0.44 | 1776 | 1.57 | 2.00 | 0.50 | 13.76 | 0.22 | 0.48 | 0.47 | 0.39 | 0.46 | 0.35 | 26.34 | 0.44 | 0.86 | 0.84 |
| Minimum | 0 | 0 | 0 | 0 | 0 | 0 | 21 | 0 | 0 | 0 | 0 | 0 | 0 | 0 | 0 | 0 | 0 |
| Maximum | 1 | 1 | 30000 | 10 | 10 | 1 | 96 | 1 | 1 | 1 | 1 | 1 | 1 | 90 | 1 | 7 | 9 |
| 1. Undermatching | | | | | | | | | | | | | | | | | |
| 2. Full-time employed | 0.02* | | | | | | | | | | | | | | | | |
| 3. Net income per month | −0.09* | 0.44* | | | | | | | | | | | | | | | |
| 4. Satisfaction with work | −0.04* | 0.09* | 0.14* | | | | | | | | | | | | | | |
| 5. Satisfaction with income | −0.05* | 0.20* | 0.39* | 0.43* | | | | | | | | | | | | | |
| 6. Female | 0.02 | −0.37* | −0.38* | −0.06* | −0.14* | | | | | | | | | | | | |
| 7. Age | −0.08* | −0.24* | 0.26* | −0.02 | 0.15* | −0.16* | | | | | | | | | | | |
| 8. Immigrant status | 0.02* | 0.00 | −0.04* | 0.02 | −0.05* | 0.03* | −0.12* | | | | | | | | | | |
| 9. First-generation | 0.10* | 0.02 | −0.02 | −0.04* | 0.02 | −0.06* | 0.12* | −0.01 | | | | | | | | | |
| 10. Highest level SE father | −0.09* | −0.03* | 0.02* | 0.02 | 0.01 | 0.04* | −0.06* | −0.03* | −0.71* | | | | | | | | |
| 11. Highest level SE mother | −0.07* | −0.01 | −0.01 | 0.02 | −0.03* | 0.06* | −0.15* | 0.01 | −0.50* | 0.46* | | | | | | | |
| 12. Highest level HE father | −0.10* | −0.02 | 0.03* | 0.02 | 0.00 | 0.03* | −0.07* | 0.01 | −0.92* | 0.75* | 0.41* | | | | | | |
| 13. Highest level HE mother | −0.07* | 0.00 | −0.04* | 0.03* | −0.03* | 0.05* | −0.18* | 0.05* | −0.56* | 0.35* | 0.70* | 0.41* | | | | | |
| 14. Occ. status parents | −0.06* | 0.01 | 0.01 | −0.02* | 0.00 | 0.01 | −0.06* | −0.05* | −0.43* | 0.49* | 0.30* | 0.49* | 0.25* | | | | |
| 15. Siblings (yes/no) | 0.02 | 0.00 | 0.02* | −0.01 | 0.01 | −0.02 | −0.01* | 0.05 | −0.07* | 0.15* | 0.11* | 0.15* | 0.10* | 0.26* | | | |
| 16. Number of brothers | −0.01 | −0.03* | 0.03* | 0.03* | 0.02 | −0.04 | 0.11 | 0.00 | −0.02* | 0.09* | 0.06* | 0.07* | 0.04* | 0.12* | 0.46* | | |
| 17. Number of sisters | 0.00 | −0.03* | 0.01 | 0.00 | 0.02 | −0.01 | 0.07* | −0.01* | −0.03* | 0.09* | 0.06* | 0.07* | 0.04* | 0.10* | 0.46* | 0.09* | |

Note: The variable "net income per month" is represented in euro (€). Variables Fulltime employed, Net Monthly income, and the two measures of Satisfaction represent average values over life per respondent.

*p < .05; N = 8,336

variables, we used linear mixed models with repeated measures, again, with undermatching as predictor and age as the within-subjects factor. The results (see Table 3.4) show a clear pattern in which the effects of undermatching are statistically significant, uniformly negative, and extending across monetary and non-monetary (psychological) dimensions.

Specifically, the average "treatment" effect associated with undermatching on net monthly income appeared to be a strong 8%, which translates in this sample to more than €3500 per year (roughly USD $3900 per year). However, the effects on the psychological measures appeared more moderate: undermatched students reported statistically significant but small 0.10 and 0.19 differences (on a 10-point scale) in satisfaction with work and satisfaction with income, respectively. Undermatching did not influence one's likelihood of being employed on a full-time basis.

TABLE 3.4    Estimated relationship between college undermatching and outcomes in adulthood

| Outcome measures | Odds ratio, $b$ | 95% CI |
| --- | --- | --- |
| 1. Full-time employed | 0.00 | [−0.03, 0.02] |
| 2. Net income per month (ln) | −0.08*** | [−0.13, −0.03] |
| 3. Satisfaction with work | −0.10* | [−0.19, −0.02] |
| 4. Satisfaction with income | −0.19** | [−0.30, −0.07] |

Note: Outcome measure 'Net income per month (ln)' is log transformed income. The estimate for outcome 1 is based on a logistic mixed model (the *Odds ratio* is reported). The estimates for outcomes 2–4 are based on linear mixed models (unstandardized coefficients, $b$, are reported). Across all models, the estimated coefficient represents the effect of undermatching.
*$p < .05$; **$p < .01$; ***$p < .001$; $N = 5,648$

### 5.2    *Moderating Influence of First-Generation Status*

Next, we estimated the same models separately for individuals who were first-generation college students and continuing-generation college students (see Table 3.5). The results indicated a negative and statistically significant effect of undermatching on net monthly earnings among first-generation students (roughly 8% less net earnings each month). Among continuing-generation students, the effect of undermatching did not reach statistical significance. In other words, any influence undermatching may have on earnings was due to random chance among continuing-generation students. Similarly, we found largely negative consequences of undermatching on levels of satisfaction

LONG-TERM CAREER CONSEQUENCES OF COLLEGE UNDERMATCHING          63

with work and satisfaction with income that were more pronounced among first-generation students than among continuing-generation students. In fact, for continuing-generation students, undermatching did not yield a statistically significant influence on any of the outcomes measured. Because roughly 63% of the sample consists of first-generation students, there is a slightly higher level of statistical power in the analyses for first-generation students compared to those for continuing generation students, leading standard errors to be smaller and increase the chances of reaching statistical significance of the estimates for the first-generation sample. However, because the continuing-students group remains substantial in size ($n$ = 2090), the differences we found are likely not solely explained by power differences.

TABLE 3.5     Estimated relationship between college undermatching and outcomes in adulthood, by students' first-generation status

| Outcome measures | First-generation | | Continuing-generation | |
|---|---|---|---|---|
| | Odds ratio, *b* | 95% CI | Odds ratio, *b* | 95% CI |
| 1. Full-time employed | 0.02 | [−0.01, 0.05] | −0.02 | [−0.07, 0.02] |
| 2. Net income per month (ln) | −0.08* | [−0.13, −0.02] | −0.06 | [−0.16, 0.04] |
| 3. Satisfaction with work | −0.12* | [−0.22, −0.01] | −0.08 | [−0.24, 0.07] |
| 4. Satisfaction with income | −0.21** | [−0.35, −0.07] | −0.16 | [−0.38, 0.06] |

Note: Outcome measure 'Net income per month (ln)' is log transformed income. The estimates for outcome 1 are based on a logistic mixed model (*Odds Ratios* are reported). The estimates for outcomes 2–4 are based on linear mixed models (unstandardized coefficients, *b*, are reported). Across all models, the estimated coefficient represents the effect of undermatching.
*$p$ < .05; **$p$ < .01; ***$p$ < .001; $N$ = 5,648

### 5.3     *Consequences of Undermatching throughout Adulthood*
Finally, we examined how the relationships between undermatching and outcomes in adulthood develop during the life course between age 25 and age 50. For each of the analytic models previously described, we added to the regression equation an interaction term for *age × undermatch*. For the full sample, results yielded a significant interaction effect between undermatching and age on net earnings, satisfaction with work and satisfaction with income (see Table 3.6). These results indicate that the negative relationships between undermatching and these career outcomes, in fact, become more pronounced with age. In addition, while undermatching did not have a significant influence

TABLE 3.6    Estimated interaction effects between undermatching and age, in general and by students' first-generation status

| Outcome measures | Full sample Odds ratio, $b$ | First-generation Odds ratio, $b$ | Continuing-generation Odds ratio, $b$ |
| --- | --- | --- | --- |
| *1. Full-time employed* | | | |
| Undermatching | 0.00 | 0.02 | −0.01 |
| Age | −0.13*** | −0.15*** | −0.07*** |
| Undermatching × Age | 0.04*** | 0.05*** | 0.02 |
| *2. Net income per month (ln)* | | | |
| Undermatching | −0.09** | −0.07* | −0.15* |
| Age | 0.41*** | 0.39** | 0.49*** |
| Undermatching × Age | −0.07*** | −0.04* | −0.20*** |
| *3. Satisfaction with work* | | | |
| Undermatching | −0.14** | −0.16** | −0.05 |
| Age | −0.10*** | −0.10*** | −0.08 |
| Undermatching × Age | −0.10* | −0.15** | 0.08 |
| *4. Satisfaction with income* | | | |
| Undermatching | −0.18** | −0.18* | −0.21 |
| Age | 0.44*** | 0.46*** | 0.51*** |
| Undermatching × Age | −0.11* | −0.10 | −0.23* |

Note: Outcome measure 'Net income per month (ln)' is log transformed income. Covariate 'Age' is standardized. The estimates for outcome 1 are based on a logistic mixed model (*Odds ratios* are reported). The estimates for outcomes 2–4 are based on linear mixed models (unstandardized coefficients, $b$, are reported). Across all models, the estimated coefficient represents the effect of undermatching.
*$p < .05$; **$p < .01$; ***$p < .001$; $N = 5,648$

on one's likelihood of being employed full-time, the interaction effects suggest that over time – the longer one is in the labor market – undermatching may somewhat dampen the negative consequences of aging on full-time employment, though the magnitude of the effect was negligible in size (0.04 on a 10-point scale).

When the interaction term was estimated separately for first-generation students and continuing-generation students, the results show that the negative influence of undermatching on net monthly earnings becomes more pronounced with age, and the size of the interaction effect is considerably larger among continuing-generation students. In other words, the negative consequences of undermatching on income grow over one's lifetime, particularly among continuing-generation students.

Regarding satisfaction with work, results indicate that only among first-generation students do the negative consequences of undermatching become stronger with age. For continuing-generation students, neither undermatching nor age nor their interaction exerted significant influence on satisfaction with work. Alternatively, for first-generation students, though undermatching has a negative effect on satisfaction with income, the effect does not appear to significantly change over time. For continuing-generation students, the negative influence of undermatching solely exists in the context of aging.

We further show the relationship between undermatching and age for net monthly earnings separated by first generation and continuing generation status in Figure 3.2. Consistent with the previous discussion, continuing-generation students who attended a matched college receive higher net monthly earnings than other students, and these differences become significant after about age 30. In addition, first-generation students who attended a matched college have higher monthly earnings than students who were undermatched, and among older individuals, the earnings differences between matched and undermatched groups appear greater for continuing-generation students. In other words, over the long term, undermatching has a larger negative influence on earnings among continuing-generations student than among first-generation students.

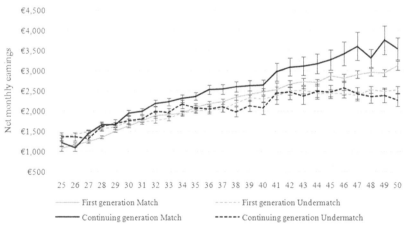

FIGURE 3.2  Net monthly earnings separated by undermatching, first-generation status and age

## 6 Discussion

Given the well-documented, long-term effects on wages and job opportunities associated with attending more selective higher education institutions (Mayhew et al., 2016) and disparate access to elite institutions among lower SES students (Deutschlander, 2017), college undermatching remains a concern among policymakers and social scientists. Yet little is known about the long-term consequences of undermatching, particularly in terms of several years following college. In this study, we begin to fill this knowledge gap by examining undermatching in relation to employment, income, and two dimensions of job-related satisfaction.

By leveraging the information contained in the German SOEP database and employing methods to reduce selection bias in our results, we were able to advance research on undermatching in several important ways. First, the large sample size allowed us to estimate the general effects of undermatching among all SOEP participants, and to estimate conditional effects by examine first-generation and continuing generation students separately. In addition, given that SOEP data have been collected every year since 1984, the sample participants ranged in age from 21 to 94, with an average time in the labour market of 18 years. This allowed us to ascertain if the influence of the long-term effects of undermatching strengthen, weaken, or remain consistent as more years pass following college graduation. As mentioned before, because of the longitudinal character of the data, people from all ages can have filled in the questionnaires in all years between 1984 and 2017. Assuming that generations are equally represented across the sample, we were able to analyze the effect of age on our outcome measures. However, we cannot rule out that societal changes across the last decades confound these age-effects.

Furthermore, because the SOEP data reflect the German context, we were able to capitalize on the well-defined and centralized German higher education system, were there are two types of higher education (highly selective and less selective), each with clearly defined admissions criteria based on the type of high school attended. Such distinctions of the German system afforded us a clear framework to determine academic undermatch, building on the recommendations of Bastedo and Flaster (2014). Finally, we have contributed important new evidence to the small number of prior studies that have focused on the consequences of undermatching (Muskens et al., 2019; Ovink et al., 2018); the large majority of prior studies of undermatching has focused on causes of – the factors predicting – undermatching in college (Belasco & Trivette, 2015; Bowen et al., 2009; Roderick, Coca, & Nagaoka, 2011; Roksa & Deutschlander, 2018; Smith et al., 2013), rather than the effects of undermatching.

LONG-TERM CAREER CONSEQUENCES OF COLLEGE UNDERMATCHING 67

Building on prior evidence, we addressed our research questions in lieu of plausible mechanisms centred on misalignment and peer effects perspectives, where the concept of social exclusion and mismatch are known to occur among lower-SES students in upwardly mobile environments (Hoxby & Turner, 2013; Jury et al., 2017; Miller et al., 2015, Muskens et al., 2019; Stephens et al, 2019). Altogether, our results point to four main findings.

First, in response to our research question on the long-term effects of under-matching, we found consistent evidence that, holding precollege and ascribed background factors equal, undermatching in college appears to have a neg-ative and lasting influence on work-related outcomes. The only exception to this finding was the lack of influence undermatching had on the likelihood of full-time employment. Across all other outcomes (including monthly income, satisfaction with work conditions, and satisfaction with income), undermatch-ing appears to have a detrimental effect. Ovink et al.'s (2018) analysis of longi-tudinal data from the U.S. roughly eight years after individuals graduated from secondary school produced similar findings to ours, within the early stages of one's career. Results from their most robust analyses (i.e., those that relied on instrumental variable approaches to account for selection bias) indicated a negative influence of undermatching on the likelihood of full-time employ-ment within the first few years of completing college. Alternatively, based on a broader view of careers over many years beyond college, our findings suggest the average effect of undermatching is not significantly related with the likeli-hood of being employed full-time. In addition, Ovink et al. found negative but not statistically significant effects of undermatching on earnings, whereas we uncovered significant negative effects of undermatching on earnings. It may be that the negative earnings effects of undermatching don't appear until several years beyond college, where undermatching reduces the odds of working full-time initially after completing college but not over the full arc of one's career.

Second, in addressing if, or to what extent, the effects of undermatching are conditional on being a first-generation student, we uncovered evidence to sug-gest that the general effects discussed above are driven by students who were first in their family to attend college. In other words, undermatching appears more detrimental for first-generation students than for their continuing-gen-eration counterparts. However, this finding should be taken with caution given that the differences in statistical significance across these two sub-populations may be partially driven by distributional properties of the samples; while the effects were similarly negative across both groups, the larger standard errors among the continuing-generation sample made those estimates less likely to reach statistical significance for a given effect size. Nevertheless, it stands to reason that continuing-generation students have access to other resources while in college and once in the labour market that may mitigate some of the negative consequences of undermatching in a less selective college.

From a status attainment perspective, if undermatching is in fact distinctly problematic for first-generation students, then greater attention should be placed on encouraging first-generation students to enrol in the most selective institution to which they are admitted. This recommendation mirrors those of other scholars – such as Roksa and Deutschlander (2018), Hoxby and Avery (2013) and Bastedo and Jaquette (2011) – who focused on the factors that predict undermatching among students from lower SES backgrounds, and supports Alon and Tienda's (2005) claim that attending a more selective institution among students from lower socioeconomic backgrounds plays a distinctly valuable role in social mobility. By illustrating that the effects of undermatching among first-generation students extend well beyond the college years, our results should be cause for increased concern about the long-term socioeconomic implications of undermatching.

Third, in terms of the interaction between the number of years since college and undermatching, we identified that the detrimental influence of undermatching becomes more pronounced with time: a statistically significant, negative interaction effect was found with respect to full-time employment, income, and both measures of job-related satisfaction. Interestingly, while undermatching did not directly influence one's likelihood of full-time employment, and while the odds of full-time employment decline with age, undermatching appears to somewhat offset the age-based declines in full-time employment, particularly among first-generation college students. No clear explanation exists to account for this finding, other than the possibility that undermatched students, because they earn less, may be particularly driven to secure (and successful in securing) full-time employment later in life out of a necessity to maintain financial security. Importantly, the negative effects of undermatching become particularly strong for older individuals who were continuing-generation students, in terms of income and feelings of satisfaction with their income, while older workers who undermatched and were first-generation students expressed distinctly lower levels of satisfaction with their overall work conditions.

Our fourth and final main finding points to the mechanisms that may explain these results. Given the consistent negative long-term consequences of undermatching, our findings do not lend support for notions of social misalignment. The social misalignment perspective centres on the mismatch among individuals from lower socioeconomic backgrounds that may lead to positive psychological outcomes being associated with undermatching (particularly among first-generation students) due to greater access to positive experiences during college and, subsequently, once in the labour market (Jury et al., 2017). To the contrary, the negative effects of undermatching were most prominent among first-generation students, which provides empirical support for the academic misalignment perspective and the peer effects perspective. Academic misalignment between and an institution and a student's capacity – as in the case of undermatching – appears to diminish satisfaction in areas of one's career. This finding supports those of Muskens et al. (2019) that were based on students during their final year of college. What's more, to the extent that work-related earnings signal differences in returns for human capital, the peer effects perspective provides explanation for the negative income effects of undermatching: if individuals who attended less selective colleges developed less human capital as a function of their institutional environment, then one would expect that enrolling in an undermatched institution may affect labour market outcomes like earnings.

Altogether, evidence clearly points to lasting negative consequences of undermatching in college. Given the lack of prior research focused on the long-term outcomes associated with college, we have contributed new empirical support for initiatives aimed at encouraging students to take advantage of being admissible to more selective higher education institutions. Put simply, matching in more selective institutions is associated with lasting positive consequence, particularly for first-generation students, and our study suggests that this relationship may be causal.

Importantly, our findings also raise some important questions regarding the long-term processes connecting higher education track and work-related outcomes and it is important to keep in mind that the PSM approach we employed, while effective at removing preexisting differences across a host of observed precollege characteristics, does not remove the potential that unobserved characteristics (e.g., preference for living close to parents, career ambition) continued to confound our results. Because it is not possible to remove selection bias caused by unobserved covariates in the absence of random assignment, we cannot rule out that our results may be partly biased by pre-existing differences between matched and undermatched students.

## 7 Implications

Ultimately, our results have implications for higher education policy by providing new empirical evidence that the higher education system may strengthen social stratification if the educational environments within selective institutions are not sufficiently inclusive for first-generation students (or, more generally, students from lower SES backgrounds). It is important to consider the practice-based strategies higher education institutions can implement to counteract these processes.

Researchers and practitioners have, for decades, experimented with new programs and policies to support higher education access and success among students from underrepresented or under resourced populations. Examples of such studies are many and too vast to cover in this chapter; for further reading on this important body of scholarship, see Bettinger and Baker (2014); Lohfink and Paulsen (2005); Wolniak, Mayhew, and Engberg (2012); Kim and Sax (2009); Fischer (2007); Harper and Hurtado (2007); Hurtado (2005); Noble, Flynn, Lee, and Hilton (2007); Scrivener, Weiss, Ratledge, Rudd, Sommo, and Fresques (2015).

On the whole, the literature points to the complex reality that no single intervention strategy will lead to meaningful and long-term improvements. Instead, multi-faceted strategies should be employed that: (1) Start early, by building college knowledge about academics and the long-term benefits associated with a high-quality college education; (2) Offer transitional support to reduce the obstacles first-generation and students from lower SES backgrounds face in acclimating to a new – particularly selective – institutional environment; and (3) Deliver sustained support centred on exposing students to academic and social integration programs, specialized learning communities, and diversity initiatives.

Furthermore, to assist in the college decision-making process, counsellors that advise and inform students during the transition from high school to higher education should be aware of the kind of evidence we have presented here, specifically that undermatching is not beneficial for low-SES students in the long run. Armed with this information, counsellors may be able to provide more informed support to help students make careful trade-offs between the advantages of undermatching (e.g., staying closer to home and friends) and the advantages of matching (e.g., higher wages and more work satisfaction on the longer term).

### References

Alon, S., & Tienda, M. (2005). Assessing the mismatch hypothesis: Differences in college graduation rates by institutional selectivity. *Sociology of Education, 78*(4), 294–315.

Bastedo, M. N., & Flaster, A. (2014). Conceptual and methodological problems in research on college undermatch. *Educational Researcher, 43*(2), 93–99.

Bastedo, M. N., & Jaquette, O. (2011). Running in place: Low-income students and the dynamics of higher education stratification. *Educational Evaluation and Policy Analysis, 33*(3), 318–339.

Belasco, A. S., & Trivette, M. J. (2015). Aiming low: Estimating the scope and predictors of undermatch. *Journal of Higher Education, 86*(2), 233–263.

Bettinger, E. P., & Baker, R. (2014). The effects of student coaching an evaluation of a randomized experiment in student advising. *Educational Evaluation and Policy Analysis, 36*(1), 3–19.

Black, S. E., Cortes, K. E., & Lincove, J. A. (2015). *Apply yourself: Racial and ethnic differences in college application* (Working Paper No. 21368). National Bureau of Economic Research. Retrieved from http://www.nber.org/papers/w21368

Carrell, S. E., Fullerton, R. L., & West, J. E. (2009). Does your Cohort Matter? Measuring Peer effects in college achievement. *Journal of Labor Economics, 27*(3), 439–464.

Deutschlander, D. (2017). Academic undermatch: How general and specific cultural capital structure inequality. *Sociological Forum, 32*(1), 162–185.

Fischer, M. J. (2007). Settling into campus life: Differences by race/ethnicity in college involvement and outcomes. *Journal of Higher Education, 78*(2), 125–161.

Grunwald, H. E., & Mayhew, M. J. (2008). Using propensity scores for estimating causal effects: A study in the development of moral reasoning. *Research in Higher Education, 49*(8), 758–775.

Harper, S. R., & Hurtado, S. (2007). Nine themes in campus racial climates and implications for institutional transformation. In S. R. Harper & L. D. Patton (Eds.), *Responding to the realities of race on campus* (New Directions for Student Services, No. 120, pp. 7–24). Jossey-Bass.

Hoxby, C. M., & Avery, C. (2013). *The missing "one-offs": The hidden supply of high-achieving, low income students.* Brookings Papers on Economic Activity.

Hoxby, C. M., & Turner, S. (2013). *Expanding college opportunities for high achieving, low income students* (SIEPR 12-014). Stanford Institute for Economic Policy Research.

Hurtado, S. (2005). The next generation of diversity and intergroup relations research. *Journal of Social Issues, 61*, 595–610.

Iacus, S. M., King, G., & Porro, G. (2009). CEM: Software for coarsened exact matching. *Journal of Statistical Software, 30*, 1–27.

Jury, M., Smeding, A., Stephens, N. M., Nelson, J. E., Aelenei, C., & Darnon, C. (2017). The experience of low-SES students in higher education: Psychological barriers to success and interventions to reduce social-class inequality. *Journal of Social Issues, 73*(1), 23–41.

Kim, Y. K., & Sax, L. J. (2009). Student-faculty interaction in research universities: Differences by student gender, race, social class, and first-generation status. *Research in Higher Education, 50*, 437–459.

Liu, X., & Borden, V. (2019). Addressing self-selection and endogeneity in higher education research. *Theory and Method in Higher Education Research, 5*, 129–151.

Lohfink, M. M., & Paulsen, M. B. (2005). Comparing the determinants of persistence for first-generation and continuing-generation students. *Journal of College Student Development, 46*(4), 409–428.

Manski, C. F. (1993). Identification of endogenous social effects: The reflection problem. *Review of Economic Studies, 60*, 531–542.

Mayhew, M. J., Rockenbach, A. B., Bowman, N. A., Seifert, T. A., & Wolniak, G. C. (2016). *How college affects students: 21st Century evidence that higher education works.* Jossey-Bass.

Miller, G. E., Yu, T., Chen, E., & Brody, G. H. (2015). Self-control forecasts better psychosocial outcomes but faster epigenetic aging in low-SES youth. *Proceedings of the National Academy of Sciences, 112*(33), 10325–10330.

Muskens, M., Frankenhuis, W. E., & Borghans, L. (2019). Low-income students in higher education: Undermatching predicts decreased satisfaction towards the final stage in college. *Journal of Youth and Adolescence, 48*(7), 1296–1310.

Noble, K., Flynn, N. T., Lee, J. D., & Hilton, D. (2007). Predicting successful college experiences: Evidence from a first year retention program. *Journal of College Student Retention: Research, Theory and Practice, 9*(1), 39–60.

Ovink, S., Kalogrides, D., Nanney, M., & Delaney, P. (2018). College match and undermatch: Assessing student preferences, college proximity, and inequality in postcollege outcomes. *Research in Higher Education, 59*(5), 553–590.

Raudenbush, S. W., & Bryk, A. S. (2002). *Hierarchical linear models: Applications and data analysis methods.* Sage Publications.

Roksa, J., & Deutschlander, D. (2018). Applying to college: The role of family resources in academic undermatch. *Teachers College Record, 120*(6), 1–30.

Rosenbaum, P. R., & Rubin, D. B. (1983). The central role of the propensity score in observational studies for causal effects. *Biometrika, 70*(1), 41–55.

Sacerdote, B. (2001). Peer effects with random assignment: Results for Dartmouth roommates. *Quarterly Journal of Economics, 116*(2), 681–704.

Scrivener, S., Weiss, M.J., Ratledge, A., Rudd, T., Sommo, C., & Fresques, H. (2015). *Doubling graduation rates: three-year effects of CUNY's Accelerated Study in Associate Programs (ASAP) for developmental education students.* MDRC.

Smith, J., Pender, M., & Howell, J. (2013). The full extent of student-college academic undermatch. *Economics of Education Review, 32*, 247–261.

Stephens, N. M., Townsend, S. S., & Dittmann, A. G. (2019). Social-class disparities in higher education and professional workplaces: The role of cultural mismatch. *Current Directions in Psychological Science, 28*(1), 67–73.

Thoemmes, F. J., & Kim, E. S. (2011). A systematic review of propensity score methods in the social sciences. *Multivariate Behavioral Research, 46*(1), 90–118.

Tiboris, M. (2014). What's wrong with undermatching? *Journal of Philosophy of Education, 48*(4), 646–664.

Wickrama, K. A. S., O'Neal, C. W., & Lee, T. K. (2016). The health impact of upward mobility: Does socioeconomic attainment make youth more vulnerable to stressful circumstances? *Journal of Youth and Adolescence, 45*(2), 271–285.

Wolniak, G. C., & Ballerini, V. (2019). Peer effects, higher education. In P. Teixeira & J. Shin (Eds.), *Encyclopedia of international higher education systems and institutions.* Springer. https://doi.org/10.1007/978-94-017-9553-1_84-1

Wolniak, G. C., Mayhew, M. J., & Engberg, M. E. (2012). Learning's weak link to persistence. *Journal of Higher Education, 83*(6), 795–823.

Wolniak, G. C., & Muskens, M (2019, April). *Undermatching and affective development during the first year of college: A longitudinal study of college students in the Netherlands.* Presented at the Annual Meeting the American Education Research Association, Toronto, Ontario.

Yoshioka, M. R., & Noguchi, E. (2009). The developmental life course perspective: A conceptual and organizing framework for human behavior and the social environment. *Journal of Human Behavior in the Social Environment, 19*(7), 873–884.

CHAPTER 4

# Between Trust and Strategic Behavior of Academic (Middle) Leaders in Higher Education: The Levels of Strategy

*Ton Kallenberg*

### Abstract

This exploratory study is part of a larger inquiry that investigates the roles and practices of academic leaders in Higher Education. This chapter explores the relationship between trust, strategic behavior of academic (middle) leaders, and their ambition to achieve personal, organizational or societal status within the organizational strategy. A key aspect in the functioning of academic (middle) leaders is the way they fulfill the role of broker: they 'knit together' organizational activities and mediate, negotiate and interpret connections between top and ground levels throughout the organization. In this way, they fulfill four strategic roles in a more or less intensive manner: championing, synthesizing, facilitating, implementing. In this chapter it is argued that relational and organizational based trust influences the strategic roles of academic (middle) leaders and their ambitions of strategic levels. Because academic leaders are in a pivotal position within a university, their behavior is an important factor in the difference between successful and unsuccessful strategies of universities.

### Keywords

academic leaders – strategic behavior – organizational strategy – strategy implementation – middle managers – relational based trust – competence based trust – organizational based trust

## 1 Introduction

There is a general consensus that the Higher Education area has become more global, complicated, dynamic, challenging, and uncertain (Toma, 2010; Pucciarelli & Kaplan, 2016; Strike, 2018). In this ever-more complex and competitive environment, universities act as strategic actors. This strategic behavior of universities well researched (Baldridge, 1983; Maassen & Potman, 1990; Rowley & Sherman, 2004; Whitley, 2008; Deiaco, Hughes, & McKelvey, 2012; Thoenig & Paradeise, 2018). It makes sense to assume that it is generally a specific group of officials within universities who play an important role in the development of the strategy. Of course, this includes the executive board and the top management, like deans (Gmelch, 2002). However, there are several indications that there is also a broad layer of other academic leaders that influence the strategic behavior of universities (Boyko & Jones, 2010; Bolden et al., 2009; Fumasoli & Lepori, 2011; Kallenberg, 2013).

This research focusses on the strategic behavior of one specific group within universities, namely the academic leaders. The vast majority of the academic leaders at universities can be referred to as academic middle managers[1] (Hellawell & Hancock, 2001; Kallenberg, 2013). These managers are in a crucial position within the organization with the ability to make or break strategies (Wooldridge, Schmid, & Floyd, 2008; Rouleau & Balogun, 2011). These academic (middle) leaders work at the interface between administration, academics and university leadership (Milburn, 2010; Whitchurch, 2008, 2018; Mcfarlane, 2011). In addition, they work within both the academic and administrative rhythms, timescales and staff, and between the organizational structure of checks and balances (Kallenberg, 2016). In their position they can neither been seen as part of the administrators nor do they belong to the academic staff (Klumpp & Teichler, 2008; Schneijderberg & Merkator, 2013). Thanks to their position, they have a number of possibilities, which allows them to exhibit strategic behavior that plays an important role in the difference between successful and unsuccessful strategies of the university (Kallenberg, 2007, 2013, 2019; Huy, 2011; Giangreco & Peccei, 2005; Wooldridge et al., 2008).

A good 'fit' between the organizational strategy and the strategic behavior of academic leaders (convergent behavior), serves the organization and the employee (Robinson & Pearce, 1988; Meyer & Herscovitch, 2001). However, in practice, this 'fit' is not self-evident, because academic leaders not only strive for the goals at organizational level and show convergent behavior. They also strive for other levels, namely their personal or societal levels that can be seen as divergent behavior with regard to the organizational strategy. Several scholars concluded that behavior of employees within organizations is more convergent, as there is more trust in each other's views and work (Ellonen et al., 2008; Zhang et al., 2008). Therefore trust is an important factor and is the basis for strong outcomes and high achievements of the organization.

Because of the position of academic leaders within the organization, the trust factor is possibly the largestinfluence on (the nature of) their strategic behavior. Academic leaders appear to be not just passive recipients, but active interpreters, mediators, and intermediaries in implementing strategic change (Balogun & Johnson, 2004). Kallenberg (2013) argued that academic leaders mediate, negotiate, and interpret connections between the universities institutional (strategic) and technical (operational) environments. The expectation in this research is that the extent to which they experience trust within and inside the organization therefore will have an influence on their strategic behavior.

This chapter is an exploratory study in the relationship between trust; strategic behavior of academic leaders; and their ambition to achieve personal, organizational or societal strategic levels. Specifically, the chapter aims to address the following questions: What kind of trust is dominant for academic leaders? How do academic leaders perceive their own strategic roles? Which level of strategy motivates the strategic behavior of academic leaders (personal, organizational, societal)? Moreover, as a central question: To which extent does the trust factor influence strategic behavior of academic leaders?

In the following sections answers to these questions will be given. The second section addresses a theoretical review of relevant literature about the three constructs (trust, strategic behavior, and strategic levels). The third section addresses the methodology and the analytical framework, and the fourth and the fifth sections present the results and the discussion and conclusions.

## 2 Concepts of Trust, Strategic Behavior and Levels of Strategy

### 2.1 *Trust*

Trust and trust relationship have been a topic of research in many disciplines for many years. There are many definitions of trust, most of which conceptualize it as a state, belief of positive expectation (McAllister, 1995; McEvily & Tortoriello, 2011; Oomsels & Bouckaert, 2014). Trust is an essential and important precondition and ingredient for friendships in social life, and for successful cooperation and effectiveness in organizations (Das & Teng, 2001). It is a conscious, interpersonal, voluntary and situational process to which two (or more) parties are committed. The process is dynamic, action oriented and non linear. It is the oil in the engine of bargaining and negotiations between organizations, economic transactions, politics and even international conflicts (Paliszkiewicz, 2011; Vlaar, Van den Bosch, & Volberda, 2007).

In this research we define trust as the belief that another party will act in such a way that it is beneficial to the trusting actor; will act reliable, and

THE LEVELS OF STRATEGY 77

will behave correspond in a predictable and mutual acceptable manner (Paliszkiewicz, Koohang, & Nord, 2014).

Trust is interpreted from the perspective of the relation between people (*relational based trust*) and in, or between, organizations (*organizational based trust*).

*Relational based trust* is the result of repeated interaction between partners in which mutually positive experiences have been gained over time, and are based on a partner's competence (i.e., technical skills, experience, and reliability) and integrity (i.e., motives, honesty, responsibility, and character) and lead to commitment and mutual interest in each other (Langfield-Smith, 2008; Palieszkiewicz, 2011; Connelly et al., 2015).

*Organizational based trust*, is based on the extent to which an individual relies on the organization's direction, result, processes, and relationships. There must be clarity about the direction (where do we go as an organization or as a team? (Topics of vision, mission, strategy and objectives); on the outcome (what performance is expected of the employees? What do we expect from each other?); about the processes (how are we going to do it?); and about the relationships (is there attention and time for the employees?). Organizational based trust includes employee loyalty, commitment and cooperative, or convergent, behavior (Aryee, Budhwar, & Chen, 2002). As there is more trust within the organization, this contributes to an open communication, healthy work relations, work pleasure and commitment of employees within the organization (Eisenberger & Stinglhamber, 2011).

It is not straightforward to securetrust between people or organizations. Similarly, in some cases or situations, such as politics (Bauer & Fatke, 2014) or psychological (Mayo, Alfasi, & Schwarz, 2014) distrust may be useful. However, especially with relational and organizational based trust, there are signals that – if there's not enough trust – an individual will have to spend more time and energy to supervise others' behavior so as to protect his own interests (Bromiley & Cummings, 1996) and also toward more strategic behavior of employees (Zoogah, 2016).

### 2.2    *Strategic Behavior of Academic (Middle) Leaders*

The academic (middle) leaders' position and the manner in which they carry out the functions of their position – the role that they play – offers them the opportunity to exert significant influence on strategic processes within the university (Kallenberg, 2015). They are part of various information flows, streaming in different directions: top-down, bottom-up, horizontal and diagonal. They are able to connect the academic and administrative domains, and they are quite close to the operational level as well as to the strategic level of the university.

This position offers them the possibility to act in a strategic way. Strategic behavior in this research is defined as: behavior that serves the interests of the actor, it is intentional (aware of the eventual negative effects for other actors), and it is camouflage-based (other actors are not allowed to see what the actor does and has in mind) (Ten Heuvelhof, 2016).

In recent years, research into the (strategic) behavior of academic leaders in universities has received more attention (i.e. Floyd, 2016; Harboe, 2013; Kallenberg, 2013, 2015, 2016; Davis et al., 2014; Preymann et al., 2015; Karlsson & Ryttberg, 2016; Marini & Reale, 2015). Several of those scholars made use of the insights of a well-known typology of strategic roles of middle managers which was described by Floyd & Wooldridge (1992, 1994, 1996, 1997) for – especially – the profit sector. Because of its proven usefulness, this typology is used in this research too.

Floyd and Wooldridge (1997) point out that middle managers take part in two types of activities. The first consists of behavioral activities (*upward* and *downward*), which depend on which directions middle managers influence organizational members. The second consists of cognitive abilities (*integrative* and *divergent*), which depend on how middle managers' activities are with the 'official' policy and strategy of the organization. Floyd & Wooldridge developed a typology of four strategic roles of middle management: championing, synthesizing, facilitating and implementing. Playing one of these strategic roles does not exclude the possibility of also playing another role. In fact, the authors believe that through time there is an optimal dynamic of strategic roles, which allows middle managers to develop improvements for themselves and for their organizations. In addition, there is a set of managerial skills that may lead to optimal performance in each strategic role. Middle management's strategic roles have to do with change: understanding the need for change (synthesizing), preparing for it (facilitating), stimulating it (championing), and ultimately, managing the process (implementing). Interpreted for academic leaders, these roles can be operationalized as shown in Figure 4.1.

*Championing* is how academic leaders promote strategic initiatives to their superiors and in the process diversify the universities' repertoire of capabilities. Championing is a form of upward influence that involves persuading the faculty or university board to alter existing priorities – to invest in something that shifts or widens the strategic focus. For example: starting a new masters or choosing for a new educational concept. This requires a foundation of support with others within the university; so, effective championing also involves influencing peers, subordinates, students and other stakeholders.

# THE LEVELS OF STRATEGY

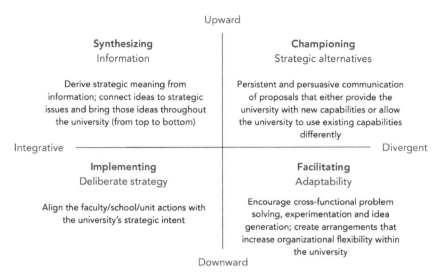

FIGURE 4.1   Strategic roles of academic leaders

*Synthesizing* is a process of giving interpreted information to the faculty or university board. The academic leader combines strategic and operational information and gives its own color through evaluation, advice and subjective interpretation (Kallenberg, 2013). Through interpretation, the academic leader influences the perception of the board and thus also the strategy (and frame it as an opportunity or threat). By doing that, – the manager keeps their gaze at the same time to the external area (new social developments, questions for renewal) as they are inward (the teacher team, which has often a demand for rest and stability).

*Facilitating* is about supporting and developing (experimental) programs and organizational arrangements that increase the flexibility of the university, stimulate organizational learning and enhance the repertoire of strategic actions. Academic leaders do this by freely sharing information and stimulating experiments and by providing sufficient resources. The resources can consist of give time in order that the scientific staff can professionalize in a new role; or search for (and find) additional funds, resources, task hours or workspace for lecturers. In addition, the facilitating role consists mainly of activities related to promote cooperation, identify and reduce barriers in the university; improve cooperation between programs or departments; and adapt processes or create a breakthrough in bottlenecks.

*Implementing* can be seen as series of interventions designed to align organizational actions with strategic intent. Implementing is based on the administrative skill of creating changes. It is a deliberate attitude, which create a change aligned with the strategic intention. Briggs (2005) refers to this role as 'making it happen'. Therefore, implementation is realizing a change; at least in the moment it is applied. Implementing deliberate strategy serves to sell faculty or university board initiatives to subordinates. This traditional role can be seen as the organizational soldier – the guards who strictly give orders based on rules – but it is during the implementation that academic leaders can really know the difficulties and realities of the environment (Kallenberg, 2013). Therefore, even in an apparently simple activity, academic leaders are prospecting realities from the future. There are academic leaders that are 'guards' who are more than simple followers of order; guards are organizational goal oriented people who use all their force to implement their psychological contract, which is aligned with the organizational plan. This is often considered to be the most important strategic role of the academic leader (Kallenberg, 2016).

An effective academic leader achieves a proper balance among the four roles and matches this to the universities strategic context. The degree, in which academic leaders play these roles, depends, beside personal strategy, also on the organizational context in which they act. This context can influence the role achievement. A certain consistency exists between the different roles. Academic leaders who can spend as much attention on all roles, will be appointed in many cases as successful, because they are skillful enough to coordinate their actions on the situation of the context. However, that is precisely what one person cannot do (Quinn & Rohrbauch, 1983). In practice, an academic leader has one or two dominant roles, but the other roles will get significant less attention. As a result, other colleagues at their level, like frontline managers, or the top management, must fulfill the other roles. In other words, when all the roles are played by top -, middle -, or frontline management, this probably contributes to good strategic processes. On the other hand, when an academic leader functions 'badly' in certain roles, this has direct its by-effects on the total strategy, when there are no colleagues who take up these roles. This can lead to issues such as stickiness in the process or even disturbances in the strategic processes. Therefore, the acting of academic leaders can be considered as necessary oil in the universities' strategy.

### 2.3 Levels of Strategy

The third concept in this chapter are *levels of strategy*. Three levels of strategy are distinguished: personal level; organizational level and societal level.

The driving force for strategic behavior on the *personal level* is determined by the answer whether the academic leader sees the subject as a personal risk or as an opportunity in achieving personal goals (basic awareness). Underneath these behaviors lie academic leaders' pre-occupations and their underlying concerns about what the process holds in stock for them personally.

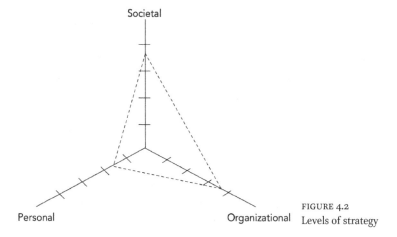

FIGURE 4.2 Levels of strategy

These personal concerns are with identity ("Do I want to be a loyal part of this new …?"), with competence ("Am I able to work in this new …?") and with stability ("Will I be still in charge for …?"). In this view, academic leaders will try to intervene in processes in order to realize something that is in line with their own interest or their own career. Conversely, this leads to behavior to stay out of the 'line of fire' with hidden agendas, evasiveness, obstruction, and looking for some pretext. For instance: While a certain innovation is to be started, and the academic leader wants to go on a holiday, (s)he tries to shift the implementation of the innovation to a later stadium in order that (s)he can go on vacation, under the guise that processes do not develop that quick and that it will not succeed.

Strategic behavior on the *organizational level* is behavior aimed at achieving the universities' goals (business awareness). This may be divergent or convergent, e.g. that an innovation is good or not good.

Strategic behavior at *societal level* is aimed at achieving socially oriented goals and ideals (global awareness).

## 3   Methodology

The findings reported in this chapter are part of a larger study that investigate the complex world and lived experience of Academic Leaders in Higher Education and how that crystallizes in certain roles and practices. In this study, the aim is to achieve an understanding of the relationship between trust, strategic behavior of academic leaders, and their aspiration to achieve personal, organizational or societal strategic levels? For that purpose, an online survey was conducted.

The online questionnaire was distributed among academic leaders of seven universities in the Netherlands during January–March 2019. This online survey was send to 840 addresses and yielded 208 respondents (24.7%). In addition to the invitation email one reminder was sent after eight days. A non-response study has not been conducted, because ...? The raw data analysis was conducted to pinpoint aspects such as normality, relationships between the research variables, missing values and outliers. This had led to the removal of several respondents for various reasons (such as incompleteness, obstruction, etc.) and resulted in a final sample population of 166 respondents for analysis. The findings do not aim at providing scientific or rational generalization, but rather seek to offer insight and provide a theoretical understanding of academic leaders' strategic roles in the Higher Education context that reflects the richness, dynamism and complexity of the data and the context, and can be useful for further investigation.

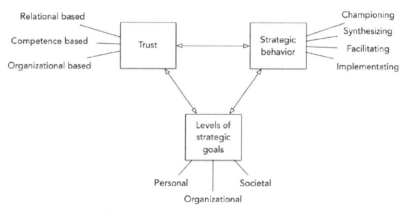

FIGURE 4.3    Framework

The questionnaire sought basic information, such as age, gender, qualifications. Furthermore respondents were asked to answer the items of two validated questionnaires, i.e. the strategic roles of middle managers (Floyd & Wooldridge, 2000) with 20 items, and relational, competence and institutional based trust (Paliszkiewicz, Koohang, & Nord, 2014) with 19 items, and additional questions about the levels of strategy. Respondents were asked how they experienced their roles, trust and levels of strategy. As this relates to their perception the reality may be different. Therefore, it is necessary to take into account that respondents may tend to respond more reddish.

The measures of all items included a 5 point Likert-type scale representing strongly agree = 5, agree = 4, neither agree nor disagree = 3, disagree = 2, and strongly disagree = 1.

THE LEVELS OF STRATEGY                                                                83

Based on what has been discussed so far, the expectation is that the extent of (relational or organizational) trust correlates with the fulfilling of certain strategic roles of academic leaders; and also that the extent of trust correlates with the motives for the levels of strategy. More explicitly, these expectations are as follows:

- the higher the relational trust, the more academic leaders will fulfill strategic roles championing and synthesizing;
- the higher relational trust, the more levels of strategy of academic leaders will be aimed at organizational goals;
- the lower relational trust, the more academic leaders will fulfill strategic roles facilitating and implementing;
- the lower the relational trust, the more the levels of strategy of academic leaders will be aimed at personal goals
- the higher the organizational trust, the more academic leaders will fulfill the strategic role 'championing'
- the higher organizational trust, the more the levels of strategy of academic leaders will be aimed at organizational and societal goals;
- the lower the organizational trust, the more academic leaders will fulfill the strategic role 'implementing';
- the lower the organizational trust, the more the levels of strategy of academic leaders will be aimed at personal goals.

## 4       Findings

The findings are based on responses obtained from 166 academic leaders. These academic leaders were mainly in positions, such as director/head of study (54), vice-deans (37), head of departments (29), academic/educational directors (31), and others (15). The features of the group consists of 51.2% male and 48.8% female respondents; their average age is 49 years old, and they are all academics with 92% of them having a PhD. During phase two, perspectives expressed during interviews were considered from 20 academic leaders employed on four different Dutch universities. The features of this group were – more or less- equal, namely 11 male and nine female; their average age was 50 years old and they are all academics with 95% PhD.

Regarding the question trust of academic leaders, it appears that academic leaders have – on average – a great deal of trust, both in relational based trust and in organizational based trust. Organizational based trust (4.03) is even larger than relational based trust (3.49). Given the low standard deviation (.58) of organizational based trust, this is a strong fact.

TABLE 4.1 Means of trust, strategic roles and levels of strategy

| | | Implementing | Synthesizing | Facilitating | Championing | Personal | Organizational | Societal |
|---|---|---|---|---|---|---|---|---|
| Relational based trust | | | | | | 3.49 (Std 1.41) | | |
| < 3.30 | 34 | 2.95 | 4.27 | 3.76 | 3.13 | 3.36 | 3.31 | 2.95 |
| 3.31–3.59 | 56 | 2.85 | 4.14 | 3.87 | 3.57 | 3.18 | 3.33 | 2.91 |
| > 3.60 | 76 | 2.73 | 4.21 | 3.85 | 3.78 | 2.97 | 3.39 | 2.84 |
| Organizational based trust | | | | | | 4.03 (Std .58) | | |
| < 3.90 | 39 | 2.63 | 4.22 | 3.91 | 3.65 | 3.17 | 2.97 | 3.13 |
| 3.90–4.09 | 95 | 2.82 | 4.14 | 3.85 | 3.58 | 3.11 | 3.39 | 2.95 |
| > 4.10 | 32 | 3.02 | 4.31 | 3.72 | 3.46 | 3.08 | 3.67 | 2.76 |
| M | 166 | 2.81 | 4.19 | 3.84 | 3.58 | 3.12 | 3.35 | 2.89 |
| Std. | | .73 | .61 | .89 | .75 | .92 | .82 | .59 |

As regards the way in which academic leaders perceive their strategic roles it shows that they are most focused on the role synthesizing (4.19) and the least on the role implementing (2.81). The roles facilitating (3.84) and championing (3.58) move in between.

The third construct in this study is 'levels of strategy', and here we see that behavior of academic leaders is most focused on the organizational level (3.35). Personal level (3.12) and societal level (2.89) follow at reasonable distance.

The central question in this chapter is to what extent does the factor trust influence strategic behavior of academic leaders?

In order to be able to sketch a more nuanced picture of this, it was decided to divide the scores of the items relational based trust and organizational based trust into three groups. The criterion for grouping is based on the standard normal distribution. This has led to the boundaries of the groups in relational based trust and organizational based trust being different.

The scores of relational based trust and the role of championing are positive correlated ($r = .74; p = .001$). If the score of relational based trust increase, the score of the role of championing increases too. This was expected. Unlike expectation, this correlation does not appear between relational based trust and the role synthesizing ($r = .21; p = .486$). Concerning the levels of strategy, relational based trust does not lead to significant changes for organizational goals ($r = .29; p = .351$) or societal goals ($r = .18; p = .437$), whereas there is a significant negative correlation with personal goals ($r = -.68; p = .002$).

Organizational based trust correlates positive with the strategic role implementing ($r = .73; p = .001$) and correlates negative with the strategic role championing ($r = -.66; p = .003$). This negative correlation with championing is opposite to what was expected.

As far as the levels of strategy are concerned, organizational goals and organizational based trust correlate positive ($r = .81; p = .000$), as expected. But, contrary to expectations, societal goals are more strongly pursued when organizational based trust decreases ($r = -.62; p = .001$). Personal goals show no significant differences in the relationship to organizational based trust ($r = -.23; p = .129$).

As for the strategic roles of academic leaders, the implementation role is least fulfilled and there is a significant correlation with both relational based trust (more relational based trust leads to less fulfillment) ($r = -.64; p = .002$) and organizational based trust (more organizational based trust leads to more fulfillment) ($r = .73; p = .001$).

The role synthesizing is most fulfilled by academic leaders and is not significant affected by the degree of trust. Unlike implementing, the role facilitating increases as relational based trust increases (people are encouraged to think differently) ($r = .69$; $p = .000$); while the role facilitating decreases as organizational based trust increases ($r = -.73$; $p = .000$). Apparently, people are less encouraged to think differently and more in line with the organization (of course this can be influenced by the academic leader being satisfied with the daily practice).

The same goes more or less for the role championing. The more satisfied with the organization the less often an attempt is made to change the mind of the organization ($r = -.66$; $p = .003$). But if relational based trust is higher, this championing role will increase ($r = .74$; $p = .001$). Apparently there's in that situation less need or freedom to propose something new.

## 5　Discussion and Conclusions

A first cautious conclusion to be drawn on the basis of this preliminary research is that the results provide indications that trust influences strategic behavior of academic (middle) leaders. It is in line with the expectation that was put forward at the beginning of this chapter. However, the results also provide indications that it is not self-evident that if the factor trust increase it, at the same time, can be assumed that all strategic roles of academic leaders increase or decrease equally.

Trust was expected to be influenced mainly by 'upwards' or 'downwards' acting, but it appears to have a particular impact on integrative or divergent actions of the academic leader. However, in contrast to my expectations, it turns out that especially the dimension integrative versus divergent acting seems to make the difference. Higher trust (relational or organizational based) leads to integrative acting (synthesizing, implementing) and to organizational goals. Therefore, there is no combination of championing and synthesizing on the one hand, and facilitating and implementing on the other. It are especially the combinations of synthesizing and implementing (because these are aimed at integrative thinking), and facilitating and championing (because these are both aimed at divergent thinking).

Finally, because trust influences the strategic actions of academic leaders, it is also interesting to discuss its impact on the organizational strategy. After all, there is a significant body of research suggesting that middle managers make significant contributions to the universities strategy (Earley, 1998; Fenton-O'Creevy, 2000; Payaud, 2003; Torset & Tixier, 2003; Davis et al., 2014). They will come forward during formal – above all informal – meetings, to take the opportunity to advocate their personal, organizational or societal levels of strategy. They then support this with notes, memos, lobby and other internal political behavior. And they have the opportunity to do so, because universities have moved away from the traditional top-down, command-and-control model of organization, toward a more decentralized, process-centered orientation where power emanates from the middle. But precisely because that relationship exists, it is relevant – from the perspective of organizational importance – that academic leaders act as convergent as possible, as Robinson & Pearce (1988) and Meyer and Herscovitch (2001) indicated earlier. In addition, for that, both personal and organizational trust is of great importance in order to prevent academic leaders from being too inclined to pursue personal strategies. After all, as this research has indicated, there is a chance that they will strive for personal levels of strategy when relational based trust and/or organizational based trust decreases. In particular, because the university context is becoming increasingly under (external) pressure and becomes more complex, and – as a result – academic leaders are becoming increasingly faced with large bureaucratic tyranny plagued with red-tape and minute-detail reporting ending into a culture of conformance and adherence to rules (Davis et al., 2014). In order to prevent that academic leaders turn into functionaries who simply carry out the decisions of their paymasters, academic leaders should be equipped with trust and autonomy. Only then, they can operate effective on the levels of strategy. This is important because academic leaders occupy a pivotal position at the center of university, from which they fulfill an important role in the determining the difference between successful and unsuccessful strategies of universities (Kallenberg, 2007, 2013, 2019; Huy, 2011; Giangreco & Peccei, 2005; Wooldridge et al., 2008).

This exploratory study has produced several interesting results. These are the first results of a more comprehensive research into the complex world and lived experience of Academic Leaders in Higher Education The results of this study must therefore be assessed from this perspective. However, they are an invitation for more research and also show that there is room for more detailed analyses.

### Note

1  Academic (middle) managers is an umbrella-term for academics who are temporarily in a managerial role, like academic dean (Wolverton et al., 2001; Vieira da Motta & Bolan, 2008), head of study (Kallenberg & Harboe, 2014), educational director (Preston & Floyd, 2016; Branson, Franken, & Penney, 2016), manager academics (Deem & Brehony, 2005), academic manager (Mercer, 2009) or program directors, course coordinators (Ladyshewsky et al., 2007).

## References

Alshammari, A. K. (2015). The perspectives of research in educational management and role of leadership. *International Journal of Science and Research (IJSR)*, 4(6) 71–75.

Aryee, S., Budhwar, P. S., & Chen, Z. X. (2002). Trust as a mediator of the relationship between organizational justice and work outcomes: Test of a social exchange model. *Journal of Organizational Behavior, 23,* 267–285.

Avolio, B. J., Walumbwa, J., & Weber, T. J. (2009). Leadership: Current theories, research, and future directions. *Annual Review of Psychology, 60,* 421–49.

Baldridge, J. V. (1983). Strategic planning in higher education: Does the emperor have any clothes? In J. V. Baldridge & T. Deal (Eds.), *The dynamics of organizational change in education* (pp. 167–185). McCutchan.

Balogun, J., & Johnson, G. (2004). Organizational restructuring and middle manager sensemaking. *Academy of Management Journal, 47*(4), 523–549.

Bauer, P. C., & Fatke, M. (2014). Direct democracy and political trust: Enhancing trust, initiating distrust – Or both? *Swiss Political Science Review, 20*(1), 44–69. https://doi.org/10.1111/spsr.12071

Bolden, R., Petrov, G., & Gosling, J. (2009). Distributed leadership in higher education: Rhetoric and reality. *Educational Management Administration & Leadership, 37*(2), 257–277. https://doi.org/10.1177/1741143208100301

Boyko, L. M., & Jones, G. A. (2010). The roles and responsibilities of middle management (Chairs and Deans) in Canadian Universities. In V. L. Meek, L. Goedegebuure, R. Santiago, & T. Carvalho (Eds.), *The changing dynamics of higher education middle management.* Springer.

Briggs, A. R. J. (2005). Middle managers in English further education colleges. *Educational Management Administration & Leadership, 33*(1), 27–50.

Bromiley, P., & Cummings, L. (1996). Transaction costs in organizations with trust. In R. Bies, R. Lewicki, & B. Sheppard (Eds.), *Research on negotiation in organizations* (pp. 219–247). JAI.

Connelly, B. L., Crook, T. R., Combs, J. G., Ketchen Jr., D. J., & Aguinis, H. (2015). Competence- and integrity-based trust in interorganizational relationships: Which matters more? *Journal of Management, 44*(3), 919–945. https://doi.org/10.1177/0149206315596813

Das, T. K., & Teng, B. S. (2001). Trust, control, and risk in strategic alliances: An integrated framework. *Organization studies, 22*(2), 251–283. https://doi.org/10.1177%2F0170840601222004

Davis, A., Jansen van Rensburg, M., & Venter, P. (2014). The impact of managerialism on the strategy work of university middle managers. *Studies in Higher Education,* 1480–1494. https://doi.org/10.1080/03075079.2014.981518

Deiaco, E., Hughes, A., & McKelvey, M. (2012). Universities as strategic actors in the knowledge economy. *Cambridge Journal of Economics, 36*(3), 525–541. https://doi.org/10.1093/cje/bes024

Eisenberger, R., & Stinglhamber, F. (2011). *Perceived organizational support: Fostering enthusiastic and productive employees.* American Psychological Association. https://doi.org/10.1037/12318-000

Ellonen, R., Blomqvist, K., & Puumalainen, K. (2008). The role of trust in organizational effectiveness. *European Journal of Innovation Management, 11*(2), 162.

Floyd, A. (2016). Supporting academic middle managers in higher education: Do we care? *Higher Education Policy, 29*(2), 167–183.

Floyd, S. W., & Wooldridge, B. (1992). Middle management involvement in strategy and its association with strategic type: A research note. *Strategic Management Journal, 13*, 153–167.

Floyd, S. W., & Wooldridge, B. (1996). *The strategic middle manager: How to create and sustain competitive advantage.* Jossey-Bass.

Floyd, S. W., & Wooldridge, B. (1997). Middle management's strategic influence and organizational performance. *Journal of Management Studies, 34*, 465–485.

Floyd, S. W., & Wooldridge, B. (2000). *Building strategy from the middle: Reconceptualizing strategy process.* Sage.

Fumasoli, T., & Lepori, B. (2011). Pattern of strategies in Swiss higher education institutions. *Higher Education, 61*, 157–178. doi:10.1007/s10734-010-9330-x

Giangreco, A., & Peccei, R. (2005). The nature and antecedents of middle manager resistance to change: Evidence from an Italian context. *The International Journal of Human Resource Management, 16*(10), 1812–1829.

Gmelch, W. H. (2002). *Deans' balancing acts: Education leaders and the challenges they face.* AACTE Publishers. Retrieved from http://files.eric.ed.gov/fulltext/ED481388.pdf

Harboe, T. (2013). *Subtil ledelse I en ny og mere insisterende form – et kvalitativt studie af studieledere ved danske universiteter* [*Subtle leadership in a new and more persistent form – A qualitative study of Heads of Study at Danish universities*] (Dissertation). University of Southern Denmark.

Hellawell, D., & Hancock, N. (2001). A case study of the changing role of the academic middle manager in higher education: Between hierarchical control and collegiality? *Research Papers in Education, 16*(2), 183–197.

Huy, Q. (2011). How middle managers' group-focus emotions and organizational social identities influence strategy implementation. *Strategic Management Journal, 32*(13), 1387–1410. http://dx.doi.org/10.1002/smj.961

Kallenberg, T. (2007). Strategy innovation in higher education: The roles of academic middle managers. *Tertiary Education Management, 13*(1), 19–33.

Kallenberg, T. (2013). *Prisma van de verandering? De rollen van academische midden-managers bij strategische innovaties in het hoger onderwijs* [*Prism of change? The roles of academic middle managers during strategic innovations in higher education*]. Boom/Lemma.

Kallenberg, T. (2015). Academic middle managers shaping the landscape between policy and practice. In R. M. O. Pritchard, M. Klumpp, & U. Teichler (Eds.), *Diversity and excellence in higher education. Can the challenges be reconciled?* (pp. 201–216). Sense Publishers.

Kallenberg, T. (2016). Interacting spheres revisited. Academics and administrators between dualism and cooperation. In R. Pritchard, A. Pausits, & J. Williams (Eds.), *From here to there: Positioning higher education institutions* (pp. 177–198). Sense.

Kallenberg, T. (2019). Shadows of hierarchy: Managerial-administrative relationships under pressure. In P. Teixeira, A. Magalhães, M. J. Rosa, & A. Veiga (Eds.), *Under pressure? Higher education institutions coping with multiple challenges*. Brill Sense. doi:10.1163/9789004398481_006

Karlsson, S., & Ryttberg, M. (2016). Those who walk the talk: The role of administrative professionals in transforming universities into strategic actors. *Nordic Journal of Studies in Educational Policy, 2016*(2–3). http://dx.doi.org/10.3402/nstep.v2.31537

Klumpp, M., & Teichler, U. (2008). Experten für das Hochschulsystem: Hochschulprofessionen zwischen Wissenschaft und Administration. In B. M. Lehm, E. Mayer, & U. Tiegel (Eds.), *Hochschulen in neuer Verantwortung. Strategisch, überlastet, divers?* (pp. 169–171). Klemens.

Langfield-Smith, K. (2008). The relations between transactional characteristics, trust and risk in the start-up phase of a collaborative alliance. *Management Accounting Research, 19*(4), 344–364. https://doi.org/10.1016/j.mar.2008.09.001

Maassen, P. A. M., & Potman, H. P. (1990). Strategic decision making in higher education. An analysis of the new planning system in Dutch higher education. *Higher Education, 20*(4), 393–410.

Marini, G., & Reale, E. (2016). How does collegiality survive managerially led universities? Evidence from a European survey. *European Journal of Higher Education, 6*(2). 111–127. http://dx.doi.org/10.1080/21568235.2015.1070676

Mayo, R., Alfasi, D., & Schwarz, N. (2014). Distrust and the positive test heuristic: Dispositional and situated social distrust improves performance on the Wason rule discovery task. *Journal of Experimental Psychology: General, 143*(3), 985–990. https://doi.org/10.1037/a0035127

McAllister, D. J. (1995). Affect-and cognition based trust as foundations for interpersonal cooperation in organizations. *Academy of Management Journal, 38*(1), 24–59. https://doi.org/10.5465/256727

McEvily, B., & Tortoriello, M. (2011). Measuring trust in organisational research: Review and recommendations. *Journal of Trust Research, 1*(1), 23–63. https://doi.org/10.1080/21515581.2011.552424

Mcfarlane, B. (2011). The morphing of academic practice: Unbundling and the rise of the para-academic. *Higher Education Quarterly, 65*(1), 57–73.

Meyer, J. P., & Herscovitch, L. (2001). Commitment in the workplace: Toward a general model. *Human Resource Management Review, 11*, 299–326.

Milburn, P. C. (2010). The role of programme directors as academic leaders. *Active Learning in Higher Education, 11*(2), 87–95. https://doi.org/10.1177/1469787410365653

Ng, T. W. H. (2015). The incremental validity of organizational commitment, organizational trust, and organizational identification. *Journal of Vocational Behavior, 88*(6), 154–163. https://doi.org/10.1016/j.jvb.2015.03.003

Oomsels, P., & Bouckaert, G. (2014). Studying interorganizational trust in public administration: A conceptual and analytical framework for administrational trust. *Public Performance & Management Review, 37*(4), 577–604.

Paliszkiewicz, J. (2011). Trust management: Literature review. *Management, 6*(4), 315–331.

Paliszkiewicz, J., Koohang, A., & Nord, J. H. (2014). Management trust, organizational trust, and organizational performance: Empiral validation of an instrument. *Online Journal of Applied Knowledge Management, 2*(1), 28–39.

Preymann, S., Ehrenstorfer, B., Sterrer, S., & Aichinger, R. (2015, August 30–September 2). *Illusion or reality? Academics and administrative middle-level managers in the same boat.* Paper presented at the EAIR 37th Annual Forum "From here to there: Positioning Higher Education Institutions", Danube University, Krems, Austria.

Pucciarelli, F., & Kaplan, A. (2016). Competition and strategy in higher education: Managing complexity and uncertainty. *Business Horizons, 59*(3), 311–320. https://doi.org/10.1016/j.bushor.2016.01.003

Quinn, R. E., & Rohrbauch, J. (1983). A spatial model of effectiveness criteria: Towards a competing values approach to organizational analysis. *Management Science, 29*(3), 363–377.

Robinson, R. B., & Pearce, J. A. (1988). Planned patterns of strategic behavior and their relationship to business-unit performance. *Strategic Management Journal, 9*, 43–60.

Rouleau, L., & Balogun, J. (2011). Middle managers, strategic sensemaking, and discursive competence. Journal of Management Studies, 48(5). 953–983. http://dx.doi.org/10.1111/j.1467-6486.2010.00941.x

Rowley, D. J., & Sherman, H. (2004). *From strategy to change: Implementing the plan in higher education.* Jossey-Bass.

Scheijderberg, C., & Merkator, N. (2013). The new higher education professionals. In B. Kehm & U. Teichler (Eds.), *The academic profession in Europe: New tasks and new challenges.* Springer.

Smith, J. A., Flowers, P., & Larkin, M. (2009). *Interpretative phenomenological analysis: Theory, method and research.* Sage.

Strike, T. (Ed.). (2018). *Higher education strategy and planning.* Routledge.

Ten Heuvelhof, E. (2016). *Strategisch Gedrag in Netwerken. Wat het is, hoe we het ontwikkelen, wat we ervan moeten vinden*. Boom.

Thoenig, J. C., & Paradeise, C. (2018). Higher education institutions as strategic actors. *European Review, 26*(1), 57–69.

Toma, J. D. (2010). *Building organizational capacity: Strategic management in higher education*. The John Hopkins University Press.

Vlaar, P. W. L., van den Bosch, F. A. J., & Volberda, H. W. (2007). On the evolution of trust, distrust, and formal coordination and control in interorganizational relationships: Towards an integrative framework. *Group and Organization Management, 32*(4), 407–428. doi:10.1177/1059601106294215

Whitchurch, C. (2008). Shifting identities and blurring boundaries: The emergence of third space professionals in UK higher education. *Higher Education Quarterly, 62*(4), 377–396.

Whitchurch, C. (2018). Being a higher education professional today. working in third space. In E. C. Bossu & N. Brown (Eds.), *University development and administration. Professional and support staff in higher education*. Springer.

Whitley, R. (2008, November 1–3). *Universities as strategic actors: Limitations and variations*. Paper presented at the Conference "The university in the market", Stockholm, Wenner-Gren Center. Retrieved from http://hdl.handle.net/10419/50654

Wooldridge, B., Schmid, T., & Floyd, S. W. (2008). The middle management perspective on strategy process: Contributions, synthesis, and future research. *Journal of Management, 34*(6), 1190–1221. http://dx.doi.org/10.1177/0149206308324326

Zhang, A. Y., Tsui, A. S., Song, L. J., Chaoping, L., & Jia, L. (2008). How do I trust thee? The employee-organization relationship: Supervisory support and middle manager trust in the organization. *Human Resource Management, 47*(1), 111–132.

Zoogah, D. B. (2014). *Strategic followership: How Follers impact organizational effectiveness*. Palgrave MacMillan.

CHAPTER 5

# Politicians and Bureaucrats in a Humboldt Type System: The Case of Italy

*Alfredo Marra and Roberto Moscati*

### Abstract

The chapter deals with the rapid increase of administrative activities in the Italian higher education system as well as in its individual university with relevant consequences on the level of bureaucratization of the academic life. The Italian system of higher education – traditionally belonging to the Humboldtian model – is characterized by an unstable but substantial role of the state. In recent decades the degree of autonomy granted to the universities went up and down while the increasing amount of rules produced more bureaucracy. The introduction of the assessment policy enacted through the Agency for Quality Assurance (ANVUR) contributed to a growing amount of rules and regulation. At the same time, the juridification of the assessment processes demonstrated the confusion between the administrative/technical rules and the political will in controlling the universities' autonomy. Meanwhile, the attempt to create a structure of governance at the level of individual university more suited with the competition among universities produced resistances from the traditional representation of scientific areas, while the growing relevance of the internal administration gave rise to a higher level of bureaucratization.

### Keywords

Italian higher education system – state bureaucracy – university autonomy – globalization – quality assurance

## 1 Introduction

One of the results of the ongoing developments in higher education systems and their social and political relevance is a rapid increase in administrative activities both within individual universities and entire systems, which

© KONINKLIJKE BRILL NV, LEIDEN, 2020 | DOI: 10.1163/9789004436558_006

has important consequences on the level of bureaucratization of academic life.

This chapter describes the phenomenon as it emerges in the Italian higher education system, which belongs to the Humboldtian model, like many others in continental Europe. The first section underscores the differences between continental European and Anglo-Saxon models and illustrates how the globalization process and development of the New Public Management approach to public administration services have whittled down these differences. The second section concentrates on the impact of this process on the Italian system, where the role of the state is substantial, but unstable. In recent decades, for example, the degree of autonomy granted to the universities has both risen and fallen, while the upsurge in rules has produced more bureaucracy. The introduction of the assessment policy via the Agency for Quality Assurance (ANVUR) has revealed the Ministry's incapacity to govern at a distance despite the ever-increasing amount of rules and regulations. In the third section the focus is on the attempt to create a structure of governance in individual universities which is more geared towards competition among the various seats. Resistance to this move has come from the traditional representatives of scientific area interests while the growing relevance of individual administrations has produced a higher level of bureaucratization.

The concluding remarks underline the absence at system level of a clear and stable political vision, so preventing the development of a coherent policy in line with the basic needs of the country today.

## 2 Recent Trends in Higher Education Systems

In order to offer some considerations on the impact bureaucracy and politics have had and continue to have on higher education systems, we always need to keep in mind the basic features which have made these systems different right from the start.

In the modern period, where the nation-state is the external power universities relate to, a continental European model can be identified in which the nation-state has become the crucial partner for universities, a result of the reforms introduced by the Napoleonic system and Humboldt's German model. Running side by side is an Anglo-Saxon model (both in Great Britain and the United States), where the state's role was initially negligible, given the private origins of the universities and their desire to remain autonomous. Indeed, in Anglo-Saxon countries, the interests of the community were not originally identified in the concept of nation-state, but in that of property individualism. From here, therefore, a different definition of community conceived in economic terms and linked to property, meaning literally common wealth (Neave, 2002, 2012). But now, however, in controlling the quality of the services offered, the state has recently begun to pull more weight in Anglo-Saxon higher education, too.

For its part, the European model has brought about the transfer of universities into the legal property of the state in order to ensure the priority of national interests, and construct around them a regulated area defined and protected by the law. The model of state control with these features was founded on the continent on the principle of 'legal homogeneity'. This centralizing logic, dear to nation-states, was developed back in the times of the 1789 French Revolution.

In this context, the relation between state and academic autonomy has taken on diverse features in response to diverse ends. The logic behind autonomy was to protect the world of training from the pressures of vested interests and inherited privileges, in the name of the universality of science and knowledge and the value of competence. This was how Wilhelm von Humboldt perceived it, back in the first half of the nineteenth century. However, the states, centralistic as they were, did not want to give up any form of control over the workings of the training system and translated this desire for control into a homogeneous structuring of teaching programs and protection of the teaching staff by making them state employees or public officials (Napoleonic style).

The traditional differences between the two models have been modified over time with the more general processes of globalization and the different relevance acquired by knowledge in society today. There are many definitions of the concept of globalization, which are at times at odds with one another. Most particularly, two definitions stand at opposition – one postulating convergence, the other divergence.

> The first emphasizes the progressive and sometime ineluctable trend toward homogenization (cultural, political, and economic). It is founded on a linear, top-down, deterministic causal explanation. The latter emphasizes the heterogeneity of globalization's effects and outcomes on the local level (national, regional and even organizational). That entails a greater prominence accorded to a bottom-up process of manipulation, localization, interpretation, mediation resistance and so on. Thus the kind of explanation is non-linear, non-deterministic, conflictual and, sometimes, voluntarist. (Vaira, 2004, p. 484)

The debate on globalization has inevitably involved higher education, given the series of new tasks attributed to universities on social, political and economic places. Tasks that have deeply affected the traditional models of internal organization, values and the whole of academic life. In brief, it can be stated that for some time now higher education has been undergoing a profound process of institutional change – characterized by resistance, conflict, tensions and attempts at adaptation, including the de-institutionalization of policies and relative values, and at the same time the institutionalization of new policies and reference values. (Clark, 1998; Delanty, 2001; Gumport, 2000).

On a theoretic level, three ways of interpreting this process of change have attempted to analyze the transformations in the diverse systems of higher education by means of three narratives reforming public services: New Public Management, Network Governance and the Neo-Weberian narrative (Ferlie, Musselin, & Andresani, 2008, p. 334). *New Public Management* (NPM) relies on (1) markets (or quasi such) rather than planning, (2) strong performance measurement, monitoring and management systems, with a growth of audit systems rather than tacit or self-regulation sectors, and (3) empowered and entrepreneurial management rather than collegial public-sector professionals and administrators (Andresani & Ferlie, 2005). Its aim is to produce a smaller, more efficient and more results-oriented public sector. *Network Governance* emerged through the concept of multi-level 'governance' allowing:

> more balance among the involved actors, more deliberative democracy and, consequently, the co-production of public policies among more numerous, more diverse and more equal actors [... consequently], a greater range of actors and interactions emerges, and the central state plays more of an influencing and less of a directing role. There is a shift from vertical to lateral forms of management [...] knowledge and 'best practice' spread across the network, based on high-trust repeated interactions and a 'clannish' culture. (Ferlie et al., 2005, p. 337)

*The Neo-Weberian narrative* "may be seen as an operationalising of the principles of democratic revitalization within public management reform" (Ferlie et al., 2005, p. 338), which represents the use for the higher education systems of some principles Weber introduced as for states applying the rule of law. These principles included the state steering the higher education sector but developing an external orientation in meeting citizens' needs; encouraging results achievement more the correct application of rules and regulations; shifting from ex ante to ex post the control system; preserving the concept of public service for HES with the protection of a tenured academic core, the upholding of academic honour code and effective self-regulation (Pollit & Bouckaert, 2004).

As these three interpretations of the governance of higher education systems represent ideal type models, they are only partly realizable. They are particularly affected by the meeting between traditional aspects – answering determined functions of higher education teaching – and new aspects – aiming at interpreting the roles and functions attributed to higher education in a society under change, defined as 'the knowledge society'. More generally, the more common needs linked to the evolution of the economy and society seem to be grafted onto national higher education systems with consolidated characteristics. Hybrid forms are produced, which are the fruit of the combination of the old and new, or even of all the three models mentioned above.

More precisely, in Continental European countries, where NPM had made a strong impact, there seems to be a greater inclination towards either Network Governance models (with new subjects involved in constructing and carrying out policies) or neo-Weberian ones. These tend to give greater importance to legal and procedural rather than economic aspects of the functions and tasks of public services, including the systems of higher education. Systems, therefore, not directed towards the market as serving the citizens. From this approach derives the commitment to make public bureaucracy more efficient and improve the state's capacity to monitor and assess rather than reduce its impact.

A summary of the process under way is proposed by the traditional structuralist model, according to which the structural characteristics of the politico-administrative system help to explain the policies behind the reform of higher education (Bleiklie & Michelsen, 2013). This approach identifies six main tendencies in the evolution of higher education systems: (i) universities are undergoing a process of hierarchization on the New Public Management Model, which gives great importance to a strong leadership and the managerial structure of the executive power at the cost of the structures elected by the academic world; (ii) a revision of financing, partly linked to performance, is under way; (iii) universities are more and more coming under assessment; (iv) a greater role is accorded to supranational players (European Union, OCSE, Bologna Process); (v) autonomy is on the rise via the greater power given to governance, but at the same time there is a greater standardization of procedures and also criteria for assessing performance.

This global trend seems to corroborate the new institutionalist thesis of increasing isomorphism (Di Maggio & Powell, 1991; Meyer & Rowan, 1977; Thomas et al., 1997), and hence the convergence thesis about globalization's processes and outcomes in the higher education sector (Vaira, 2004). However, on the other hand, these theories seem excessively deterministic since they underestimate local reactions to these kinds of macro-processes. In fact, policies, national and local cultural and economic features, tend to metabolize this global tendency in the light of specific historical traditions, needs, practices and institutional structures (Bradley et al., 2000; Burbles & Torres, 2000; Vaira, 2004). It follows that (i) national policies still play an important role in organizing higher instruction in relation to national culture and social/economic needs (Marginson, 2002); but also (ii) individual seats have particular characteristics that condition in specific forms the modalities of reaction to external pressure for change. To sum up on a theoretical level, it seems that two levels of analysis can be distinguished. The new institutionalist approach – with especially the principle of isomorphic change can be usefully applied to macro-structural dynamics, while "strategic and translation approaches are well-suited to analyze the micro-level dynamics and actions ... but it is still difficult to make these two levels communicate to each other" (Vaira, 2004, p. 497).

## 3 Politicians and Bureaucrats in the Italian Higher Education System

### 3.1 *Premise*

In the preceding analysis of the relation between political and administrative elements in higher education systems, the differences between Anglo-Saxon and Napoleonic models are very clearly marked. An interesting case is the Italian system, which belongs to the Napoleonic model, with some variations on the historically more important French version.

In order to understand how the relations between politicians and bureaucrats have developed and what their respective roles are within the Italian system, some clarifications need to be made over terminology. In this chapter, for example, the term bureaucracy will be used in two senses. First of all, it will identify the bureaucrats tasked with carrying out public policies. In fact, while politicians are called on to identify public interests, the role of the bureaucrats is to look after such interests in concrete terms, in this way implementing political policies. In this first meaning, therefore, bureaucracy is a synonym for public administration and bureaucrats, who are the alter egos of politicians. The latter, in turn, are identified in our case with governments and in particular with Ministers of Education.

Secondly, the term bureaucracy will be used in the Weberian sense to identify the type of organization founded on a legal-rational model, whose functioning is governed by a system of written rules. From this point of view, an excessive or disorganized increase in the rules governing the workings is by itself an increase in bureaucracy as well as in the power of the bureaucrats called on to implement these rules. Finally, a disproportionate increase in the activity of the organizations in respect to the development of their typical missions (in the case of universities – research, teaching, transfer of knowledge) stands for what will here be called bureaucratization, or "the growth of the part of the organization that does not directly carry out the work but which regulates, supervises and supports those who do" (Gornitzka, Kyvik, & Larsen, 1998).

### 3.2    *Politics and Bureaucrats in the Italian University System*

A first affirmation to make is that for forty years after the Constitution of the Italian Republic was introduced, politics played an insignificant, if not quasi-inexistent, role in the development of a specific public policy for universities (Capano, 1998, p. 211). Proof of this lies in the fact that there are very few systematic laws in relation to higher education in the whole history of the State, and the few that there are, are sectorial, almost always dictated by emergencies. Indeed, faced by one of the most important factors of change in higher education, i.e. the increased social demand for education in the late 1960s and early 1970s, the political answer was simply to open up access, where in other countries structural reforms, at times and importantly, differentiating training courses, were quickly put in place.

On the margins of the over-arching schooling policy, higher education was contained within the Ministry of Public Instruction, which held the role of decision-maker in the whole system. In other terms, for the whole period of the Republic right up to the early 1990s, bureaucrats in the Ministry carried out the governance of the university system. Far more than the Minister in office, in fact, the favourite contact for official and unofficial academic bodies was the General Direction of University Instruction (Capano, Regini, & Turri, 2017, p. 54). Its excessive formalism and bureaucracy ever present since the unification of Italy have been highlighted by the literature (Melis, 1994, p. 187).

Over the last twenty-five years, however, in Italy as in all main European countries, profound changes have taken place. Inspired by the ideas of New Public Management, they have substantially modified the structure of the higher education. The beginnings of this transformation coincide with Law no. 168/1989, which finally recognized the autonomy of universities, solemnly affirmed by the Constitution but which had remained on paper. It also provided for the institution of a specific Ministry of the University, Scientific Research and Technology (MURST), based on the supposition that only a strong centre capable of governing from a distance would be able to guarantee the conditions for the single university seats to become autonomous. The Law was one of the first on devolutionary reforms, which characterized the 1990s.

However, there was no linear development to the university autonomy for a series of reasons. In the first place, the Ministry had a tormented life, conditioned by needs outside those of higher education. We just need to mention that after only ten years, another law merged it with the Education Ministry. Later, for exclusively political reasons of balance, the Ministry was again separated for two years (2006–2008), and then definitely merged with Education. Secondly, in its twelve or so years of life, eight different Ministers were sworn into office. Too many, evidently, and for periods too short to be able to develop any overall, long-term policy. Finally, and this is the most significant fact, the progressive recognition of university autonomy took place by means of an enormous, specifically governmental, production of primary legislation, plus secondary government and ministerial regulations (Monti, 2007, p. 94). More generally, the legislation that has gradually extended the spaces of university autonomy is fragmentary in nature, always awaiting organic change. They are also incremental, i.e. with new legislation added to the old, creating an effect of stratification, ever extending the regulated area, even more tangled up and difficult to interpret (Cassese, 2001).

This situation has obviously consolidated the role of the bureaucrats as well as increased the weight of CRUI (the Rectors' conference). Bureaucrats and rectors now form a priestly class, in that they are the main depositaries of the power to select, interpret and apply legislation. Emblematic of this transformation is the failure, due to the Rectors' Conference and the tacit consent of the then Minister, of the publication of a single text of university legislation in the moment in which it was ready to be approved (Cassese, 2002). In brief, it can be said that the season of autonomy, as realized, has brought less bureaucracy – because the Ministry has been deprived of the penetrating powers it possessed before 1989 – to the advantage of university autonomy. However, at the same time it has also brought more bureaucracy, as the effect of the uncertainty because of the exponential increase in regulations.

The situation has indeed, worsened in recent years. Since 2010, Italian universities have undergone an important reform (law 240/2010) realized by means of 50-odd implementary decrees (between legislative, government and ministerial decrees). Yet again, however, instead of taking the place of the previous regulations, new ones are often added on, with the effect of thickening the layers of legislation and increasing the margins of interpretation for those called upon to apply it (Barbati, 2014). It must also be added that like all public administrations, universities have found themselves with a phenomenal number of rules which may be financial – designed to curtail expenditure post economic crisis – or organizational, aiming at reinforcing impartiality and contrasting corruption. The effect of these mostly administrative legislative interventions is to produce further administrative and procedural burdens.

According to some studies (e.g. Vesperini, 2013), in the decade 2004–2013, the legislator intervened in university matters over 120 times, an average of more than once a month. In most cases the interventions were made by the Government and not Parliament, which bears witness to the way the executive power interferes heavily in university affairs. Besides primary sources, there is an enormous quantity of variously prescriptive acts (regulations, decrees, notes etc.) dictated from the centre by the Ministry and ANVUR, the governmental evaluation agency operating since 2011. It needs to be noted that in many cases, the acts are not limited to specifying the content of the law so that it can be applied, but they absolve a function that is both executive and at the same time substitutive of the Law. The latter, in fact, signs a blank approval for the acts of the Ministry or the Agency.

Overall, in recent years the weight of bureaucracy has been significantly increased by the stratification of legislation, with the result that the model of autonomy, only timidly put into place from the 1990s onwards, has clearly been scaled back, at least in substance, to the advantage of a progressive re-centralization. This can only partly be explained as an effect of the financial crisis and the consequent need to centralize mechanisms for controlling the organization costs and the operations of autonomies. In reality, the new centralization of higher education also depends on other factors.

(a) Primarily, it was a political reaction to the poor show that the universities made of themselves in the season of autonomy. At the same time, however, it must not be forgotten that the irresponsibility of the universities was, if not encouraged, at least facilitated by the Ministry's incapacity to carry out its function of governance at a distance. This incapacity was in turn due to the limits of a political class too often incapable of going "beyond a stereotyped vision of the university" as well as a ministerial bureaucracy substantially unaware of the real mechanisms of functioning "of the institutions it would be called upon to direct, monitor, assist, govern" (Capano, 2011, p. 169; Capano, Regini, & Turri, 2017, pp. 29–59).

(b) Secondly and especially, centralization was the result of the creation of ANVUR and its activity involving almost all moments of university life, from the evaluation of research and teaching results, to the accreditation of courses and seats, from the procedure for the National Scientific Qualification to the distribution of finances.

The creation of the Agency was a difficult process. Originally thought of as a genuine authority unconnected to politics, in line with what had been established by the European Association for Quality Assurance in Higher Education (ENQA), ANVUR was set up as a ministerial agency. However, right from the beginning, a certain ambiguity was evident in its relations with the Minister and the Ministry, with regard to both its structural and procedural profiles (Marra, 2014).

From an organizational point of view, the Minister's power to appoint the Council members is not in line with the logic calling for evaluators to be apolitical (Pinelli, 2011). But then, following the logic of evaluators being independent from the evaluated, the scarce transparency shown in the way the board members choose the members of the groups of evaluating experts (GEV) is even less satisfying.

From the point of view of procedure, the two practices evaluating research quality (VQR) and the procedures for national scientific qualification (ASN) reveal a grave state of confusion in the roles between Ministry and Agency. Evaluative methods and instruments are read as real parameters of judgment and incorporated in ministerial decrees, resulting in evaluation being absorbed 100% into the administrative world and in this way causing it to ossify (Cassese, 2012).

The notation – 'juridification of the assessment' – is particularly important in the light of this chapter. It is the outcome, perhaps foreseeable, of the transfer of institutions and instruments belonging to Anglo-Saxon countries into the Italian context, which is fully inserted in the paradigm of legal homogeneity. It should not therefore be surprising that assessment is reached via an exponential increase in administrative procedures, which determine a rise in the power of the bureaucracy defining and directing procedures. A bureaucracy which no longer has the face of the traditional ministerial administration and no longer deploys the typical 'command and control' instruments – but resorts to the apparently neutral one of technology. All things considered, it is a new techno-bureaucracy which uses rigid articulated procedures aiming at introducing administered competition to direct and conform university activity especially for the attribution of state funds, without however insuring – above all with the assessment of research – the full guarantee of transparency and publicity typical of administrative procedure (Ramajoli, 2014).

There again, the ambiguous relation between Agency and Ministry has meant that the effective government of the system has been progressively moving from the Ministry to Agency (Barbati, 2014). Added to this, the fact that the Ministry is the only body not to have been updated after the Reform, and, as we have seen, its political upper echelons already show signs of weakness. Since, in fact, by law the assessment results go to make up the basis of almost all the enactment procedures of the 2010 Reform, those who organize and manage assessment procedures are in a position to condition all the organizational and functional moments in university life, directing and/or moulding them.

The result is that not only does the Agency replace the Ministerial bureaucrats, but also assessment "occupies the spaces that should belong to the choices made by the political-administrative position, therefore making itself the governing instrument of the system and not only for its government" (Barbati, 2014).

In this confusion of roles between Ministry and Agency, the results of ANVUR's actions have been perceived as the fruit of only apparently technical choices, in reality guided by a precise political will coming from the Government, which, with the help of a limited academic elite, aims at re-dimensioning the university system and introducing a "top-down differentiation" (Viesti, 2016, 2018). Whether or not they are the product of a conscious political choice, the consequences of the technical decisions taken up to now have had a considerable political effect, having determined a significant increase in territorial imbalances. In fact, the differences between university seats in the north centre, south and the islands (Sicily and Sardinia) are greater, and more and more students from the south and the islands transfer to the north. Up to now, there has been no reaction at a political level.

## 4　University Dimensions

At the level of the individual seats, the subject of the relation between politics and administrations can be developed along two trajectories.

In a first sense, the political/administrative relation can be delineated as that between two distinct moments of making the reforms (politics) and putting them in place (administration). Since the universities are the recipients of policies dictated by the centre, it is the way policies are received and implemented that makes for their success. In a second sense, the politics-administration relation can be examined by looking at the way in which competences are divided between teaching and administrative staff.

In the first case, it must be said that, as frequently happens in any reform process with a public administration, attempts to introduce changes have always come up against the difficulties inherent in an inelastic context with consolidated ways. In detail, more resistance to reform has come from the teaching staff than the administrative section. Teaching staff have generally complained about a lack of information on the dynamics of the innovations, but are less oppositional where the latter are accompanied by a sticks and carrots mechanism linked to the coming into effect of the national system of assessment. By contrast, university administrations quite often reveal a greater readiness to implement the reforms. In the case of the Bologna Process, for example, they mostly understand the aims of the reform and uphold its feasibility, even if it means a greater work load collocated in widespread organizational difficulties (Dosso, 2010; Denti & Moscati, 2008; Moscati, 2006). This contrast in attitude is probably explained by the different sense of belonging of teaching and administrative/technical staff. The former mostly have a sense of belonging more to a scientific community than to an academic seat/institution.

There are some aspects to highlight with regard to applying the principle of distinction between politics and bureaucracy in universities. On one hand, in fact, the bodies governing universities do not really represent political positions in general, but are the expression of the scientific and teaching interests of the academic community, in line with an idea of autonomy primarily understood as self-government. On the other hand, the handling of the teaching and research, characterized by a high technical/specialist content is, as stated by the Law, entrusted directly to the academics without any role accorded to the bureaucrats.

In spite of these distinctions, the dividing line between politics and administration mentioned above should also be applied to universities, however hard it is to establish how it should operate. According to some (Capano, 2008), this difficulty led before the 2010 reform to a fairly unhappy division in responsibilities, determining an overload of work for the governing bodies (and scarce awareness in decision-making), and an under-used and de-responsibilized managerial class.

The problem was not solved with the reform of governance brought about by the 2010 law. Although the new set-up of governing bodies enhancing the rector and marginalizing the senate appears to be more suitably structured for taking decisions on strategies and planning, the functional differentiation between political and administrative bodies does not appear to be sufficiently delineated. The law limited itself to renaming the executive director 'registrar' (general director), and tasking him/her with the overall management and organization of the services, instrumental resources and techno-administrative personnel. Thus creating a trend towards a governance diarchy with the registrar flanking the rector. Nevertheless, the relations have not yet been clearly defined between governing and bureaucratic bodies with each university seat, and there is much uncertainty about the managerial duties to accord to the administration, and likewise the tasks and functions to reserve to academics. The division of tasks and the control area in the formation of policies and their enactment has often given rise to unstable equilibriums.

Furthermore, in Italy as elsewhere, adaptation to reforms, developing assessment processes and multiplying relations with the outside world have pushed universities towards a process of redefining internal organizational mechanisms. At the present moment, differently from in the past, the universities need to develop strategies and their own policies for trying to achieve the best performances possible in order to obtain resources from the State, unlock further external resources via other financing forms (European projects, third mission, etc.), and also answer outside pressures from the social context. This has led to the increasing importance of management and internal administration, i.e. an increase in bureaucratization (Gornitzka, Kyvik, & Larsen, 1998). Differently from elsewhere, the bureaucratization of the Italian university has not led to an increase in administration personnel. On the contrary, over the last ten years, the number with life tenure has suffered a drastic cut, by about 16%. However, the drop in academics on life tenure is even greater (24%), which means that the higher costs of the increase in bureaucratic expenses is paid for mostly by the teaching staff.

## 5 Concluding Remarks

The Italian system of higher education is characterized by the processes of change common to systems particularly influenced by the neo-liberal approach of New Public Management. The interweaving of this approach with the Humboldt/Napoleonic model has caused transformations in the functioning of the system and the relation between the political sphere (ministers) and the administrative one (bureaucrats), which have much in common with other systems with the same political and cultural origins. In the present process of evolution of the functions and tasks of the university, the balance between meritocracy, democracy and bureaucracy is unstable, at both the level of system and individual institutions, in Italy and various other contexts (Gornitzka, Kyvik & Larsen, 1998). In the case of Italy, furthermore, the particular complexity and inefficiency of the central administrative system is added to uncertainty about both the level of autonomy of the individual universities and state intervention, which in recent times has been increasingly expressed via the control and direction operations of the agency tasked with assessment (ANVUR).

In particular, the absence of a system policy, which clearly defines the general objectives, makes it difficult to define university policies, and with the establishment of a definition it would be useful to have an assessment system incentivizing going after such objectives (Capano et al., 2017). In Italy – where there are deep social and economic inequalities between different parts of the country – it is difficult to reach a balance between merit, excellence and equality. There are evident difficulties in applying central assessment models tending to standardization in a very uneven system of higher education.

Given the above considerations, it is therefore possible to affirm that in the Italian system of higher education, the development of transition processes concerning the university calls, today more than ever, for a political guidance capable of sustaining and directing the change.

Put into perspective, therefore, the new starting point is above all re-thinking the centre of the system and redefining the roles to be covered by political decision-maker, assessment agency and individual universities. To do this, however, changing the legislation – as often happens in order to avoid critical issues – is a necessary step, but by itself not enough. What is needed is a serious renewal of the ministerial set-up, a separation between higher education from primary and secondary, plus a minister of the university with adequate technical and professional competences. What is indeed missing today. It would also be useful to stimulate in individual seats policies aiming at rewarding a progressive achievement of institutional performances defined via forms shared by internal and external stakeholders.

### References

Andresani, G., & Ferlie, E. (2006). Studying governance within the British public sector and without: Theoretical and methodological issues. *Public Management Review*, *8*(3), 415–432.

Barbati, C. (2014). Il governo del sistema universitario: soggetti in cerca di un ruolo. *Rivista trimestrale di diritto pubblico, 2*, 337–360.

Bleiklie, I., & Michelsen, S. (2013). Comparing HE policies in Europe. Structures and reform output in eight countries. *Higher Education, 65*, 113–133. doi:10.10007/s10734-012-9584-6

Bradley, H., Erickson, M., Stephenson, C., & Williams, S. (2000). *Myths at work.* Polity Press.

Burbules, N. C., & Torres, C. A. (Eds.). (2000). *Globalization and education. Critical perspectives.* Routledge.

Capano, G. (1998). *La politica universitaria.* Il Mulino.

Capano, G. (2008). Il governo degli atenei. In R. Moscati & M. Vaira (Eds.), *L'università di fronte al cambiamento: realizzazioni, problemi, prospettive* (pp. 117–142). Il Mulino.

Capano, G. (2011). Un centro organizzato per non governare? In C. Bologna & G. Endrici (Eds.), *Governare le università. Il centro del sistema* (pp. 157–174). Il Mulino.

Capano, G., Regini, M., & Turri, M. (2017). *Salvare l'università italiana. Oltre i miti e i tabù.* Il Mulino.

Cassese, S. (2001). L'autonomia e il testo unico sull'università. *Giornale di diritto amministrativo, 5*, 515–524.

Cassese, S. (2002). Introduzione. In S. Cassese (Ed.), *Il testo unico delle norme sull'università*. Clueb.

Cassese, S. (2013). L'ANVUR ha ucciso la valutazione. Viva la valutazione! Lo stato delle università e la valutazione della ricerca. *Il Mulino, 1*, 73–179.

Clark, R. B. (1998). *Creating entrepreneurial universities. Organizational pathways of transformation*. Pergamon.

Delanty, G. (2001). *The university on the knowledge society*. Open University Press.

Denti, F., & Moscati, R. (2008). Strutture formative e relazioni sociali: la riforma degli ordinamenti didattici nell'università italiana. *Rassegna Italiana di Sociologia, 4*, 515–546.

Di Maggio, P. J., & Powell, W. W. (1991). The Iron Cage revisited: Institutional isomorphism and collective rationality. In W. W. Powell & P. J. Di Maggio (Eds.), *The new institutionalism in organizational analysis* (pp. 165–187). Chicago University Press.

Dosso, C. (2010). L'attuazione amministrativa della riforma degli ordinamenti didattici: le valutazioni del personale tecnico-amministrativo. In R. Moscati (Ed.), *Come e perché cambiano le università in Italia e in Europa* (pp. 65–91). Liguori.

Ferlie, E., Musselin, C., & Andresani, G. (2008). The steering of higher education system: A public management perspective. *Higher Education, 56*(3), 325–348.

Gornitzka, Å., Kyvik, S., & Larsen, I. M. (1998). The bureaucratization of universities. *Minerva, 36*, 21–47.

Gumport, P. (2000). Academic restructuring: Organizational change and institutional imperatives. *Higher Education, 69*, 67–91.

Marginson, S. (2002). Nation-building universities in a global environment: The case of Australia. *Higher Education, 43*(3), 409–428.

Marra, A. (2014). La valutazione del sistema universitario e il ruolo dell'ANVUR. In G. Piperata (Ed.), *L'università e la sua organizzazione. Questioni ricorrenti e profili evolutivi* (pp. 115–138). Editoriale Scientifica.

Melis, G. (1994). Alle origini della Direzione generale per l'istruzione superiore. In I. Porciani (Ed.), *L'università tra Otto e Novecento: i modelli europei e il caso italiano* (pp. 187–208). Jovene.

Merloni, F. (2009). *Dirigenza pubblica e amministrazione imparziale. Il modello italiano in Europa*. Il Mulino.

Meyer, J. W., & Rowan, G. (1977). Institutionalized organizations: Formal structure as myth and ceremony. *American Journal of Sociology, 83*, 340–363.

Monti, A. (2007). *Indagine sul declino dell'università italiana*. Gangemi.

Moscati, R. (2006). Italy. In J. J. F. Forest & P. G. Altbach (Eds.), *International handbook of higher education* (Vol. II, pp. 811–827). Springer.

Neave, G. (2002). The stakeholders perspective historically explored. In J. Enders & O. Fulton (Eds.), *Higher education in a globalising world* (pp. 17–37). Kluwer.

Neave, G. (2012). *The evaluative state. Institutional autonomy and re-engineering higher education in Western Europe. The prince and his pleasure.* Palgrave Macmillan.

Pinelli, C. (2011). Autonomia universitaria, libertà della scienza e valutazione dell'attività Scientifica. *Munus*, 567–578.

Pollit, C., & Bouckaert, G. (2004). *Public management reform: A comparative analysis.* Oxford University Press.

Ramajoli, M. (2014). Stato valutatore, autonomia universitaria e libertà di ricerca. *Giornale di diritto amministrativo, 3*, 313–321.

Vaira, M. (2004). Globalization and higher education organizational change: A framework for analysis. *Higher Education, 48*, 483–510.

Vesperini, G. (2013). Iperregolazione e burocratizzazione del sistema universitario. *Rivista trimestrale di diritto pubblico, 4*, 947–966.

Viesti, G. (Ed.). (2016). *Università in declino. Un'indagine sugli atenei da Nord a Sud.* Donzelli.

Viesti, G. (2018). *La laurea negata. Le politiche contro l'istruzione universitaria.* Laterza.

# PART 2

## *Higher Education Systems: (Responsible?) Practices and Policies*

∴

CHAPTER 6

# University Mergers in Austria: Experiences and Future Scenarios for Organizational Development in Higher Education

*Attila Pausits*

### Abstract

University merger has been a major trend in higher education development for almost 40 years. Competition, positioning, economies of scale but also defragmentation and better control or efficiency considerations are often central arguments for such initiatives and systemic and institutional changes. Today, almost all countries in Europe have experience with mergers in higher education. In this chapter, international trends and drivers for mergers will be used to reflect and discuss possible scenarios of the Austrian higher education system. Even though, mergers have already taken place in Austria, the country is lagging behind in the application of models as well as the use international standards in the application and use of such models by international standards. This exploratory contribution examines possible scenarios of mergers in higher education and shows opportunities and limitations from an institutional perspective.

### Keywords

mergers – Austria – organizational development – defragmentation – merger types – hybrid mergers – cross-sectoral mergers

## 1 Introduction

Today, reforms in higher education at the system as well as institutional levels are driven more and more by international trends. Shifts from a formerly "elitist model" to broader access, global competition, and the need to position single institutions are the driving forces in recent higher education development initiatives (D'Ambrosio & Ehrenberg, 2007). Differentiation, both vertically

© KONINKLIJKE BRILL NV, LEIDEN, 2020 | DOI: 10.1163/9789004436558_007

(hierarchy, reputation) and horizontally (profile, positioning, organizational culture) (Marginson, 2016), is requested by different stakeholders. Ministries are looking for incentives and models to improve higher education systems; rectorates are looking for the strategic advantages of their own universities; academics are searching for better framework conditions for their own research and teaching; and students are searching for good study programs and better educational services.

In recent years, the higher education landscape has been significantly influenced by rankings and other forms of (quality) measures to evaluate institutional performance (Hazelkorn, 2011). Systemically and systematically, the expectations on higher education institutions have increased and been partly redefined by different stakeholders. In addition to the original tasks of research and teaching, for example, the third mission as a set of services for new communities and as a vehicle of broader societal responsibility, has enlarged core missions (Pinheiro et al., 2015). At the same time, besides this complexity and task 'expansion', the dissatisfaction of various stakeholders with higher education has increased. The notion of accountability has redefined the concept of public funding. Efficiency and effectiveness in the use of public funds have become driving forces of university development (Altbach & Peterson, 2007). Therefore, indicator-driven assessment of achievements and performances, valued by international comparisons and benchmarks, became in vogue. Evidence based policy formation and decision-making processes are supported by new measures and tools. Relying on rankings, getting better at economies of scale, or simplifying university governance are often mentioned in the literature, used by decision makers, or discussed through the media as possible development measures (Dixon & Coy, 2007; Mahrl & Pausits, 2011; Mortimer & Sathre, 2007). However, these developments also lead to a large number of questions: Which models are suitable in a given system? What evidence has been provided in the scientific literature so far? What insights and evidence are there between expected and real effects of mergers? Or simply, what are the success factors of a merger in the initiation or implementation phase?

Mergers in higher education became an especially popular and widely used tool to lead changes and develop higher education for the better (Curaj et al., 2015). Although mergers in higher education are not a new phenomenon, they have become recently a global instrument for system and organizational development (Bennetot & Estermann, 2015).

In this article, a general overview of models and findings on mergers in Europe and elsewhere will be presented through a literature review. Relying on these experiences, possibilities and limits of mergers in Austria will then be discussed. This chapter focuses on an exploratory perspective and discusses possible scenarios of mergers – vertical and horizontal – and their implications for the higher education system in the country. Both, international experience and national framework conditions will be reflected; sectoral diversity and possible cross-sector mergers discussed and intra-sectoral scenarios elaborated. Finally, several organizational and legal aspects influencing mergers will be presented. Thus, the article provides a theoretically founded and generally practice-oriented approach, and discusses possible implications and challenges of mergers in Austria.

## 2 University Mergers in Europe: Drivers and Models

The competitive pressures on systems, institutions, and also research units have increased and led to new solutions but also new perspectives regarding performance. Economies of scale, excellence, and efficiency are the new buzzwords in higher education. Today, higher education takes advantage of different scenarios of this co-competition. Universities cooperate in one field, for example through a joint master's program in teaching, and compete for research funding elsewhere. Fighting for the brightest minds, best students, third party funding, research infrastructure, as a few examples of the competition, confront higher education institutions with new demands and challenges. The race for scarce resources leads to diverse ways of cooperation. These can take different forms from loose connections to formal collaboration (Harman & Meek, 2002). Alliances, consortia, networks and much more are examples of this diversity. The new target systems in which higher education institutions find themselves are characterized by a steadily increasing influence of a growing number of stakeholders. As a logical consequence of this demand orientation, the search for structures and forms in order to exploit potential synergies, institutional and system leaders pursue cooperative arrangements to improve their institutions' strategic and operational positions and to withstand the mounting pressures (Harman & Harman, 2008). Due to different positioning among institutions, as related to levels of research, teaching or both, higher education systems have become more differentiated in many countries such as Romania, Finland and Austria (Curaj et al., 2015).

This differentiation has led not only to clarity about the tasks and possible profiles of these institutions, but to a further discourse on the timeliness, function and possible change of their profiles (Pausits, 2015). This is often accompanied by modifications in the framework conditions, institutional developments, and the status quo within a higher education system. The increasing size of higher education systems, the autonomy of single institutions proposed by the New Public Management model, and the habitus and interests of individual actors, make future higher education reforms and changes more complex. Many governments aim to reduce the number of institutions, create larger units and take advantage of economies of scale. At the same time, and in addition to national approaches, initiatives of the European Higher Education Area lead to further harmonization (Curaj et al., 2015). The best known and most far-reaching is the Bologna Process. In addition, there are more recent initiatives to foster institutional cooperation. Probably the most discussed one is the 'European Universities' program of the European Commission, wherein the cooperation of individual universities is supported not only on content (individual research projects) but also at the strategic level, such as the coordination of the entirety of university research strategies.

The first major wave of higher education mergers in Europe took place in the 1980s and 1990s. A review and theoretical modeling of these was documented from the end of 1980 through a variety of publications (Goedegebuure, 1992; Harman & Meek, 2002; Pinheiro et al., 2016). In general, the mergers in the UK (OECD, 2017), the Netherlands (Goedegebuure, 1992) and Norway (Kyvik, 2002) are examples of the first wave (Rocha et al., 2018). After 2000, a spread of mergers to other European countries followed. Not surprisingly, the first wave was mainly driven and supported by initiatives of national governments and aimed to establish larger comprehensive universities and to overcome further fragmentation of higher education systems. For example, in the Netherlands from the mid-1980s to 1999, mergers reduced the number of universities of applied sciences from almost 350 to 58 (Goedegebuure, 1992). Often, as in Hungary or Ireland, university mergers have been embedded in significant educational reforms and have been used as tools to achieve overall system-wide goals (Harman & Harman, 2008). In most cases, these mergers have coincided with the expansion of the tertiary sector. Thus, mergers can also be seen as measures of systemic transition from an elite to a mass higher education system (Georghiou & Cassingena Harper, 2015).

The national ambitions to improve structures, to prepare for international competition, and develop higher education institutions as engines of knowledge creation, led to a significant increase of mergers in many countries. Governments often used ranking results as an impetus to initiate mergers or to underline the importance of structural as well as institutional improvements within a higher education system (Hazelkorn, 2011). In France and Russia, for example, the position of individual universities in rankings was used as an argument to justify the creation of a new higher education institution. However, other international examples outside Europe, such as in China, South

Africa, and Australia, show that mergers require investment in structures and systems by the public sector first (Rocha et al., 2018). Regardless of which objectives are pursued with a merger, it cannot be assumed that all parties will benefit from a merger. Often, the overarching goals such as harmonization, defragmentation, synergies or even a place among the top 25 in the Shanghai Rankings define the framework conditions and rationale of such mergers (Harman & Harman, 2008).

The large number of different types of mergers in higher education display various merger options within the sector. Mergers can be voluntary or obligatory. A classification of mergers in higher education may also refer to the size of the participating universities (large, medium and small) or to their profile, for example, a comprehensive or a specialized niche university. However, the combination of different types within tertiary education (university, university of applied science or teacher's college) can be used to differentiate between horizontal or vertical, cross-sectoral or intra-sectoral mergers (Harman & Harman, 2003). Of course, there are additional examples like between universities and non-university research institutions. One of the best-known examples of this type in German-speaking countries is the establishment of the Karlsruhe Institute of Technology from the University of Karlsruhe and the Karlsruhe Research Center. Mergers are often used to consolidate structures (for example, in the Netherlands) or as takeovers (Goedegebuure, 1992). Frequently, they are driven by politics related to changes in legal frameworks. One of the most prominent examples of this is the University of Duisburg-Essen, which was established through a merger of the University of Duisburg and the University of Essen by changing the corresponding state law in 2002.

The number of institutions involved in such processes may vary but a minimum of two institutions need to be involved. According to Harman and Harman (2003), a merger is a combination of two or more institutions (e.g., universities, university of applied sciences, non-university research institutions). It is important that at least one institution involved in the merger and/ or the newly created organization belong to the higher education sector. The new institution is in charge of all management tasks, control, assets and liabilities. In some cases, a new institution is created by the merger in other cases (smaller, in some cases even the bigger) merging parts go into an already existing organizations (takeover). In summary, the reasons for the merger for the first wave from the 1980s, according to Pinheiro et al. (2016) can be justified as follows:
– Rationalization of higher education and scientific networks.
– Restructuring of higher education systems.
– Cost optimization and economies of scale.

Today, in contrast to this first wave, mergers in different countries are supported in particular by the following drivers:

- Global competition and positioning of individual higher education institutions as 'lighthouses of science' (Rocha et al., 2018).
- Excellence initiatives (Georghiou & Cassingena Harper, 2015).
- Improved ranking in national and especially global rankings (Hazelkorn, 2011).

Besides the different institutional types and characters, it is also notable that mergers face different challenges in research and teaching. Heterogeneous institutional educational portfolios with different subjects can stimulate each other and new interdisciplinary combinations can emerge (Georghiou & Cassingena Harper, 2015). In institutions with homogeneous profiles including similar teaching portfolios the synergies, even if this was a clear objective of the merger, will hardly be effective or will only take effect after a few years. A survey of four university mergers in Finland, including Alto University, has shown that goals regarding synergies in teaching and learning are rather general while benefits in research through a merger are more precise (Ursin et al., 2010). For example, a greater geographical distance between the merged institutions including academics teaching in different locations with significant travel time, led to models of blended or distance learning instead of rigorous elimination of parallel offers.

Higher education institutions and especially universities are among the oldest forms of organizations. Their lasting influence on the economy and society is undisputed. When and how the changes in these institutions can or should be effective is highly controversial. Changes brought about by higher education policy are often planned for short- or medium-term effects (Huisman et al., 2015). International examples and scientific literature are frequently limited to a few indicators. Improvement in the Shanghai Ranking and increase in overall third-party funding share are common forms of evidence that are repeatedly presented. Yet, extensive longitudinal studies looking at the effects of mergers are lacking. Thus, some studies report initially positive effects, for example in research (Ursin et al., 2010). However, after a few years, due to the lack of sustainable cohesion of the newly created organization, these effects deflagrate (Mao et al., 2009). As a result, mergers are subject to high (political) expectations in the short and medium perspective, but are often valued only on key objectives such as rankings. A comprehensive assessment driven by goals, but also by other contextual factors such as synergies in teaching, impact development on the third mission etc., are missing in most of the existing research (Rocha et al., 2018). Commonly used research and evaluation methods are benchmarking between existing mergers or qualitative studies relaying on employee surveys and interviews (Pinheiro et al., 2016). Comprehensive analysis is only available in a few cases. For example, in Denmark these are mainly connected to system wide and systematic use of mergers as triggers of system improvements and developments (OECD, 2017).

Nevertheless, many countries have decided to follow concentration and consolidation approaches. In anticipation of added value, many higher education institutions have given up their independence. Under pressure between political forces and institutional initiatives, today there is a wealth of national experience with mergers. Outside Europe, this includes mainly Australia, Canada, China, South Africa and the USA. In Europe, Britain, Norway, and the Netherlands have already gained experience in mergers with the first wave in the 1980s. A real wave of mergers then followed in the 2000s in the Scandinavian countries. Thus, mergers were carried out in Denmark and Finland. The most recent merger in Finland was completed in late 2018 in Tampere. Three higher education institutions merged: Tampere University of Technology, Tampere University and Tampere University of Applied Sciences. Currently, the University of Tampere is the largest university in the country. But mergers also took place in France, Russia, Poland, Hungary, Romania, Croatia and Slovakia, to name a few other examples.

As in other European countries, mergers also occurred in Austria. Similar to Germany, Belgium, and Ireland, non-university research institutions have been integrated into universities systematically. These were justified by policy makers in particular by economic benefits. According to a comparative study by the European University Association, in the Austrian case cost reduction effects, increasing efficiency, financial scarcity and, ultimately, better chances of survival of the research organization were highlighted as key drivers (Bennetot & Estermann, 2015). Another example is the establishment of teacher training colleges in Austria. These tertiary institutions have arisen from the merger of several educational institutions. Thus, until 2007, the so-called Pedagogical Academies were responsible for teacher training at general compulsory schools. In addition, the teacher training institutes were responsible for continuing education and training of teachers. Together with the vocational education academies, these institutions were established as colleges through a merger in the tertiary sector. In this sense, part of the higher education system in Austria has already been reshaped through mergers.

Due to the almost 'comprehensive merger movement' of the last 40 years with a significant increase of mergers in the recent years in Europe, as well as the experience with mergers of the non-university research institutions and the colleges of teacher education, it seems convincing to discuss further possible mergers in Austria.

## 3 Possible Scenarios in Austria

As already mentioned, higher education mergers are often initiated by system performance improvements, ranking results, institutional positioning, or excellence programs. Such excellence initiatives have already led to university mergers in Russia and France. Today, it is uncertain whether mergers in Austria, for example, through such an excellence initiative will be initiated. Possible mergers emerged several times on the political agenda at the national and regional levels. Technical universities, higher education institutions in Vienna and specialized universities, to give a few examples, have been the subject of theoretical considerations. Vienna as a higher education hub is the most important and largest 'higher educational area' in Austria. Not only because the oldest and largest university is located here but also because 16 other higher education institutions operate in the capitol city of Austria. Perhaps that is why a few years ago the issue of mergers was repeatedly raised by political actors. Through study trips and invited experts, the ministry responsible for higher education discussed mergers looking at framework conditions, effects on institution performances and international good practices. In all these, it is repeatedly pointed out that Austria has a high number of higher education institutions in terms of its population and in relation to other 'similar' countries and regions (Wolfensberger, 2015). International references such as to the Netherlands, Finland or Bavaria are frequently mentioned in media and policy papers. In light of this, the following four possible theoretical scenarios in Austria will be considered: (1) The merger of two universities, (2) the merger of two universities of applied sciences, (3) the merger of a university and a university of applied sciences. It is obvious that other possibilities and combinations are possible. However, these would go beyond the scope of this work. The chapter aims to discuss basic conditions and considerations by highlighting the most interesting and likely scenarios. Although the following scenarios are discussed with the help of legislative and legal frameworks, the systemic perspective remains as the core focus in the following section.

### 3.1 *University – University*
The Universities Act 2002 (National Council of the Republic of Austria, 2002) is a milestone in higher education development in Austria regarding institutional autonomy including merger of universities. The act explicitly regulates the possibilities and framework conditions between universities. According to the higher education act, as in many other countries, the establishment of a (new) university in Austria is regulated in a federal law. Similar to the establishment, for example, of the University of Duisburg-Essen in Germany (in

that case due to the higher education system in Germany, a provincial law), a merger is explicitly covered by the higher education act and defined practically in the sector including appropriate legal steps but also regulations. These initiatives can be carried out in a bottom-up manner by two or more universities or emanate from the constitutionally envisaged path of federal legislation, and also from the Federal Minister himself. The last option is clearly a top-down process. It is remarkable that such mergers in Austria can only take place at certain times or in a certain period. The Universities Act defines that a merger, and thus creation of a new university, can take effect only after the beginning of a new performance agreement period.

Each university has a development plan covering six years. This period is divided in two performance agreement periods of three years each. Following the regulation, merger can only take place in Austria every three years. Strictly speaking, such considerations of legal entity changes must already be taken into account in the development plans. For example, in the first performance agreement period, the preparation for a merger could take place and, with the start of the following performance agreement period, the newly established university could start operations.

The described process may look rigid as it gives limited timeframes and strict procedures. Most likely, it has its roots in Austrian university funding and related budget plan procedures of the government. The university system and single universities are governed and managed by the performance agreements. Thus, it also becomes clear that a public university without a performance agreement cannot be (re)-established. Of course, through more flexible arrangements and shortened performance agreement periods, the establishment of a merged university would be possible, but not desirable. A fundamental argument in favor of a strict scheduling is the fact that there is no legal regulation for the termination of existing performance-agreement obligations. If two or more universities merge at a time when there are ongoing commitments under the current performance agreements, it would be unclear – also in financial terms – how to interpret the agreements. In contrast to §6(4) Universities Act, it can therefore be assumed that in Austria a new university, based on an agreement between two or more universities (bottom up), can only be possible following the performance agreement periods and terms in every 3 years. Possible delays in the merger (e.g. missing the start of the performance period) would then have considerable effects on the merger process and start. In the worst case, the result would be a delay of another three years. The higher education act thus provides an exact planning model, at the same time it does not allow deviations or accept a delay. The Universities Act also covers essential internal elements and tasks such as name, organization and resource plan as well as committees and different institutional bodies. These are core and required areas for a transition period also. Thus, there are, strictly speaking, no transitional arrangements for a merger in Austria as far as structure and organs are concerned. Ultimately, this should also safeguard university operations.

Accordingly, the higher education act specifies how and when mergers can be implemented in Austria. Although universities have a high level of autonomy, as presented in the first part of this chapter, policy initiatives like consolidation of universities can arise and drive such organizational development processes as a top-down initiative. The case where the government but not the targeted universities are in favor of the merger is not defined in the higher education act. In individual cases, it can be assumed that merger without the approval of the involved university leadership and management is not possible. In line with international examples, a merger through policy makers is only conceivable through holistic and systemic decisions affecting the entire higher education system.

### 3.2    *University – University of Applied Science*

As in many other countries, collaboration between universities of applied sciences (UAS) and universities in Austria has been repeatedly discussed, for example, toward PhD studies. Universities still protect the domain of PhD studies within the higher education sector. Even though cooperation with UASs is recommended by the ministry, only few examples exist so far. However, there are many other examples of cooperation like in study programs and the use of teaching staff. Nevertheless, issues related to the positioning of the two sectors has become an important area of higher education policy discussions in the country (Pausits, 2016). This includes, for example, the shift of study programs such as business administration from universities to UASs. Although the original main task of the UAS sector is to offer teaching, research at UAS in not forbidden nor adequately rewarded but tolerated in the system. The basic tension leads again and again to critical voices and opinions in both directions of the higher education sector. Therefore, it is unlikely that a merger between a university and a UAS can be expected in the near future. However, international examples such as the University of Tampere, as we have already seen, or other international cases since the 1980s, where new universities have emerged, are examples of such developments.

With cross-sectoral mergers, the diverse legal framework conditions often make a merger challenging. In Austria, as presented above, the Universities Act provides important details for the merger of the university, but little guidance for such a 'hybrid' merger. As highlighted above by international examples and discussed in the literature, merger in the higher education sector is initially an 'upgrade'. Thus, UASs have always become universities through mergers. An inverse example that a university became a UAS through a merger is not known. The strategic factor of incentive modeling of mergers proves that core drivers are key for the success of a merger. Often the university status means better position.

Unlike other countries such as Germany or Finland, UASs in Austria have only regulations for their studies but not organizational forms. With the *Fachhochschulstudiengesetz*, the legislature has created a set of regulations for the implementation of study programs and the necessary structures and organizational frameworks in order to implement such programs. A specific organization law only for UASs does not exist. Rather, the legal form of the organization of a UAS provides the legal basis. Thus, UASs in Austria are organized as a limited liability company, associations or non-profit private foundations.

Other key issues relate to the takeover of personnel. The collective agreement gives for the universities a precise legal framework. The contract conditions of employees and their related tasks requires special attention. In this context, Frank Chantelau examined in the example of the merger of the University of Lüneburg with the University of Applied Sciences Northeast Lower Saxony in 2005, the transfer of UAS professors into university professorships (Chantelau, 2015). This revealed the complexity of such a cross-sectoral merger from constitutional to higher education law issues. This might be the reason why in the case of the Tampere University, the joining UAS kept the institution's original legal form and did not go through a full merger regarding staff legal issues. In the case of Austria such a scenario might be also a good example to overcome legal issue complexities. However, most likely this would be not that attractive for UAS's academic staff. The working conditions including teaching workload, and salary regulations, as well as the status to be employed at a university might be considered better at universities then at UASs.

It is nonetheless to be expected that such a merger would entail significant additional costs for federal funding and would increase the budget of the higher education sector (Bennetot & Estermann, 2015). This is less due to the collective agreement of the universities, but rather to the cost of the merger, which is partially rooted in existing parallel structures (Pinheiro et al., 2016). Some possible scenario to take into consideration for Austria can be found in Belgium and Finland. Although such mergers were carried out there, UASs remained as legal entities including staffing issues (Bennetot & Estermann, 2015). However, harmonization and coordination of working conditions within the structures, following social compatibility and equality, have been mentioned in the literature as one of the key elements of a cross-sectoral merger (OECD, 2017; Rocha et al., 2018). Studies also show that cost benefits through streamlining bring positive results in the short term, due to the different organizational cultures they often evaporate in the medium term (Mao et al., 2009). The possible timing of intersectoral mergers is also problematic. In line with the Higher Education Act with regard to the establishment of a 'new' university, the period of a UAS development plan (five years) provides possible 'dates' for leaving the sector as well. Since the five years are considered as a planning period, a coincidence of the two models (six- or five-year periods) and thus simultaneous planning is hardly possible. In addition, there are several recommendations, such as from the OECD, but also in strategic government planning documents such as 'future university' to expand the UAS sector. However, such a cross-sectoral merger would automatically lead to a reduction in the number of UASs. Thus, the expansion would be still possible by a shift of study programs and places to other UASs. The existing dual model with two pillars needs further revision. From today's perspective, a dominant inter-sectoral positioning strategy could be extended and hybrid models added to the existing two institutional types.

### 3.3 University of Applied Science – University of Applied Science

The UAS sector is rather small and fragmented compared to other countries such as Finland, Germany, Switzerland or the Netherlands. Although UASs have been established since 1994, about 20 years later than in other countries, it is noticeable that the university system in Austria is primarily dominated by universities (Pausits, 2016). There are 21 UASs and 22 public universities in Austria. The difference is not reflected in the number of institutions but rather in student numbers. Over 50,000 study at UASs and around 280,000 at universities (Unidata, n.d.). The size of a single UAS is rather small by international standards. Thus, on average, 352 (FTE) persons work at UASs. The largest UAS has just over 1000 (FTE) employees. In contrast, a comparative number for a university is around 9800 including 6800 scientific staff (Unidata, n.d.). One of the reasons for possible merger is the fragmentation of a higher education system and the expected scale effect of the created size after a merger. Thus, the consolidation of the UAS sector in Finland took place only after the Parliament granted (Bennetot & Estermann, 2015) UASs more freedom in particular with regard to their dependence on regional policy in 2014. Based on critical mass considerations, synergy possibilities as well as redundancies and overlap in subjects and field of studies, several mergers were carried out. This was not only lead by geographic proximity, but also as related to profiles and context.

The model of the public-private partnership in Austria has increased the influence of regional politics in the higher education sector since the 1990s. Today, the maintainers are also political actors, interest groups, and other organizations. As such, they have substantial power in strategic decisions. Of course, there are incentive mechanisms via subsidies or additional funding for further study places through federal funds. Realistic opportunities for this model of merger between UASS are institutional initiatives. A purely top-down process is unlikely due to the complex ownership, influence, and control mechanisms.

A look at the legal forms shows that UASS have different models. Thus, UASS are predominantly organized as limited companies. In addition, there are associations and private foundations as organizational models. The only exception among the UASS is the Theresian Military Academy with the Federal Ministry of Defense as provider. In general, the merger of two or more UASS depends on the different organizational models of the merging institutions and the final form after the merger. Here, there are a number of different options based on the large diversity of the sector.

## 4    Conclusions and Outlook

Mergers have been used worldwide since the 1980s for the further development of higher education. The reasons as well as the challenges around such mergers are manifold: defragmentation, economies of scale, and efficiency considerations are often used as supporting arguments (Harman & Harman, 2003). In addition, mergers as the result of excellence initiatives or international rankings are often used. In the last decade, Austria has also gained experience with mergers in higher education. As one example, the emergence of teacher's colleges through a merger of several institutions lead to a new type of higher education institution. In addition, several non-university research institutions joined universities some years ago. A systematic debate about possible further mergers within higher education or through hybrid solutions in not on the top of the higher education agenda in the country. However, such considerations are repeatedly taken up by political actors. Even though there is no clear commitment to mergers in general nor in particular sectors in higher education, international examples provide fruitful cases to be reviewed in relation to Austria. Due to the size, number and types of institutions in Austria, as well as the noted international trends, a strategic, systematic and institutional examination of mergers is useful.

Mergers can be driven both from inside and outside of the sector. However, incentives, the role of governments, and institutional leaders remain core issues. Especially the role of the leadership including the ability to manage change processes is crucial. It is obvious that university mergers, for example, are clearly defined by law, while a cross-sectoral merger remains more challenging. At the same time, hybrid models, beyond the well-known and much-quoted justifications about critical mass in research or synergies in teaching, can produce good complementary organizational models (Bennetot & Estermann, 2015; OECD, 2017; Rocha et al., 2018). In addition to the merger of non-university research institutions, there are a variety of organizations involved in teaching and training outside the higher education sector, which could be considered as potential subjects with synergy effects, for example, in third mission activities. These include, for example, regional development institutions, incubators but also facilities for minorities, disadvantaged groups or adult education organizations.

One of the driving forces behind mergers remains efficiency. However, the financial effects of mergers in higher education have not yet been established. Research on mergers always emphasizes the importance of contextualization and of the relevant indicators (Pausits, 2015). Increasing the third-party funding ratio while at the same time increasing expenditure on teaching through geographical distances have different effects. In practice, mergers are in most cases implemented for a small number of objectives. Simplified framework conditions make mergers, especially at the beginning, less complex.

The illustrated models are primary considerations and a first mapping of the 'merger landscape' in Austria. There are many good arguments why one university should merge with the other university, and just as many good arguments against it. Mergers often signify the beginning of a journey with the first known destinations of this journey at the beginning. However, where the journey leads at the end and which risks and opportunities are still recognized during this journey is often uncertain. Changes bring opportunities and risks. University mergers are not new phenomena and have been practiced again and again for nearly 40 years. As a result, merger will continue to exist as an organizational development approach or even as a system development tool. Whether and how Austria prepares for this journey and join other countries, remains to be seen.

### References

Altbach, P. G., & Peterson, P. M. (2007). *Higher education in the new century: Global challenges and innovative ideas*. Sense Publishers.

Bennetot, P. E., & Estermann, T. (2015). *Define thematic report: University mergers in Europe*. European University Association.

Chantelau, F. (2015). Der verfassungsrechtliche Rahmen für Fusionen von Universitäten und Fachhochschulen: Die Fusion der Universität Lüneburg mit der Fachhochschule Nordostniedersachsen. *Lünerburger Schriften zum Wirtschaftsrecht* (Vol. 28). Nomos.

Curaj, A., Georghiou, L., Harper, J., & Egron-Polak, E. (Eds.). (2015). *Mergers and alliances in higher education: International practice and emerging opportunities.* Springer International Publishing.

Curaj, A., Matei, L., Pricopie, R., Salmi, J., & Scott, P. (Eds.). (2015). *The European higher education area: Between critical reflections and future policies.* Springer.

D'Ambrosio, M., & Ehrenberg, R. G. (2007). *Transformational change in higher education: Positioning colleges and universities for future success.* Edward Elgar.

Dixon, K., & Coy, D. (2007). University governance: Governing bodies as providers and users of annual reports. *Higher Education, 54*(2), 267–291.

Georghiou, L., & Cassingena Harper, J. (2015). Mergers and alliances in context. In A. Curaj, L. Georghiou, J. Cassingena Harper, & E. Egron-Polak (Eds.), *Mergers and alliances in higher education: International practice and emerging opportunities* (pp. 1–14). Springer International Publishing.

Goedegebuure, L. C. J. (1992). *Mergers in higher education: A cooperative perspective.* Lemma.

Harman, G., & Harman, K. (2003). Institutional mergers in higher education: Lessons from international experience. *Tertiary Education and Management, 9*(1), 29–44.

Harman, G., & Harman, K. (2008). Strategic mergers of strong institutions to enhance competitive advantage. *Higher Education Policy, 21*(1), 99–121.

Harman, K., & Meek, V. L. (2002). Introduction to special issue: "Merger revisited: International perspectives on mergers in higher education". *Higher Education, 44*(1), 1–4.

Hazelkorn, E. (2011). *Rankings and the reshaping of higher education: The battle for world-class-excellence.* Palgrave Macmillan.

Huisman, J., Boer, H. de, Dill, D. D., & Souto-Otero, M. (2015). *The Palgrave international handbook of higher education policy and governance.* Palgrave Macmillan.

Kyvik, S. (2002). The merger of non-university colleges in Norway. *Higher Education, 44*(1), 53–72.

Mahrl, M., & Pausits, A (2011). Third mission indicators for new ranking methodologies. *Evaluation in Higher Education, 4*(1), 43–65.

Mao, Y. Q., Liu, J. J., & Du, Y. (2009). The effects of university mergers in China since 1990s: From the perspective of knowledge production. *International Journal of Educational Management, 23*(1), 19–33.

Marginson, S. (2016). High participation systems of higher education. *The Journal of Higher Education, 87*(2), 243–271.

Mortimer, K. P., & Sathre, C. O. B. (2007). *The art and politics of academic governance: Relations among boards, presidents, and faculty.* Praeger Publishers.

National Council of the Republic of Austria. (2002). *Universities act 2002*. Retrieved February 12, 2020, from https://www.uibk.ac.at/index/finanzabteilung/ug2002_englisch.pdf

OECD. (2017). *Collaboration, alliances, and merger among higher education institutions* (Working Papers No. 160). OECD.

OECD. (1992). *The measurement of scientific and technical activities: The 'Frascati manual'*. OECD.

Pausits, A. (2015). The knowledge society and diversification of higher education: From the social contract to the mission of universities. In Curaj, A., Matei, L., Pricopie, R., Salmi, J., & Scott, P. (Eds.), *The European higher education area: Between critical reflections and future policies* (pp. 267–284). Springer.

Pausits, A. (2016). The Austrian reform of the Fachhochschulen. In J. Huisman, H. de Boer, D. F. Westerheijden, M. Vukasovic, M. Seeber, & F. File (Eds.), *Policy analysis of structural reforms in higher education* (pp. 31–51). Springer.

Pinheiro, R., Langa, P., & Pausits, A. (2015). One and two equals three? The third mission of higher education institutions. *European Journal of Higher Education, 5*(3), 233–249.

Pinheiro, R., Geschwind, L., & Aarrevaara, T. (2016). *Mergers in higher education: The experience from Northern Europe* (1st ed., Vol. 46, Higher Education Dynamics). Springer.

Rocha, V., Teixeira, P. N., & Biscaia, R. (2018). Mergers in European higher education: Financial issues and multiple rationales. *Higher Education Policy* (Advance online publication). https://doi.org/10.1057/s41307-017-0076-2

Unidata. (n.d.). Retrieved February 12, 2020, from https://www.bmbwf.gv.at/Themen/Hochschule-und-Universit%C3%A4t/Hochschulsystem/Hochschulstatistik---unidata.html

Ursin, J., Aittola, H., Henderson, C., & Välimaa, J. (2010). Is education getting lost in university mergers? *Tertiary Education and Management, 16*(4), 327–340.

Wolfensberger, M. V. C. (2015). Austria: A rapidly expanding higher education sector. In M. V. C. Wolfensberger (Ed.), *Talent development in European higher education: Honors programs in the Benelux, Nordic and German-speaking countries* (Vol. 4, pp. 213–227). Springer.

CHAPTER 7

# What Does It Mean to Be a Responsible 21st Century South African University?

*Denyse Webbstock*

## Abstract

This chapter explores three themes underlying debates on South African universities with respect to responsibility.

The first is the dichotomy of the global versus the local in defining university identity and purpose. The second discusses the binary necessities to widen access, and to ensure sustainability, where achieving an appropriate balance often requires hard policy choices to be made. The third theme relates to a responsible curriculum, and here the debates on what should be taught are explored. These range from the need for decolonization, to the need to be more future-focused in preparation for participation in the fourth industrial revolution.

The chapter concludes that the application of a consistent set of principles to making the difficult choices, tempered with significant pragmatism, will lead to a responsible higher education sector.

## Keywords

responsibility – curriculum – identity – decolonization – global vs local – fourth industrial revolution – universities – South Africa

## 1 Introduction

The theme of responsibility is particularly apposite in relation to universities placed at the southern tip of Africa. While universities in South Africa are faced with many of the same challenges experienced by higher education elsewhere, the issues that are raised in relation to the responsibility of universities globally are magnified in the context of a developing country, particularly one that is emerging from a complicated history with all the legacy issues that that

© KONINKLIJKE BRILL NV, LEIDEN, 2020 | DOI: 10.1163/9789004436558_008

entails. Simultaneously, it is also attempting to bring about rapid change and to forge a new identity.

While many global debates apply, the specificity of the location of South African universities geographically and historically, twenty-five years after the introduction of democracy and the re-entry of South African universities to the international community, demands careful consideration. Three binary tensions that underlie an examination of what it means to be a responsible university, given these contextual factors, are explored in this chapter.

## 2 Responsibility and Focus

The first major issue is the question of how South African universities should navigate the need to be both locally relevant and globally competitive at the same time. It's a question of the appropriate gaze – internal or external. It is also a question of fundamental purpose – do universities see themselves primarily as contributing to the economic and social development of a new democratic order and the national priorities of South Africa, or do they have aspirations to participate in the global knowledge producing community, with an implied emphasis on research productivity? While these are not necessarily mutually exclusive ends, resource constraints and limited capacity often mean that the emphasis is heavier on one end of the scale.

South Africa currently has 26 public universities, of three types: traditional universities that see themselves as research-intensive; comprehensive universities that straddle the divide between theoretical and applied studies; and universities of technology that, as their name implies, focus on technological studies. All are degree-granting institutions, although the proportion of diploma offerings is higher in the latter two categories, and all are expected to produce research to varying degrees. The highly-regulated private sector is expanding, but from a very small base; the enrolments in the private sector constitute about a tenth of the higher education system.

The public higher education system has, until recently, really been thought of as the university sector described above, which is comparatively small relative to other countries in terms of the participation rate (although having grown exponentially since 1994).[1] The further education and training sector, with particular post-school training colleges (now known as Tertiary Vocation Education and Training (TVET) colleges), is smaller still, and relatively under-developed, and has only in the last few years come under the purview of the Department of Higher Education and Training which is re-conceptualizing the system as one that encompasses 'post-school education and training'. This chapter focuses on the university sector within the post-school system.

The university sector is largely an undergraduate one, with only a few institutions offering substantial proportions of postgraduate offerings. Of just over a million students in the system as a whole, 83% are studying at the undergraduate level (CHE, 2019, derived from fig. 52). It has been described as a low participation, high attrition system in that the Gross Enrolment Rate (GER) is roughly 21%, but student completion rates remain low (approximately 30% in regulation time for a 3-year degree, and 55% after five years) and they are sharply skewed by race and prior education.[2]

In the national policy debates, university education has been regarded as a public good in the main, but the funding system is based on both governmental subsidies or block grants, and individual private tuition fees, which have increased as subsidies have declined. To increase access, there is a National Student Financial Aid Scheme (NSFAS) that provides financial aid to financially needy students in the form of bursaries and loans. The funding regime indicates thus that higher education is seen de facto as both a public and a private good, and this of course has a bearing on the way the fundamental purpose of higher education is conceptualized.

While the sector is small enough to be cohesive, it belies a fragmented and uneven past, and twenty-five years into democracy, the scars of inequality still run deep. As noted in a review of higher education (Webbstock, 2016, p. 6):

> The sector's cohesiveness also masks continuing levels of inequality for students and differences in quality of education within the sector, with some institutions focused on climbing the international rankings while others have been placed under administration as government intervenes to rescue them from particular governance and management crises.
>
> The cohesion and integration have also left unresolved the question of potential institutional differentiation, with continuing contestation about the nature and identity of higher education and its fundamental purpose – or whether there are multiple purposes to be achieved in different ways.

The question of what is a responsible university in this context can therefore have different interpretations, depending on the institutional vantage point. Nevertheless, the institutions are all confronted with similar dilemmas and the same policy, economic and social context that frames such a discussion.

Most obviously, the question of fundamental orientation plays itself out in the question of whether our universities should participate in international rankings systems or focus more deliberately on finding solutions to local social and economic challenges.

The ranking systems are particularly controversial in a situation of deep inequality. There are widespread perceptions that ranking systems are biased towards research output and favour institutions that are established and well-endowed, to the detriment of those institutions that are more focused on a teaching mission and which are geared to producing so-called 'work-ready' graduates to help drive the economy and social development. Underlying this critique is an idea that 'blue skies' research is a luxury in some situations, whose benefits may take a long time to reach application stage, while the needs of the country are more immediate and pressing – the need for engineers, professionals, artisans, teachers, nurses and other medical personnel, is acute and pressing, suggesting a focus on teaching and training. While acknowledging the reality of rankings systems, the Minister of Higher Education and Training (Nzimande, 2019) in his previous term noted:

> But there are many dangers with ranking systems. What is a particular concern to us is the potential to reproduce or even widen inequalities. Both within and between countries, institutional ranking systems tend to reinforce existing hierarchies and can lead to lack of development of university systems at a national level, as resources are siphoned off to support a few institutions to become more highly ranked in the globally competitive arena.

Having outlined the particular ways in which ranking indicators can perversely drive a system towards particular goals, he makes a strong argument that,

> International rankings drive behaviour, and they are unlikely to go away. Universities in the developing world should identify areas of excellence where institutions can be supported through national and continental collaboration and support to compete within the global knowledge economy, strengthening a differentiated system as well as individual institutions. We should energetically promote and develop a field-specific ranking system to stand alongside the more traditional approaches that make unfair comparisons between very different kinds of institutions, and at the same time we must continue to challenge the mainstream ranking systems, in terms of what they are measuring, how they are measuring, and what the effects of this measurement are on systems.

The reality in South Africa is that less than half of the 26 institutions feature in the ranking systems, and where they do, in terms of research output, they tend to perform very well. However, in terms of measures such as staff: student ratio, they cannot even begin to compete, as the universities are largely teaching institutions for many students with a relatively small core of academic staff responsible for both teaching and research. The introduction of the Times Higher Education Impact Rankings based on the United Nations' Sustainable Development Goals has provided an avenue for South African universities to compete on an entirely different set of indicators denoting more socio-economic ends, such as reduced inequalities, or gender equality, or poverty reduction, which some argue are more apposite to the developmental context in which these universities are situated than purely research-related indicators alone.

So what constitutes a responsible focus for a South African university? After decades of a gaze towards the colonial north, one that influenced not only the idea of what constitutes excellence in higher education, but that determined in large part the curriculum of universities, it makes sense for institutions now to be immersed in developing the knowledge required to address local challenges, particularly, as is often argued, such universities are largely government funded. Clearly, from this perspective, the subsidizing of universities must lead to improved socio-economic outcomes for the country as a whole, implying a focus on locally-applicable knowledge and skills. Yet too inward a gaze can subvert the very intent to harness global knowledge to this end, and lead to a more parochial purpose and perhaps venture towards mediocrity in the long term. This is a difficult tension for South African institutions to navigate.

The University of Johannesburg, a relatively young university born of a merger in 2005 between an Afrikaans-speaking university, a so-called 'technikon', and the Soweto and East Rand campuses of a former distance institution, has chosen to navigate this tension by focusing its strategy on preparing its students to participate meaningfully in the fourth industrial revolution (4IR). The critique sometimes voiced is that the implication is a research focus on advanced technology and a global gaze that belies the importance of the grassroots challenges of the metropolitan area of Johannesburg and the rural areas from which many of its students originate. Such a focus is also sometimes seen to be in opposition to the political imperative of 'transformation', which in its South African meaning, implies not only radical change in the demographic composition of the staff and student bodies of universities, but also in the fundamental role of universities to focus more squarely on national goals. As expressed in a review of higher education (CHE, 2016, p. 22),

> In short, the vision and goals of the founding post-apartheid policy statements related not simply to the achievement of an equitable demographic composition of the student body in terms of access and success,

the achievement of equity in the staff body and improvement in research outputs and the production of high-level skills for the economy, but to a higher education system that would play a significant role in helping to build an open, democratic, post-apartheid society and an informed, critical, and socially aware citizenry.

As an example of concern about a focus on the fourth industrial revolution, the Minister of Higher Education and Training has raised the specter of job losses through the disruptive effects of the introduction of advanced technologies, and warned against a focus on 4IR resulting in deepening inequalities (Nzimande, 2019). Similarly, Gillwald (2019) warns that,

> The adoption by South Africa of 4IR models and policy designed by WEF (World Economic Forum) partner consultants is based on a number of assumptions that don't apply to developing countries. These include mature, competitive markets and functioning democracies, capable institutions and educated and healthy populations. As a result, the proposed policies are unlikely to contribute to economic growth, job creation and the empowerment of women ...
>
> The layering of advanced technologies over existing inequalities won't contribute to digital inclusion. It will simply worsen inequality within and between nations. How quickly South Africa is able to redress existing inequalities will determine the degree to which it is able to harness the potential benefits of advanced technologies for equitable development.

However, she also argues that,

> To this end public investment in universities is needed. This will enable knowledge and skills to be developed to undertake research and implement policy.

In this context, there is a strong argument that the responsible South African university, while being cognisant of current inequalities, would indeed be future-focused, and take advantage of global research developments precisely to advance the local development agenda.

The global gaze is important for local ends. As Xing and Marwala (2017, p. 14) write,

> First, with its hybrid innovation strategy, higher education practitioners need to have a global perspective. The trend of world technology

development should be well-perceived and thus appropriate plans need to be made. Each stream of innovation resources, internally, locally, regionally, and globally, should be utilized properly. Second, by having various development strategies and incentive policies across different departments, the connectivity among them should be optimized to avoid potential overlapping. Third, the speed of technology transfer needs to be raised to boost the economic and social development.

Excellence in this understanding is relative; it cannot be an 'empty referent' as Readings (1997) once argued, but it must relate to the academic project of the context in which a university is situated.

What does this mean in practice? For a responsible university, it means having the ambition and the courage to compete in international rankings systems while preparing students to journey from humble beginnings to be equipped to participate in a technology-mediated future. It means focusing energies on a few well-chosen areas for excellence in research which is apposite to the country rather than trying to cover all areas, and, as argued below, it means leap-frogging in terms of stages of curriculum development to ensure relevance, appropriateness and a situated excellence.

## 3 Responsibility and Participation

Not only is it important for responsible institutions to navigate the tension between the global and the local contexts, but the question of deciding who participates in higher education is acutely felt in the South African higher education context. Questions of access to higher education have been central to a developing democracy – as noted above, the higher education system, despite having more than doubled in size from the half a million in 1994 to more than a million currently, remains small in relation to demand, a demand that emanates from a population that had been denied access in the past.

Responsibility in this regard requires navigating the tension between widening access to accommodate that demand, and ensuring that the higher education system is sustainable. Universities in South Africa rely to differing extents (i.e. between 30% and 80%) on subsidy funding, and have varying success in generating third-stream income (some as little as 3%, others as much as 46%). Tuition fees make up the difference, and in order to keep universities sustainable, these have risen sharply in recent years. However, the fee-paying base is very small and the majority of students require financial aid in order to attend. The financial aid scheme has grown dramatically in recent years, particularly following a spate of student protests in 2015–2016, from R6 billion (South African Rand) in 2012 to R12 billion in 2017 (CHE, 2019, fig. 158).

The extensive and ongoing student protests around funding and financial aid have engendered major national debates around the best models for ensuring that financially needy students gain access in a sustainable way. A National Commission of Inquiry into Higher Education (Fees Commission, 2017) sat for many months in 2016–2017 to consider the potential solutions, but in the end their advice was overtaken by an announcement by the then President that the income level at which students become eligible for financial aid would be raised substantially to allow for more poor students to attend university. At the same time, the system became largely a bursary-granting scheme rather than a loan scheme, requiring the national Treasury to find an extra unbudgeted R57 billion over three years, and raising questions about the scheme's[3] long-term sustainability.

The solution was only partial, however, as it catered only for those students below the threshold level, whereas the reality is that the proportion of students whose parents can afford the fees is very small indeed, and the rest find themselves in what has become termed the 'missing middle': too rich to qualify, too poor to pay the fees. Despite the development of a separate scheme to raise funding for this group, there are already signs that there are large numbers of such students who are only partially funded, and struggling to cope, or who are being excluded from participation altogether. This is one of the main areas for continual monitoring as part of institutional research.

In addition to the above, the decision to extend the financial aid scheme according to the particular model chosen was taken without sufficient regard to some of the factors affecting student success in the system. Mention was made above of a long history of poor throughput rates in minimum time across the system, some of which could be attributable to students' financial difficulties, but which are more clearly related to an 'articulation gap' between school and university, which results in students being insufficiently prepared academically for higher education study in a variety of different ways.

The Council on Higher Education (CHE) conducted an extensive study in 2013 that focused on the barriers to student success, which culminated in advice provided to the Minister of Higher Education and Training regarding what could be done to alleviate the situation (CHE, 2013). The study concluded that the most significant contributing factor to poor throughput rates was a systemic one; i.e. that the parameters within which South African degree curricula are designed have become rigid and out of sync with the current student body and its needs. In other words, the majority of South African students take much longer than the three-year regulation time to complete a degree, and thus it makes sense to extend the regulation time and to redesign the curriculum to cover four years, and to allow space in the curriculum for the developmental work to be undertaken to address the under-preparedness – which takes different forms in different fields. In essence, while some of the financial aid issues are being addressed, the students are being funded to gain access to a system that is inefficient in facilitating students to graduate in the time for which they are funded. In addition, to find the resources for the financial aid scheme, subsidies to universities are already beginning to be cut, which, in the longer term, will have an effect on the quality of the system through reduced staffing levels and lack of maintenance of infrastructure.

Balancing the tension between increasing access and ensuring sustainability is difficult; however, the Fees Commission's recommendations may have been the more responsible route to resolving this tension than what in fact transpired. The Fees Commission argued that the funding of university students needed to be considered in the context of education overall – from early childhood development, schooling, and the very underdeveloped tertiary vocational and community education sectors – and not privilege only a very small proportion of youth overall who are admitted to universities. It also recognized that curriculum reform was necessary to address high dropout rates and to ensure the maintenance of quality in the system. Arguing that higher education has both public and private benefits, it advocated a cost-sharing model to pay for university tuition; subsidies to universities needed to increase to 1% of GDP, while student fees could be covered by an income-contingent loan scheme for all, with the provision that those graduates whose future income did not meet a certain threshold would not be required to repay. In effect, the students' repayment terms would be dependent on their own future income, rather than the past income of their parents or guardians, providing all academically qualifying students with the opportunity to study.[4] The decision that was taken instead is that there is a bursary scheme for students whose parents' income is below a certain threshold, while all others do not qualify. The Fees Commission's recommendations prioritized the sustainability not only of the financial aid scheme, but of higher education itself, while it can be argued that the decision that was actually taken to introduce free education for some was politically expedient, and responded to immediate demands, while paying less regard to future sustainability.

## 4 Responsibility and Curriculum

The theme of responsibility underlies not only the questions of the internal and external orientation of institutions in terms of purpose, and the tension between widening access and ensuring sustainability, but it is echoed in debates about what is to be taught. There are enduring discussions about what kind of curriculum is appropriate in a South African university in the 21st Century. At the heart of student protests in 2015 and 2016 was a call to 'decolonize' the curriculum, and in most narratives this implied a refocusing of what is taught, from a preoccupation with knowledge derived from the former colonial powers, to foregrounding indigenous knowledge systems, local content, and specifically African ways of understanding the world.

There are a number of different strands to the decolonization narrative. In some versions, the view is that the content of what is taught needs to be replaced – that a particular Eurocentric 'canon' of works should be reoriented towards locally-produced texts, examples and applications of knowledge in a bid to Africanize the curriculum.

A related version concerns not only what is taught, but how it is taught – there is a need to move away from a conception of the learner as 'decontextualized', towards recognizing his or her social embeddedness in order to prevent alienation and facilitate better access to the hidden codes and meanings of disciplinary knowledge.

A third strand attacks what is perceived to be dominant western rationality and the scientific paradigm underlying conceptions of knowledge itself, and proposes a fundamental transformation of the university as an institution in an 'ontological project' to reassert what it means to be African (Njamnjoh, 2016).

Curriculum is intensely political, and different views on what should constitute an appropriate curriculum for a South African university have resonance with the first theme of this chapter, i.e. the local versus the global vantage point for establishing institutional identity and purpose. As Badat (2017) notes,

> It is clear that curriculum is connected with large and fundamental questions, and that the issue of its decolonisation involves tackling simultaneously and concertedly the question of the core purpose and goals of South African universities. It should also be clear that curriculum is connected with profound questions of values, epistemology, ontology and knowledge making and dissemination, in a context of unequal social relations.

All of the versions of the decolonization debate sketched above turn the gaze inward and set themselves against a particular past. They are sometimes seen as being in tension with more externally-focused and future-oriented narratives that insist on a global gaze in the readying of students for active participation in an international world of scholars, such as those strategies that focus on the fourth industrial revolution. The latter view implies embracing and harnessing knowledge from wherever it is produced, and contributing to its global currency from a unique standpoint.

A 'large and fundamental question' facing responsible universities in South Africa therefore, is how they will be prepared for the fourth industrial revolution in a context in which the hallmarks of the third industrial revolution – digital access and connectivity, and the skills that enable that – are very unevenly distributed. Curriculum in the third industrial revolution is highly influenced by the immediate and increasingly free access to information, mediated through a changing pedagogy that favours group-work, problem-solving in project teams and peer learning, often in blended modes – yet much of the curriculum in South African universities is still informed by traditional methods of delivering knowledge in ways in which the learner essentially remains a passive recipient. Access to information is dependent on access to technology, reliable digital and other infrastructure and digital literacy, yet these are not ubiquitous in the South African context.

The fourth industrial revolution, which is characterized by the "integration and compounding effects of multiple 'exponential technologies', such as artificial intelligence (AI), biotechnologies and nanomaterials ..." (Penprase, 2018) demands a leap in curriculum development for South African universities to be able to participate meaningfully in the brave new world, or risk being relegated to onlookers and recipients of received technologies developed elsewhere, on others' terms.

Penprase (2018, p. 217) puts it thus,

> The need for higher education to respond is urgent as the power of 4IR technologies for either positive social impacts or devastating environmental damage is upon us, as is the potential for irreversible loss of control over networks of powerful artificial intelligence (AI) agents with increasing autonomy within financial sectors and within urban infrastructure. Substantial changes to the science and technology curriculum will be required to allow for students to develop capacity in the rapidly emerging areas of genomics, data science, AI, robotics and nanomaterials.

Obviously this implies a need to increase a focus on the technological disciplines, but, as importantly, the context, conditions and use to which technological advances are put requires graduates with a much broader understanding across disciplinary boundaries, who are flexible and adaptable, and who have a capacity to innovate. How universities achieve that is dependent on the appropriateness of the shape, form, mode, and quality of their curriculum. Penprase (2018) continues, noting that,

> Any effective 4IR education strategy must also include in equal measure a deep consideration of the human condition, the ways in which new technologies and shifting economic power impact people of all socioeconomic levels, and the threats that exist within a world that is increasingly interconnected, in a way that fosters deep intercultural understanding and an abiding respect for freedom and human rights. Such approaches favor an interdisciplinary and global curriculum in a residential context, such as is found in many liberal arts institutions. These approaches maximize the development of intercultural and interpersonal skills, which will be a hallmark of the future 4IR workplace.

A responsible university in South Africa needs to be adept in positioning itself between the poles of the debate between decoloniality and an interconnected world, finding ways to be rooted in its context and taking account of the specificity of its historical and geographical location, while inserting itself into global conversations and contributing and competing on a more equal footing.

## 5    Conclusion

The three themes explored in this chapter indicate that achieving responsibility in institutional terms lies in navigating careful paths between various dichotomous standpoints. There are no clear guides to achieving an optimal balance between the competing ideas in each of the three themes. However, the consistent application of a set of a priori principles, implemented with pragmatism and good sense is important in this regard. Achieving a balance of priorities is essential, with due regard to principles of equity and fairness, as well as transparency and quality, to ensure a credible, stable and sustainable higher education system that is appropriate for its context, but able to perform on the global stage. Responsibility in this context is a complex, situated concept that makes governance and leadership especially challenging.

### Notes

1   In terms of UNESCO's Gross Enrolment Rate, South Africa at 21% is below the average of 29% for developing countries, and far below the 74% for developed countries (UNESCO 2016, table 5, p. 436).

2   UNESCO's indicator of participation, the Gross Enrolment Rate or GER, i.e. the total headcount enrolled in some form of higher education over the national population of 20–24 year-olds of the population (CHE, 2019, p. iv; fig. 7; fig. 132).

3   According to the then Minister of Finance in his budget speech in February 2018, an additional R57 billion over the next three years would need to be allocated to fund free education for students who come from poor or working-class families with a combined income of R350,000. This is on top of the R10 billion which was provisionally allocated in the 2017 budget (Mail & Guardian, 2018).

## References

Badat, S. (2017, April 10). *Trepidation, longing and belonging: Liberating the curriculum at universities in South Africa*. Public lecture. University of Pretoria.

CHE. (2013). *A proposal for undergraduate curriculum reform in South Africa: The case for a flexible curriculum structure*. CHE.

CHE. (2016). *Advice to the minister of higher education and training on fee increases for South African universities for 2017*.

CHE. (2017). *Advice to the minister of higher education and training on fee regulation for South African universities*.

CHE. (2019). *VitalStats 2017*. Pretoria.

Commission of Inquiry into Higher Education and Training (Fees Commission). (2017). Report, (pp. 540–554), Commission of Inquiry.

Gillwald, A. (2019, October 3). South Africa must harness digital technology in a way that helps fix its problems. *The Conversation*.

Nyamnjoh, F. B. (2016). *#RhodesMustFall: Nibbling at resilient colonialism in South Africa*. Langa.

Nzimande, B. E. (2016, September 4). Challenging rankings systems. *Independent Thinking, 11*.

Nzimande, B. E. (2019, September 19). *The role of a transformative higher education in a developmental state and its response to the challenges and opportunities posed by the 4th Industrial Revolution*. UNISA Founders' Lecture.

Penprase, B. E. (2018). The fourth industrial revolution and higher education. In N. W. Gleason (Ed.), *Higher education in the era of the fourth industrial revolution*. Palgrave Macmillan.

Readings, B. (1997). *The university in ruins*. Harvard University Press.

UNESCO. (2016). *GEM report 2016* (2nd ed.). Statistical tables. UNESCO.

Webbstock, D. (2016). Overview. In CHE (Ed.), *Higher education reviewed: Two decades of democracy*. CHE.

Webbstock, D. (2016). Overview. In *Higher education reviewed: Two decades of democracy* (p. 22). CHE.

Webbstock, D. (2018). *A monitoring brief on decolonising the curriculum*. BrieflySpeaking. CHE.

Xing, B., & Marwala, T. (2017). Implications of the fourth industrial age on higher education. *The Thinker, 73*, 14.

CHAPTER 8

# The Central Government in Higher Education: Defining Areas of Responsibility between State Ministry and Governmental Agencies in Austria and Norway

*Philipp Friedrich*

### Abstract

In their attempt to redefine the relationship between state and higher education institutions by the end of the century, national administrations in Europe underwent changes in their organizational format and governance approach toward the sector. This chapter presents parts of a doctoral thesis that examined closely the governance changes taking place in Austrian and Norwegian HE in the early 2000s. Central to the thesis were organizational transformations at the ministerial level and the creation of governmental agencies in the area of quality assurance and internationalization, using organizational autonomy and capacity as analytical dimensions. Based on statistical data, legal frameworks, policy documents, and expert interviews, the thesis shed light on how governments in higher education transformed against the backdrop of substantive governance reforms. The Austrian approach included capacity reductions at the ministerial level, and a cautious approach toward the empowerment of governmental agencies. The Norwegian approach involved stable capacity developments at the ministerial level, while similarly expanding autonomy and capacity of governmental agencies.

### Keywords

administrative reorganization – agencification – higher education governance – public sector reforms

© KONINKLIJKE BRILL NV, LEIDEN, 2020 | DOI: 10.1163/9789004436558_009

## 1    Introduction

The central government in higher education (HE), that is the state ministry with its subordinate agencies, plays a decisive role in European HE systems. It defines the structural setup of the overall governance structure and is politically accountable for the actions of universities and colleges[1] (Austin & Jones, 2015). However, given the increased complexity of the HE policy arena with its various actors, different governance levels, and numerous policy issues (Chou et al., 2017), finding effective governance arrangements presents a considerable challenge. Two developments stand out that have added to the increased challenge in rearranging the governance of European HE in the past decades.

The first development refers to the enhancement of institutional autonomy,[2] which was considered to unlock the potential of higher education institutions (HEIs), and which would make them more effective in adapting to society's needs (Maassen & Musselin, 2009). It was also considered to release the ministry from administrative overload and provide it with the opportunity to steer from a distance (Capano, 2011; Kickert, 1995). The second development refers to the establishment of governmental agencies during administrative reorganization within the HE bureaucracy[3] (Bach et al., 2012). Agencies cover parts of the ministerial mandate in specific policy themes such as quality assurance (QA), student affairs internationalization, and digitalization. They enjoy some discretion in their scope of actions, but remain legally and financially bound to the ministry (Christensen & Lægreid, 2007).

However, especially the latter remains an understudied aspect in HE governance. While some scholars addressed the issue of agencies as buffer organizations in the early 1990s (e.g., de Boer, 1992 or El-Khawas, 1992), a more systematic approach about the agencies' governance relationship to the ministry is still missing. Yet, in order to understand the consequences of systemic governance shifts, e.g. caused by enhanced institutional autonomy and governance reforms, it is important to turn attention to how the role of the central government is developing. The latter is the aim of this chapter.

The chapters suggests an analytical framework that captures changes at the central government based on autonomy and capacity developments. The framework also assesses ministerial effectiveness, and discusses various autonomy and capacity arrangements in relation to the agencies. The chapter is in essence a synopsis of a dissertation project that studied these developments in light of university reforms and during the establishment of governmental agencies in the areas of QA and internationalization. Two cases, the Austrian and Norwegian central government in HE, and their development in the past two decades functioned as empirical examples.

The remainder of the chapter is as follows: first, agencification processes in HE are elaborated upon before presenting a conceptual and analytical approach to study administrative reorganization in HE. Then the empirical contexts (Austria and Norway) are outlined paired with methodological considerations. Some empirical results will be presented, before discussing their implications for the governance of HE. The chapter concludes by outlining limitations and future research avenues in the study of the central government in HE.

## 2 What Do We Know so Far about Agencification in Higher Education?

The creation of governmental agencies, often described as agencification, is by no means a new phenomenon in the study of administrative reorganization (see e.g., Bach et al., 2012; Pollitt et al., 2001; Verhoest, 2012). It is, however, compared to other public sectors, a more recent phenomenon in the HE area, with limited attention from the research community (notable exceptions are e.g., Beerkens, 2015; Capano & Turri, 2017; Jungblut & Woelert, 2018).

Agencies are commonly understood as public sector organizations that remain subordinate to a ministry, yet enjoy considerable discretion in their assigned policy fields. Thus, they are often labelled as semi-autonomous agencies/organizations, as the parent ministry has the authority to substantially alter the budgets and main goals of the agency (Pollitt et al., 2001). Agencies are usually led by civil servants appointed by the ministry, while the ministry remains politically accountable for the agency's actions (Bach et al., 2012).

The establishment of governmental agencies is part of the structural devolution of monolithic state bureaucracies, which started around the 1980s with the introduction of New Public Management (NPM) inspired reforms (Ferlie et al., 2008). Even though earlier forms and concepts of governmental agencies can be already found in various countries at that time, their number and function has enhanced dramatically in the time after (Christensen et al., 2008).

What was new with the reforms from the 1980s was the increased focus on managerial and business-like aspects in public administration, in which agencies were supposed to play a crucial role in the future. The general assumption was that agencification leads to improved public sector performance

(Christensen & Lægreid, 2007) as agencies have to operate in more market-oriented environments with more business-like character (Van Thiel et al., 2012). This was expected to lead to more competitive behavior, closer relationship to customers and their needs, and higher efficiency in providing public services.

This development within the broader public administration domain also spilled over to the administering of HE, and at that time was subsumed under the concept of steering-at-a-distance (Van Vught, 1989). The concept describes a governance relationship in which the ministry abstains from micro-managing HE institutions, and focuses on output steering instead. Moreover, public agencies were increasingly established and functioned as buffer organizations in the growing gap between ministry and the HE institutions. A body of literature from the early 1990s discusses this changing relationship between the state and universities at that time, as well as the first experiences with HE buffer organizations/agencies in countries at the forefront of this development, such as Great Britain and the Netherlands (e.g., de Boer, 1992; El-Khawas, 1992).

However, the HE reform wave in Western Europe by the end of the 1990s/ early 2000s brought forth a new generation of agencies, which were tighter linked to ministry yet also enjoyed considerable discretion and capacity for governing specific policy themes. Yet, their changed function and standing in the governance relationship with the ministry and the sector came with certain implications. As seen in other public sectors, a number of challenges emerge between ministry and agencies in how to define areas of responsibility. These challenges typically include questions of organizational autonomy, political control, organizational performance, sector outcome, accountability, or policy coordination (Bach et al., 2012; Christensen & Lægreid, 2007; Van Thiel et al., 2012). While these issues have been addressed for various other policy sectors (see e.g., Maggetti & Verhoest, 2014), it remains unclear how ministry and agencies in HE define areas of responsibility.

A relevant factor in these adaptation processes are represented by the institutional framework conditions under which HE operates (Maassen et al., 2018). The specific politico-administrative traditions are argued to play an important role in understanding administrative reorganization and reform outcomes since they frame in what kind of environment ministry and agencies interact with each other (Painter & Peters, 2010). For instance, some contexts might have had more experience with governmental agencies than others had, and therefore developed different forms political control and agency autonomy. It is argued that because of these varying framework conditions, administrative reorganization and agencification has played out differently across policy sectors and national contexts (Van Thiel et al., 2012).

# 3 Presenting a Conceptual and Analytical Framework for Studying Administrative Reorganization in Higher Education

Central to administrative reorganization with subsequent agencification is the question of how areas of responsibility within HE are now defined, for instance, regarding QA and internationalization themes. In order to have simple yet powerful approach, a multi-functional framework was developed, inspired by discussions about bureaucratic effectiveness (Aberbach & Rockman, 1992; Fukuyama, 2013; Holmberg & Rothstein, 2012).

The first analytical angle (or function) of the framework suggests that the effectiveness of the bureaucracy can be broken down into two dimensions – autonomy and capacity – and their interplay with each other (Fukuyama, 2013). Autonomy refers to organizational autonomy, which defines in essence the scope of actions of an organization as defined in the legal framework. Capacity refers to the resources (e.g., budget, personnel) that the organization holds in order to implement its mandate (Egeberg, 2003; Fukuyama, 2013).

The organizational scope can be measured by differing autonomy degrees. An important conceptual distinction thus has to be made between ministry and agency. Formally, both can be considered as organizations with a different degree of autonomy. However, when it comes to their relation with each other, one has to keep in mind that an agency is formally subordinated to the ministry. For instance, the ministry has the power and legitimacy to define the scope of actions for its agencies, which means that there is a natural hierarchical difference between the two. There are, of course, also examples in which some agencies enjoy considerably more organizational autonomy than other agencies, often at the expense of ministerial influence. However, in order to have a clear conceptual distinction, organizational autonomy is henceforth described as authority in the case of the ministry, and as autonomy in the case of the agency.

In order to assess how effective an organization can implement its mandate, capacity presents the other central analytical dimension, which will be labelled as bureaucratic capacity given the study's focus on administrative reorganization and bureaucratic procedures. Powerful capacity indicators are, for example personnel numbers and the operational budget (Fukuyama, 2013; Wu et al., 2015). The basic assumption is that the more resources an organization possesses, the more tasks it can perform. An immaterial capacity indicator can be the working skills that the personnel possesses, e.g., defined as their educational backgrounds and experience. Here as well, the expectation is that the higher the degree and the more experience a civil servant holds, the higher the quality of the governmental services.

The second analytical angle of the framework (second function) suggests that the interplay between authority/autonomy and capacity and the varying arrangements between them are an important indication of the actual effectiveness of governance arrangements. Organizations with a broad mandate preferably hold high levels of capacity (both qualitatively and quantitatively), whereas an organization with a limited mandate might be in need of lower capacity levels. This depends, however, also on the complexity (or the "quality") of the tasks. If we only take the sheer number ("quantity") of bureaucratic procedures into consideration, fewer tasks would require less capacity and vice versa. For instance, if an internationalization agency has been assigned an encompassing mandate but is equipped poorly, it might not be able to carry out the intended policy objectives. In the opposite case (many resources, but a limited mandate) the agencies' work might lead to redundancies or a performance outside of the actual scope of the organization's mandate.

These are not only intra-organizational aspects (e.g., within the ministry/agency, see Table 8.1) but can be also considered inter-organizationally (between ministry and an agency, see Figure 8.1). A ministry that established a powerful agency in a specific policy field such as QA might want to reduce its own mandate and capacity accordingly. Too much autonomy on both sides might result into aggravated turf wars, too little capacity on both sides in practically no policy development at all. These are by no means the only scenarios, but just examples of different autonomy and capacity arrangements within and between organizations.

Table 8.1 shows intra-organizational arrangements between autonomy and capacity, and describes potential implications of the different arrangements (for more information see also Friedrich, 2019). Growths in autonomy and capacity lead to an expanding organization, whereas reductions in both dimensions to contraction. Different variations occur, if only one of the dimensions change. If, for example, organizational autonomy is enhanced/stays the same but capacity levels remain unchanged or diminish, then the organization is expected to perform more efficiently (efficiency type 1, hyper-efficiency, and efficiency type 2). In the opposite cases, an organization would in essence have more resources to focus on a rather limited mandate (potency type 1, hyper-potency, potency type 2).

Figure 8.1 feeds these intra-organizational aspects into a framework that examines the governance relationship between ministry and agencies. One

THE CENTRAL GOVERNMENT IN HIGHER EDUCATION 147

TABLE 8.1    Autonomy-capacity arrangements for bureaucratic organizations (1st function)

| | Capacity | | |
|---|---|---|---|
| **Autonomy** + | = | − | |
| + | *Expansion* The mandate of the organization has been enhanced, as well as its resources | *Efficiency* (*type 1*) The organizational mandate has been enhanced, but the resources remain unchanged | *Hyper-efficiency* The organizational mandate is enhanced but at the same the resources have been reduced |
| = | *Potency* (*type 1*) The organization holds the same mandate but receives additional resources | *Status quo* Unchanged autonomy and capacity | *Efficiency* (*type 2*) Similar to type 1; the organization holds the same mandate capacity is being reduced. |
| − | *Hyper-potency* The organizational mandate has been limited, but resources have increased | *Potency* (*type 2*) Similar to type 1; the organizational mandate has been limited while capacity remains unchanged | *Contraction* The organization is experiencing limitations in both its mandate and its resources. |

important aspect is, for example, how authority/autonomy and capacity is distributed between ministry and agencies. Figure 8.1 provides the opportunity to position an agency within these two dimensions. If the position of an agency is marked with a dot, different statements about its relative strengths and governance effectiveness can be made, dependent on its location in the figure. An agency located within the A-quadrant has rather limited influence due to low autonomy and capacity levels. An agency in the B-quadrant enjoys moderate levels of autonomy and capacity, whereas an agency in the C-quadrant is already at the brink of pursuing agendas decoupled from the ministry.[4]

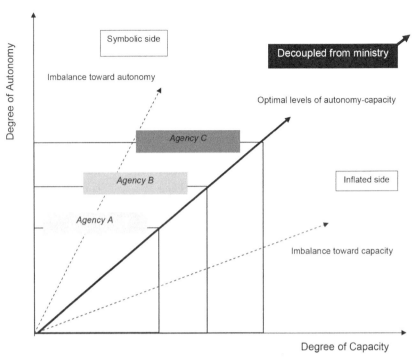

FIGURE 8.1   Autonomy-capacity arrangements for HE agencies in relation to ministry (2nd function)

Generally, the more autonomy and capacity an agency enjoys the more powerful and influential it can be considered in relation to the ministry. Agencies with ever-increasing autonomy and capacity have the potential to become increasingly decoupled from the ministry, whereas a development towards the zero-point would theoretically imply a structural incorporation back into the ministry.

Within the quadrants, a position close to the autonomy or capacity axes implies ineffectiveness for the agencies mandate, whereas placements close to the linear function imply optimal balances of autonomy and capacity. Thus, as long as a mandate can be pursued with appropriate amount of resources, also a less influential agency (type A) can be effective within its area of responsibility.

The underlying expectation in both analytical angles is the existence of an optimal balance between autonomy and capacity, both within and across the organizations, which eventually equals effective governance arrangements. The next section presents the contexts in which these expectations were tested empirically.

THE CENTRAL GOVERNMENT IN HIGHER EDUCATION                    149

## 4    A First Empirical Application: The Austrian and Norwegian Context

### 4.1    *Research Design and Case Selection*

The dissertation project underlying this book chapter is designed as a comparative case study and employed a qualitative research strategy in studying organizational changes at the central government in HE. Special interest was given to cases embedded in mature and complex HE systems, undergoing a comprehensive reform process in terms of university autonomy and administrative reorganization, and which are rooted in different politico-administrative traditions.

Austria and Norway can be considered representative contexts to which these criteria would apply (Seawright & Gerring, 2008). Austria is part of the Germanic administrative tradition, whereas Norway belongs to the Scandinavian families (Painter & Peters, 2010). Both systems experienced substantial governance changes at the early 2000s (University Act 2002 in Austria, Quality Reform 2003 in Norway). A by-product of the latest major HE reform from the early 2000s was the establishment of governmental agencies, among other things in the area of QA and internationalization. In the dissertation project, special attention was given to the two countries' HE ministries (the Austrian Federal Ministry of Education, Science and Research, and the Norwegian Ministry of Education and Research),[5] and their relationship to two subordinate agencies each, which are responsible for QA and internationalization. The agencies are the Agency for Quality Assurance and Accreditation Austria (AQ Austria) and the Norwegian Agency for Quality Assurance in Education (NOKUT), and the Norwegian Centre for International Cooperation in Education (SIU) and the Austrian Agency for International Cooperation in Education and Research (OeAD).[6]

## 5    Data Collection and Analysis

The data material collected for this study are
- Statistical data on organizational developments (personnel numbers and operational budget of the organizations), extracted from national databases and annual reports
- Policy and legal documents such as national laws and regulations, internal documents on working procedures, etc.

150 FRIEDRICH

– Expert interviews with bureaucrats, politicians and academics (see Table 8.2).

The statistical data were analyzed in a descriptive and non-inferential way (Bryman, 2016), documents and interviews were analyzed thematically

TABLE 8.2    Overview empirical material

| Austria | Norway |
| --- | --- |
| ***Legal framework*** | |
| – University Act 2002 (*Universitätsgesetz 2002*) | – Lov om universiteter og høyskoler (universitets- og høyskoleloven) |
| – The Act on Quality Assurance in Higher Education (*Hochschul-Qualitätssicherungs-gesetz*) | – NOU 2000:14 (Mjøs) |
| | – NOU 2003:25 (Ryssdal) |
| | – NOU 2008: 3 (Stjernø) |
| – Education Documentation Act (*Bildungsdokumentationsgesetz*) | – Quality reform (St.meld.nr.27, 2000–2001) |
| – Federal law on the establishment of the OeAD-GmbH (*Bundesgesetz zur Errichtung der „OeAD-Gesellschaft mit beschränkter Haftung" (OeAD-Gesetz – OeADG)*) | |
| ***Organizational documents*** | |
| *Austrian Federal Ministry of Education, Science, and Research* | *Ministry of Education and Research* |
| – Distribution of functions for the years 2000 until 2018 (*Geschäftseinteilung*) | – Allocation letters to NOKUT (for the years 2014 until 2018) and SIU (for the years 2011 until 2018) |
| *AQ Austria* | *NOKUT* |
| – Annual reports for the years 2012 until 2017 | – Annual reports for the years 2003 until 2017 |
| *FHR* | |
| – Annual reports for the years 2000 until 2010 | |
| *ÖAR* | |
| – Annual reports for the years 2000 until 2012 | |
| *AQA* | |
| – Annual reports for the years 2005 until 2012 | |
| *OeAD* | *SIU* |
| – Annual reports for the years 2000 until 2017 | – Annual reports for the years 2001 until 2017 |

(Krippendorff, 2013; Saldaña, 2016). The various data sources covered different aspects of interest. For instance, statistical data revealed organizational capacity developments over the past 20 years, documents and legal texts indicated how areas of responsibility between ministry and agencies were regulated, whereas expert interviews provided insights in how the actual bureaucratic practices developed over time. By relying on multiple sources of evidence and collecting rich data (Patton, 2014; Yin, 2014), the study performed methodological triangulation (Denzin, 2006), which provides a holistic and multi-dimensional picture of organizational change at the central government in HE.

In the following, both contexts and cases will be presented separately. The first part of each case study provides an overview for country-specific developments. This is followed by a presentation of organizational change at the particular central governments. The case studies conclude with a description of the interactional dynamics between ministry and agencies. Of central interest is how areas of responsibility are defined, based on national developments in authority/autonomy and capacity.

### 5.1    *The Austrian Case*

The most recent and substantial HE reforms in Austria led to the University Act 2002. This law was primarily about enhancing the autonomy of Austrian universities and colleges. For this reason, central administrative tasks were transferred to the institutional level and the institutions strengthened as organizational actors. The institutional leadership became more influential which meant more decision-making competencies in e.g., personnel affairs and financial matters.

The developments were embedded in overall political change processes that considered enhanced institutional autonomy as a necessary reform step. The first were ongoing Europeanization processes, in which the harmonization of European HE presented a central element (as e.g., seen in the Bologna reform). Institutional autonomy was considered a possibility to unleash the untapped resources of European universities against the background of increasing global competition.

The second important driver at that time was the changing political climate in Austria. The new conservative-populist government favoured a slim bureaucracy, leaning toward a stricter NPM induced reform approach. Enhanced institutional autonomy thus presented a favourable option to reduce bureaucratic workload. As central administrative tasks were transferred to the institutions, the ministry reduced its bureaucratic capacity accordingly. For instance, the personnel numbers at the section responsible for HE dropped at about

40–50% compared to original numbers before the University Act 2002 was implemented.

Further, strengthening the agency level as a supplement to reduced ministerial capacity played a less important role in Austria. QA was not organized coherently for the whole sector but was separated into three different assurance agencies. This tri-partite system had different implications for the different institutional types (public institutions, universities of applied sciences, and public universities). For instance, public universities were not as strictly regulated as the private institutions or the universities of applied sciences (Fiorioli, 2014). It was not before 2012 – when the three assurance organizations merged into AQ Austria – that national QA began to play an increasing role, especially for public universities.[7] Since it started its operations in 2012, the AQ Austria had moderate staff number and operational budget developments; from 26 to 32 employees between 2012 and 2017, and from 1.66 million € to 2.54 million € in the same period.

The Austrian Agency for International Cooperation in Education and Research (OeAD) has a long organizational history, and was most of the time organized as an association closely linked to the universities. In 2009, the OeAD turned into a limited liability company (LLC), 100% owned by the ministry, which makes it effectively a governmental agency. The OeAD's mandate covers internationalization, exchange and mobility issues in tertiary education. A large part of their mandate concerns the implementation of European mobility programs. In recent years, the OeAD also became responsible for such matters in secondary education. The mandate expansions led to substantial growths regarding personnel and budget: from 100 employees in 2000 to 228 in 2017, with an increased budget (from 4.95 million € to 14.02 million €) during the same period.

Classifying the Austrian case according to the frameworks as presented in Table 8.1 and Figure 8.1, leads to following categorization. Taking the situation of the agency-level right after the reforms in 2002 into account, the Austrian ministry would be located in the efficiency (type 2) category, close to the contraction category, given its capacity reductions and limitations in the mandate (no agency structure to cover up as well as autonomous institutions). The agencies were strengthened only with some delay and quite unevenly in the years after (OeAD in 2009 and AQ Austria in 2012). From then on, AQ Austria can be categorized as expanding, given its slight capacity increases and mandate extensions. The OeAD is expanding rather dramatically but also here with some delay.

### 5.2 The Norwegian Case

Norwegian HE experienced similar challenges as most of other European HE sectors at the turn of the century: enrolment numbers increased steadily,

# THE CENTRAL GOVERNMENT IN HIGHER EDUCATION

TABLE 8.3    Austria

| Year | Capacity development (personnel numbers) | | Autonomy – capacity arrangement |
|---|---|---|---|
| | 2000 | 2017 | |
| Ministry (HE section) | 225 | 113 | Efficiency (type 2) |
| AQ Austria | –a | 32 | Expanding (with delay) |
| OeAD | 100 | 228 | Expanding (with delay) |

a  No number available (AQ Austria was founded in 2012).

overall expenses grew, and politics increasingly expressed efficiency concerns. These concerns called into question the traditional governance approach between the HE bureaucracy and the sector.

An expert commission installed by the Norwegian ministry at the end of 1990s, received the mandate to look into pressing issues in Norwegian HE at that time. After numerous consultations with the institutions and other relevant actors from the sector, the commission came up with a number of suggestions that would eventually lead to the Quality Reform 2003 and a revised HE law in 2005. Many of these suggestions were in line with the general European reform ambitions in which institutional autonomy was further enhanced, while ministries further developed a distant steering approach. Consequently, the leadership at university level was strengthened and central administrative tasks in personnel affairs, budgetary matters, and organizational structures transferred to the institutions. The ministry, however – or more precisely the ministerial department responsible for HE – did not reduce its staff numbers but applied a new governance mode toward the universities and used their remaining capacity to follow up newly established agencies.

In the area of QA that was the Norwegian Agency for Quality Assurance in Education (NOKUT), which was founded in 2003.[8] NOKUT is in essence responsible for institutional and program accreditation, and has become an important stimulator in quality development and enhancement in Norwegian HE over the years. Mandate and capacity have been expanded accordingly, starting with 34 employees and an operational budget of 25.83 million NOK in 2003 to 126 employees and a budget of 152.32 million NOK in 2017.

The Norwegian Centre for International Cooperation in Education (SIU) took over important governance responsibilities in internationalization matters at the turn of the century.

SIU started as a program association linked to the University of Bergen in 1991 but became a governmental agency in 2004. Since then it developed into a major and influential actor in Norwegian HE. Its main responsibility is the support and development of international academic collaboration in HE. Over the years, it also received more responsibility for coordinating collaboration and exchange in secondary education. Staff numbers and operational budget grew accordingly: from 21 employees and a budget 21 million NOK in 2000, to 101 employees and 116.29 million NOK in 2017.

Classifying the Norwegian case according to the frameworks (see Table 8.1 and Figure 8.1) leads to following categorization. Taking developments at the agency level into account, the Norwegian ministry would be located in the potency (type 2) category close to the hyper-potency category in Table 8.1, because its capacity remained unchanged and its mandate in parts was transferred to the agency level. The agencies themselves can be located in the expansion category since both NOKUT and SIU experienced enhancing mandates with substantial resources during the past two decades.

TABLE 8.4    Norway

| Year | Capacity development (personnel numbers) | | Autonomy – capacity arrangement |
| --- | --- | --- | --- |
| | 2000 | 2017 | |
| Ministry (HE department) | 67[a] | 61 | Potency (type 2) |
| NOKUT | 34[b] | 126 | Expanding (continuously) |
| SIU | 21 | 101 | Expanding (continuously) |

a  Number from 2002.
b  Number from 2003 (when NOKUT was founded).

## 6      Discussion and Conclusion: Comparing the Austrian and Norwegian Approach

### 6.1    *Discussion*

Austria and Norway show significant differences in their approach to reorganize the HE bureaucracy. In Austria, one can see substantive capacity reductions at the ministerial level, with no cover up at the agency level. Strengthening the agency level occurred gradually, through revisions in the legal framework (OeAD law in 2009, Act on Quality Assurance in Higher Education in 2011), and by establishing governmental agencies in the area of QA and internationalization. Based on the findings, AQ Austria can be considered a type A agency, due to its rather optimal levels of autonomy capacity but its relatively constrained mandate and standing in relation to the ministry (see Figure 8.2). Given OeAD's encompassing mandate and capacity, it can be considered a type C agency. Its slight disposition to capacity is based on the perception that it is perceived rather instrumental and occasionally constrained in its autonomy (also when compared to the Norwegian agency SIU).

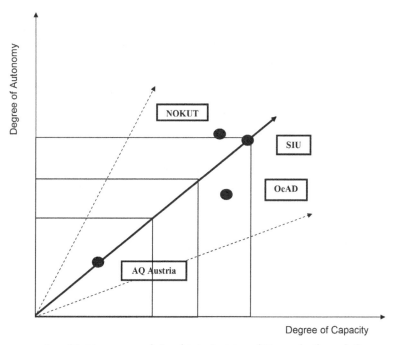

FIGURE 8.2  Ministry-agency relationship in Austria and Norway by the end of 2017

In Norway, the situation is somewhat different. After the reforms, ministerial capacity remained unchanged, in addition to a continuously strengthened agency level. Given that the agency-level (at least in the areas of QA and internationalization) grew stronger over time, different kind of governance challenges have occurred in the Norwegian context. For instance, controlling the agencies, despite unchanged capacity levels in the ministry, became more challenging due to their relative strength and increasing self-confidence. Based on the findings both agencies can be considered type C agencies (see Figure 8.2) given their continuous autonomy and capacity extensions and their standing in relation to the ministry. The difference between NOKUT and SIU in terms of autonomy is based on indications that NOKUT has become too autonomous (from the perspective of the ministry) thus also going beyond its assigned capacity levels. SIU is becoming increasingly looser-coupled from the ministry in terms influence but is also perceived as having appropriate autonomy-capacity levels.

Another reason why the Austrian and Norwegian governmental agencies have a different standing, might be also rooted in the different politico-administrative traditions of Austria and Norway. As earlier indicated, both countries belong to different administrative families (Painter & Peters, 2010). The HE governance reforms in Austria appeared to favor an approach that sees the state as part of the problem and is more in line with the core values of NPM reform discourses. Governmental capacity in the Austrian case was therefore reduced accordingly. The HE governance reforms in Norway encouraged high levels of governmental capacity, an approach that favors the state as part of the solution and is based on a different interpretation of NPM-style reforms.

From that perspective, if one considers the potential implications for institutional autonomy, the years after the new law from 2002 in Austria can be interpreted as system-level policy vacuum: reduced bureaucratic capacity with enhanced institutional autonomy but little systemic cohesion when it comes to governing the whole sector. Institutional autonomy in Norway can be considered to be more limited by rather powerful bureaucratic actors such as the ministry and the agencies but with more systemic cohesion.

TABLE 8.5    Summary of main differences between cases

| The Austrian case | The Norwegian case |
| --- | --- |
| – Reform approach: state as part of the problem | – Reform approach: state as part of the solution |
| – Efficient ministry | – Potent ministry |
| – Expanding agencies (with delay) | – Expanding agencies (continuously) |
|   – National QA constrained |   – National QA encouraged |
|   – Instrumental view of agencies |   – Autonomous view of agencies |
| – Institutional autonomy less constrained | – Institutional autonomy more constrained |
| – Little cohesion in systemic governance | – High cohesion in systemic governance |

The overall findings have shown that capacity developments are decisive in how effectively policy themes are governed in HE, but that the bureaucracy can perceive its own role quite different in relation to enhanced institutional autonomy. While it might be difficult to establish direct causalities between organizational changes at ministry/agency level and the way universities operate, it would be careless to assume that there are no reciprocal effects at all between administrative reorganization and enhanced institutional autonomy.

## 7    Conclusion

This chapter set out to propose an analytical framework for the study of organizational changes in the HE bureaucracy. The benefit such framework is the identification of effective governance arrangements between ministry and agencies based on autonomy and capacity developments. The chapter built on work from a dissertation project that examined these change processes empirically in Austria and Norway against the background of comprehensive sector reforms. The findings revealed different authority/autonomy and capacity developments at ministerial and agency level, which eventually had implications for systemic governance and the way university autonomy played out. The Austrian institutions, for instance, had a more radical and far-reaching interpretation of autonomy in the initial phase of a revised legal setting. In contrast, the Norwegian institutions experienced a much tighter governance approach, where governmental agencies were used largely to preserve the public mandate of the ministry.

The contribution of the study for research into HE is that it highlighted a so far understudied aspect of institutional autonomy, namely how the bureaucratic apparatus (especially ministerial and agency level) transformed in light of governance reforms. The suggested framework provides a simple yet powerful approach to examine this transformation process with the aim to identify effective governance arrangements between ministry and agencies. Its first empirical application can be seen as a productive test-run, as the frameworks surfaced distinct differences concerning autonomy and capacity developments. The Austrian case can be situated in the "efficiency (type 2)" –category, in which the subordinate agencies expanded with delay. The Norwegian case can be classified as "potency (type 1)", with two expanding agencies.

The study does have, however, some limitations. The suggested framework and the empirical findings face the same underlying challenge that every qualitative research approach naturally is confronted with: to which extent are the findings relatable to a broader population? In which way does it explain change processes in other HE bureaucracies? From this point of view it might help to keep in mind that case study designs and a qualitative research approach usually aim at analytical rather than statistical generalization (Eisenhardt, 1989; Maxwell, 2013). In other words, what is more important here is the development of a conceptual and analytical framework that can in essence be applied to different contexts (i.e. different bureaucracies/politico-administrative systems).

This presents also an argument for why it is important to study other HE bureaucracies as well, in order to enhance our understanding of how the bureaucracy develops in relation to university autonomy. In this way, the proposed framework would be further developed in a meaningful way, and provide valuable insights into change processes of the HE bureaucracy.

## Notes

1   Alternatively also described as Higher Education Institutions (HEIs) in this chapter.
2   In here now and then also referred to as "university autonomy".
3   The terms "bureaucracy" and "public administration" are used synonymously unless stated differently.
4   The location of the agencies in the quadrant is still a relative categorization, dependent on the sample. For instance, an agency with 200 employees is not necessarily a large agency per se, but appears to be large if compared to an agency that has only 20 employees.
5   Strictly speaking, the focus is on the internal ministerial section/department responsible for HE. When referring to "Austrian ministry" and "Norwegian ministry", this concerns the respective HE section (Austria) or HE department (Norway).
6   Name of the organizations in German and Norwegian respectively:
    – The Agency for Quality Assurance and Accreditation Austria = *Agentur für Qualitätssicherung und Akkreditierung Austria (AQ Austria)*.
    – The Austrian Agency for International Cooperation in Education and Research = *Österreichischer Austauschdienst (OeAD)*.
    – The Norwegian Agency for Quality Assurance in Education = *Nasjonalt organ for kvalitet i utdanningen (NOKUT)*.
    – The Centre for International Cooperation = *Senter for internasjonalisering av høyere utdanning (SIU)*.
7   Based on the Austrian Act for Quality Assurance in Higher Education from 2011.
8   NOKUT is the successor of *Norgesnettrådet*, a consultative association to the ministry in matters of quality assessment.

## References

Aberbach, J. D., & Rockman, B. A. (1992). Does governance matter –And if so, how? Process, performance, and outcomes. *Governance, 5*(2), 135–153.

Austin, I., & Jones, G. A. (2015). *Governance of higher education: Global perspectives, theories, and practices*. Routledge.

Bach, T., Niklasson, B., & Painter, M. (2012). The role of agencies in policy-making. *Policy and Society, 31*(3), 183–193.

Bryman, A. (2016). *Social research methods*. Oxford University Press.

Capano, G. (2011). Government continues to do its job. A comparative study of governance shifts in the higher education sector. *Public Administration, 89*(4), 1622–1642.

Chou, M.-H., Jungblut, J., Ravinet, P., & Vukasovic, M. (2017). Higher education governance and policy: An introduction to multi-issue, multi-level and multi-actor dynamics. *Policy and Society, 36*(1), 1–15.

Christensen, T., & Lægreid, P. (2007). Regulatory agencies? The challenges of balancing agency autonomy and political control. *Governance, 20*(3), 499–520.

Christensen, T., Lie, A., & Lægreid, P. (2008). Beyond new public management: Agencification and regulatory reform in Norway. *Financial Accountability & Management, 24*(1), 15–30.

de Boer, H. F. (1992). Walking tightropes in higher education. *Higher Education Policy, 5*(3), 36–40.

Denzin, N. K. (2006). *Sociological methods: A sourcebook*. Aldine Transaction. Retrieved from https://books.google.no/books?id=ll4KYoRptYoC

Egeberg, M. (2003). How bureaucratic structure matters: An organizational perspective. In *Handbook of public administration* (pp. 116–126). Sage Publications.

Eisenhardt, K. M. (1989). Building theories from case study research. *Academy of Management Review, 14*(4), 532–550.

El-Khawas, E. (1992). Are buffer organizations doomed to fail? Inevitable dilemmas and tensions. *Higher Education Policy, 5*(3), 18–20.

Ferlie, E., Musselin, C., & Andresani, G. (2008). The steering of higher education systems: A public management perspective. *Higher Education, 56*(3), 325.

Fiorioli, E. (2014). Entwicklungslinien und Strukturentscheidungen der Qualitätssicherung in Österreich. In *Handbuch Qualität in Studium und Lehre* (pp. 103–120). DUZ Verlags- und Medienhaus GmbH.

Friedrich, P. E. (2019). Organizational change in higher education ministries in light of agencification: Comparing Austria and Norway. *Higher Education Policy*. https://doi.org/10.1057/s41307-019-00157-x

Fukuyama, F. (2013). What is governance? *Governance, 26*(3), 347–368.

Holmberg, S., & Rothstein, B. (2012). *Good government: The relevance of political science*. Edward Elgar.

Kickert, W. (1995). Steering at a distance: A new paradigm of public governance in Dutch higher education. *Governance, 8*(1), 135–157.

Krippendorff, K. (2013). *Content analysis: An introduction to its methodology*. Sage Publications.

Maassen, P., & Musselin, C. (2009). European integration and the Europeanisation of higher education. In A. Amaral, G. Neave, C. Musselin, & P. Maassen (Eds.), *European integration and the governance of higher education and research* (pp. 3–14). Springer Netherlands.

Maassen, P., Nerland, M., & Yates, L. (2018). Reconfiguring knowledge in higher education: Emerging themes and research avenues. In P. Maassen, M. Nerland, & L. Yates (Eds.), *Reconfiguring knowledge in higher education* (pp. 187–202). Springer International Publishing.

Maggetti, M., & Verhoest, K. (2014). Unexplored aspects of bureaucratic autonomy: A state of the field and ways forward. *International Review of Administrative Sciences, 80*(2), 239–256.

Maxwell, J. A. (2013). *Qualitative research design: An interactive approach: An interactive approach* (3rd ed.). Sage Publications.

Painter, M., & Peters, B. G. (2010). Administrative traditions in comparative perspective: Families, groups and hybrids. In M. Painter & B. G. Peters (Eds.), *Tradition and public administration* (pp. 19–30). Palgrave Macmillan UK.

Patton, M. Q. (2014). *Qualitative research & evaluation methods: Integrating theory and practice*. Sage Publications.

Pollitt, C., Bathgate, K., Caulfield, J., Smullen, A., & Talbot, C. (2001). Agency fever? Analysis of an international policy fashion. *Journal of Comparative Policy Analysis, 3*(3), 271–290.

Saldaña, J. (2016). *The coding manual for qualitative researchers* (3rd ed.). Sage Publications.

Seawright, J., & Gerring, J. (2008). Case selection techniques in case study research: A menu of qualitative and quantitative options. *Political Research Quarterly, 61*(2), 294–308.

Van Thiel, S., Verhoest, K., Bouckaert, G., & Lægreid, P. (2012). Lessons and recommendations for the practice of agencification. In K. Verhoest, S. Van Thiel, G. Bouckaert, & P. Lægreid (Eds.), *Government agencies: Practices and lessons from 30 countries* (pp. 413–439). Palgrave Macmillan UK.

Van Vught, F. (1989). *Governmental strategies and innovation in higher education*. Jessica Kingsley.

Verhoest, K. (2012). *Government agencies: Practices and lessons from 30 countries*. Palgrave Macmillan.

Wu, X., Ramesh, M., & Howlett, M. (2015). Policy capacity: A conceptual framework for understanding policy competences and capabilities. *Policy and Society, 34*(3–4), 165–171.

Yin, R. K. (2014). *Case study research: Design and methods* (5th ed.). Sage Publications.

CHAPTER 9

# External Accountability in Ethiopian Public Higher Education

*Solomon Gebreyohans Gebru*

### Abstract

This chapter examines the actors involved, the purpose, orientation, types, mechanisms, consequences and challenges of external accountability in the Ethiopian public higher education. Data were generated from literature review, relevant government documents and interviews conducted with key informants at several federal institutions that have a stake in the accountability of public higher education institutions (HEIs). The analysis shows that there is a trend towards result-oriented accountability in the sector and Ethiopian public HEIs are accountable to multiple external stakeholders, particularly through political, administrative and academic types of accountability. The study also demonstrates that although the external system of accountability utilizes various types, mechanisms and consequences of accountability, it is characterized by a number of challenges. Several recommendations are forwarded to minimize the challenges and to enable Ethiopian public HEIs attain their mission.

### Keywords

Ethiopia – external accountability – higher education

## 1 Introduction

In higher education (HE), 'accountability' for the use of public money and justification for research findings have always been there. Over time, however, the notion of accountability has become more pervasive and explicit to external stakeholder agendas, particularly since the 1980s and 1990s (Yamamoto, 2011). For example, citation tracking and performance data collection are among the newly emerging avenues of accountability (Kivistö et al., 2019). Partly, this is

© KONINKLIJKE BRILL NV, LEIDEN, 2020 | DOI: 10.1163/9789004436558_010

explained by the shift (since the 1980s) in the state's role in the governance of higher education institutions (HEIs) from detailed regulation to steering from a distance, which resulted in making HEIs more autonomous (Huisman, 2018; Hazelkorn, 2018). In other words, "Governments, alongside granting autonomy, introduced *ex post* evaluations (through quality evaluation and assurance policies) and asked institutions in return for autonomy to account for their activities (through annual reporting, spending reviews, and performance reporting)" (Huisman, 2018, p. 2). In Ethiopia too, following the adoption of the 2003 HE proclamation (HPR, 2003), public HEIs have become relatively more autonomous in terms of recruitment and promotion of their staff, allocation of internal funding, development of academic programs, construction of buildings, etc. (Asgedom & Hagos, 2015; Tamrat, 2012).

The following are among the specific driving factors behind strengthening external accountability in HE over time: continuous increases in the cost of HE and the perception of poor quality of learning output/outcome following HE massification and other factors. Further, the rise of the global knowledge-based economy and strong belief in the contribution of HE to societal well-being; avoiding mismatch between the education of the work force and the jobs that need to be filled; ensuring efficiency of resource utilization and transparency and the satisfaction of stakeholders or good governance in general are part of the driving factors. Since the end of the 20th century, the focus of accountability has shifted from evaluating inputs and activities toward results (output, impacts and outcomes); from improve to prove, and toward driving and monitoring the behaviors of institutions (Kivistö et al., 2019; Hazelkorn, 2018; Huisman, 2018; Yamamoto, 2011; Vidovich & Slee, 2001).

Since the end of the 1990s, Ethiopia's HE has been rapidly expanding. However, HEIs have been criticized, including by the government, for poor quality of education, low research quality and productivity, low engagement with community and industry, and administrative malpractice (see MoE, 2017; Salmi et al., 2017; Kahsay, 2017; Akalu, 2016). Although there could be several other factors for this (including lack of necessary inputs), the low performance can be partially attributed to lack of an effective system of accountability. The contemporary conception of accountability is primarily expressed in external terms (Yorke & Vidovich, 2016). To our knowledge, there are only few related research works on external accountability in the public HE of Ethiopia (see Dea & Zeleke, 2017; Asgedom & Hagos, 2015; Tamrat, 2012); none of them deal with types and mechanisms of external accountability. In fact, the notion of accountability is the most advocated but least analyzed concept in HE (Burke et al., 2004, as cited in Yamamoto, 2011). This chapter intends to examine the purpose, orientation, types, mechanisms, consequences and challenges of *external* accountability in Ethiopian public HE. In light of this, the chapter specifically aims to address the following questions. Who is involved in the external accountability of public HEIs in Ethiopia? What are the purposes, orientations, types and mechanisms, consequences and challenges of external accountability in the public HE of Ethiopia?

The remainder of this chapter consists of three sections. Sections 2 and 3 present the conceptual framework and methodology, respectively. Section 4 describes and analyzes the purpose, orientation, types and mechanisms, consequences and challenges of external accountability in the public HE sector of Ethiopia. The chapter ends with concluding remarks (Section 5).

## 2 Conceptual Framework

### 2.1 *Accountability Defined*

Although the concept of *accountability* remains an essential element of governance in human history, so far, there is no consensus about what it constitutes. It is multifaceted and ambiguous, allowing a range of interpretation, and thus it remains challenging to define it in precise terms (Bovens, 2007; Asgedom & Hagos, 2015; Kivistö et al., 2019; Han & Demircioglu, 2016). Its meaning has been extended in a number of directions (Mulgan, 2000). For example, the focus of accountability in HE during the 1980s was on the quality of teaching and learning. In the 1990s, however, it "expanded to include productivity and various measures of institutional effectiveness" (Leveille, 2006, p. 6). Generally, the notion of accountability remains "complex and ill defined" and a close scrutiny of the pertinent literature "reveals many different and sometimes opposing views on the definitions, typologies and mechanisms of accountability" (Yorke & Vidovich, 2016, p. 42).

Nevertheless, a close inspection of the literature also shows that all authors who provided definitions for the concept share one thing in common: they define it in *relational* terms. In its traditional sense, accountability involves three core elements: (a) a higher authority vested with the power of oversight, (b) an explicit reporting mechanism for conveying information to the higher authority, and (c) a measure or criterion used by the higher authority to assess compliance by subordinate institutions (Kearns, 1998, p. 144). Lindberg (2013, p. 8) identifies the following five defining characteristics of any form of accountability:

1. An agent or institution who is to give an account (A for agent);
2. An area, responsibilities, or domain subject to accountability (D for domain);
3. An agent or institution to whom A is to give account (P for principal);
4. The right of P to require A to inform and explain/justify decisions with regard to D; and
5. The right of P to sanction A if A fails to inform and/or explain/justify decisions with regard to D.

Considering the above defining characteristics, the definition provided by Bovens (2007), which is seen as a relatively comprehensive one (Huisman, 2018) is adopted by this chapter. Bovens defines *accountability* as the "[...] relationship between an actor and a forum, in which the actor has an obligation to explain and to justify his or her conduct, the forum can pose questions and pass judgment, and the actor may face consequences" (p. 450). The type of the relationship and consequences would vary depending on who is the actor (agent) and who is the *forum* (principal). For example, the actor could be an individual (elected or appointed official or a professional) or a legal entity (for example, HEIs) and the forum could be a Ministry/Agency, a Parliament, an audit office, a professional association, etc.

Accordingly, understanding accountability requires addressing the following five fundamental questions: *Who is to be held accountable, for what, to whom, through what means and with what consequences* (Trow, 1996; Romzek, 2000; Bovens, 2007). In the context of HE, the question of who is accountable to whom involves complex relationships since there are various competing stakeholders, with varying degrees of interest in the sector (Salmi, 2009). Watty (2006, as cited in Yorke & Vidovich, 2016) classifies these stakeholders into *supply* and *demand* side. The supply side includes governments (national, provincial, municipal), quality assurance agencies, HEIs and academics. On the demand side, we have students, parents, employers and the society. Cognizant of this, Zumeta (2011, p. 133) defines accountability as "responsibility for one's actions to someone or to multiple parties as a result of legal, political (in the best, constitutive sense), financial, personal, or simply morally based ties". Similarly, institutional accountability in HE is defined as "the myriad expectations-some tangible, others intangible-that are applied to colleges and universities by diverse stakeholders" (Kearns, 1998, p. 40). Here, it is noteworthy that the stakeholder to whom HEIs may be accountable varies from country to country. However, one thing that has become a common phenomenon is that HEIs are accountable to multiple external forums.

In the context of external accountability in HE, the answer for '*who is to be held accountable*' is HEIs (as an entity), represented by the Board or the

President. *'For what'*? For performance (against mission) and compliance (against laws, policies, standards, etc.). In an attempt to answer the question for what, Graycar (2016) identifies three things: money, process and outcomes. Similarly, Alach (2016) posits that "... organizations are commonly held to be accountable for their use of inputs, internal processes and the delivery of outputs; however, they are generally held to only influence impacts and outcomes" (p. 39).

The question *'for what'* concerns the *domain* of accountability. It is "... the conduct about which information is to be provided" (Bovens, 2007, p. 545). Domain emanates from the mission of institutions. In HEIs, the main components of institutional mission include teaching/learning, research and services (to industry & community). However, HEIS too are responsible for administrative issues, which include finance, property, human resource and crosscutting issues such as gender, disability, environment, etc. Here, it is important to note that the focus of accountability even within a specific domain may vary depending on the mandate of the forum. For instance, take teaching/learning as one of the domains. In this regard, if the forum is a Ministry in charge of HE, its focus of accountability could be on *results* (such as students' completion rate. If the forum is a national quality assurance agency, however, the focus could be on *inputs* such as the availability and quality of laboratories and curriculum, faculty profile, etc.

*To whom*? Since HEIS are accountable to multiple stakeholders, addressing the question for *what* determines the line of accountability (to whom). For example, if the domain of accountability is *academics*, then the line of accountability will go to the Ministry in charge of HE, other relevant government agencies and professional organizations. Nevertheless, if the domain is *finance*, it may go to the Ministry in charge of finance or other appropriate bodies. The domains of accountability also determine the *mechanisms* of accountability. For example, if the domain is *teaching*, it may include accreditation of academic programs, quality audit, reports on degree completion rates, tracer study about the employability of graduates, etc. If it were finance, it would involve internal and external audits. Generally, public institutions "... are accountable to a plethora of different forums, all of which apply a different set of criteria" (Bovens, 2007, p. 455).

Finally, the *consequences* to that would also vary depending on the *domain* of accountability. For example, if it is teaching, failure to comply with the standards of quality audit could result in closing an academic program. Generally, the consequence of accountability could be either *rewarding* achievement and/or *punishing* failure. One important issue that arises in relation to consequence is the *purpose* of accountability. Why do we hold institutions accountable? Though accountability has various purposes (economic, political, social, etc.), its main goals can be broadly grouped into two: *improving performance and ensuring compliance.*

### 2.2    *Types of Accountability in Higher Education*
Different authors have provided different *typologies* of accountability, albeit they are not usually mutually exclusive (see, for example, Romzek, 2000; Romzek & Ingraham, 2000; Bovens, 2007; Lindberg, 2013; Yorke & Vidovich, 2016; Vidovich & Slee, 2001). One of the main shortcomings observed in the literature is lack of clarity on the criteria used to develop the typologies (Lindberg, 2013). In this regard, to our knowledge, the typologies developed by Trow, (1996); Romzek (2000); Bovens (2007); Lindberg (2013) and Corbett (1996, as cited in Yorke & Vidovich, 2016) are informative.

For example, based on the *source of control*, Romzek and Lindberg classified accountability into two: *external* and *internal* (see also Trow, 1996). The fundamental question here is whether the accountability holder (the forum) is *external* or *internal* to the one being held to account (the actor). If the source of control to HEIs comes from outside the institutions (for example from national quality assurance agency), then it is *external* type, and if the control emanates from within (example from the Rector), then it is *internal*. While the subject of external accountability is the institution as a legal entity (for example HEIs), the subjects of internal accountability can be sub-institutional units (like academic units) or individuals. The source of control also implies the standards or criteria to be used "… as to what constitutes responsible conduct" (Bovens, 2007, p. 555). Based on the *source of control*, Bovens identified five sub-types of external accountability common to public institutions (see Table 9.1).

TABLE 9.1    Sub-types of external accountability

| External accountability subtypes | Forum |
| --- | --- |
| Political | Voters, legislators, ministers, political parties, media |
| Legal | Courts |
| Administrative | Inspectors, auditors and controllers |
| Professional | Professional peers |
| Social | Interest groups, charities and other stakeholders |

SOURCE: BOVENS (2007)

Romzek (2000) and Lindberg (2013) also differentiated types of accountability based on the *degree of control* the forum has over the actor or the degree of *autonomy* the actor has vis-à-vis the forum. Accordingly, while some types of accountability involve "... extremely detailed control based on specific rules and regulations" (Lindberg, 2013, p. 11), others give, for example "... the discretion to decide whether and how to respond to key stakeholder concerns" (Romzek & Ingraham, 2000, p. 242). Based on the source and degree of control, Romzek and Ingraham (2000) identified four sub-types of accountability (see Table 9.1).

TABLE 9.2    Types of accountability relationships

| Degree of autonomy (of the actor) | Source of control | |
|---|---|---|
| | Internal | External |
| Low | Hierarchical | Legal |
| High | Professional | Political |

SOURCE: ROMZEK AND INGRAHAM (2000, P. 242)

Besides the *source* and *degree* of control, Lindberg (2013) added one criteria to develop his typology: *spatial direction*. If the forum is hierarchically superior to the actor or has the right to impose sanctions directly over the actor, accountability relationship runs *vertically* upward. Generally, vertical accountability manifests in the form of principal-agent relationship. A typical example here is the line of accountability between a public university and the Ministry in charge of HE (*external vertical*) or the form of accountability between a universities President and his subordinates (*internal vertical*). However, if the forum is somehow legally on equal status with the actor, accountability runs *horizontally*. An example here is a public university giving an account to a national auditor (*external horizontal*) or a budget center of asub-university unit giving an account to an internal auditor (*internal horizontal*) (Lindberg, 2013). Under horizontal accountability, the forum may not have the power to put sanctions over the actor; it can do so by taking the matter to the court or to other superior government bodies such as the legislature (if external) or to the top management of the institutions (if internal). For example, an ombudsperson may receive a plea from a staff member accusing his university for mistreatment. If the ombudsperson finds it true, she can take it to the prosecutor for adjudication. Externally, horizontal responsibility involves the capacity of state institutions to check abuses by other public institutions or the requirement for public institutions to report sideways. Using the three criteria, Lindberg identified 12 types of accountability. Four are internal vertical, two are internal horizontal, four are external vertical and two are external horizontal. Some of the types of accountability that are applicable to HEIs include legal, political, fiscal, reputational and societal (for details, see Lindberg, 2013).

Corbett (1996, as cited in Yorke & Vidovich, 2016) provided a slightly different version in relation to *spatial direction*. Corbett identified the following *four* types of accountability: 'upward', 'outward', 'downward' and 'inward'. While both 'upward' and 'outward' accountability are externally oriented, the former is vertical and is towards government and the latter is horizontal and involves responsiveness to the wider community (with social and economic/market orientation). 'Downward' accountability is part of internal accountability, which particularly focuses on managers being accountable to subordinates. Finally, 'inward' accountability focuses on meeting professional and ethical standards.

Finally, Bovens (2007) distinguished accountability based on the *aspect of conduct.* The analytical descriptor here is the focus of accountability or about what the actors are required to explain and justify. It can be about how money is spent (*financial accountability*), the legality of procurement procedures (*procedural accountability*), or the efficiency and effectiveness of institutional policy, such as student completion rates (*product accountability*). This type of classification often concurs with the classification made according to type of forum. The classification on the aspect of conduct evidently involves the domain of accountability. Daigle and Cuocco (2002) classified accountability based on domain as *programmatic accountability*, which concerns whether public institutions have met publicly stated goals and objectives. In HE, this will refer to *academic accountability, where HEIs are expected to render account to all concerned bodie*s.

As noted in the introduction (see also Section 3 below), the focus of this chapter is on external accountability in HE. The type of external accountability in HE may vary from system to system, depending on which responsibility is allocated to which type of forum and on the mandates/missions allocated to the HEI in question. From the foregoing discussion, the following *three* types of accountability are identified as pervasive in the HE sector in general and are particularly relevant to the context of Ethiopia. They are *political, administrative* and *academic accountability*. We briefly present a description of each and subsequently use them as tools of analysis to the context of Ethiopia.

*Political accountability* is a type of external accountability. It encompasses "... being responsive to the concerns of key stakeholders, such as elected officials, clientele groups, and the general public" (p. 27). Under political accountability, the government may act on behalf of other stakeholders to safeguard their interest. Thus, from a wider perspective, political accountability includes elements of *social accountability*, which involves rendering account to the wider society (Kivistö et al., 2019). Political accountability also involves being responsive to politically *salient* issues, which are not necessarily prescribed by law or administrative orders. It is about responsiveness to political pressures and, unlike legal accountability, the accountability standards and to whom institutions must answer, may not be precise. Examples include issues such us tackling environmental pollution, sexual harassment, political activism on campus, etc.

*Administrative accountability* involves a wide range of quasi-legal forums, which include auditors, inspectors, controllers, etc. This forum exercises independent regular financial and administrative scrutiny, often on the basis of specific statutes and prescribed norms. Audit offices, ombudspersons, inspector generals, anti-fraud offices are among the agencies involved in conducting administrative accountability. Depending on the mandate of the forum, the subject of accountability could be finance, human resources, property, etc., and the focus accountability may include inputs, activities, procedures, outputs or outcomes, or a combination of them. For example, the mandate of audit offices has been broadening from scrutinizing the probity and legality of public funding to evaluating the efficacy and effectiveness of public institutions (Bovens, 2007). From the perspective of *spatial direction*, administrative accountability runs horizontally. In some cases (like financial auditing), the degree of control is typically high and very detailed (Lindberg, 2013). As pointed out earlier, administrative accountability is exercised based on "an explicit standard of performance, operational procedure, output measure, or reporting requirement ..., [which] are formally codified and, therefore, carry the force of law" (Kearns, 1998, p. 147). Thus, failure to comply with administrative requirements can lead to *legal accountability*, in which the court is the forum.

Finally, *academic accountability* refers to giving an account or being held to account about teaching, research and services (to community and industry) activities, process, outputs and outcomes (Trow, 1996; Chineze & Olele, 2012).

## 3    Methodology

This chapter focuses on external accountability in Ethiopian public HE for two reasons. First, owing to its consequences, public institutions give much attention to external accountability (see Yorke & Vidovich, 2016; Vidovich, 2018; Huisman, 2018) and, internal accountability is meant to reinforce the former. In the 21st century, the "emphasis is increasingly on accountability which: **answers** to external authorities ..." (Vidovich, 2018, original emphasis). Thus, this chapter intends to contribute to the debate on external accountability in HE in general and within Ethiopia in particular. Note that this is not to undermine the importance of internal accountability for the success of institutions. Second, the concept of accountability is amorphous and internal and external types of accountability have several sub-types and, thus the page limit does not allow us to cover both.

The study followed a qualitative approach and since studies on external accountability in Ethiopian public HE are scarce, we employed an exploratory design. Data were gathered through review of relevant literature and document analysis of proclamations, regulations and directives as well as strategic and annual plans that concern Ethiopian public HE. Likewise, feedback was provided by the federal Parliament standing Committee that oversees HE, that is, Human Resources and Technology Standing Committee (HRTSC) on the plans and reports of HEIS.

Data were also gathered through interviews with staff from state institutions that have a stake in the external accountability of HEIS. Ethiopia is a federal state and although its higher education proclamation (HEP) allows regional governments to establish HEIS (HPR, 2019), so far the sector remains, mainly, under the control of the federal government. Though the degree varies, currently, 13 federal agencies are involved in the external accountability of public HEIS. They include: the Ministry of Revenue, Institution of the Ombudsman, Anti-corruption and Ethics Commission, General Prosecutor, Court, Police, Office of the Federal Auditor General (OFAG), the Ministry of Science and Higher Education (MoSHE), the Ministry of Finance and Economic Cooperation (MoFEC), the Civil Service Commission (CSC), the Higher Education Relevance and Quality Agency (HERQA), and the Procurement and Property Administration Agency (PPAA). However, only the last seven agencies, which have relatively more frequent accountability relationships with HEIS, were consulted for this study.

Two key informants from HERQA and one key informant each from the other six institutions were purposefully selected for interviews, which were conducted in April 2019. They include senior officials (some of them at the level of directorship), who oversee public HEIS in their respective institutions. For example, the key informant from the CSC is a director who oversees the administrative structure and issues related to administrative staff (who are treated as civil servants) of public HEIS. The questions listed below were forwarded for all key informants. We did a pilot test on the interview protocol and the questions at the MoSHE and made minor modifications.

1.  In the domain that concerns your institution:
a   What is the *purpose* behind making HEIS accountable?
b   What are the *focus* areas in rendering HEIS accountable?
c   What *mechanisms* are used to ensure that HEIS areaccountable?
d   What *consequences* does your institution put on HEIS following accountability?
e   What are the *challenges* faced in making HEIS accountable?

Interview results were transcribed and analyzed against selected thematic areas (drawn from the interview checklist). The overall technique of analysis relies on the conceptual framework developed in the above. Finally, note that key informants gave consent in exchange for anonymity, and thus they are cited anonymously.

## 4   External Accountability in Ethiopian Public Higher Education

### 4.1   *External Accountability Framework*

As indicated earlier, about a dozen Federal institutions are involved in the external accountability of public HEIS. First, like any other federal institutions, federal public HEIS are budget centers (their budget is directly approved by the Parliament). Accordingly, they are subject to legislative oversight by the Federal Parliament through the HRTSC. Second, except sectoral HEIS (such as the university college of defense), all other public HEIS are directly accountable to MoSHE.[1] MoSHE is the main regulatory body of the sector and has primarily responsibility to ensure the accountability of HEIS. Third, HERQA is in charge of accreditation and quality audit (both institutional and program level). Unlike private HEIS, public HEIS and their regular programs are not accredited, thus HERQA's role in public HEIS is limited to quality audit. Fourth, the higher education strategy center (HESC), is mandated with ensuring that the strategic and annual plans of HEIS are in line with the national HE macro strategy and plan, and with following up their implementation, preparing budget allocation formula to individual HEI and monitoring its implementation. Although HERQA and HESC are designated as autonomous bodies, they are both accountable to MoSHE (HPR, 2019). If an HEI has a teaching hospital, the Ministry of Health is also involved in the accountability framework.

Further, four other federal bodies play an important role in the external accountability of HEIS, particularly in the administrative wing. The Civil Service Commission (CSC) is authorized to approve HEI's administrative wing organizational structure, which is a form of proactive accountability. It also plays a role in reviewing administrative staff grievances that HEIs failed to resolve. The Office of the Federal Auditor General (OFAG) plays an important role in the accountability of HEIs by conducting financial, property and performance audits and reporting the findings to all concerned bodies. MoFEC regulates HEIs in relation to financial issues. Finally, public HEIs have functional accountability to the Procurement and Property Administration Agency (PPAA), in relation to procurement and property administration. For example, certain types of procurement and disposal of properties may require the approval of PPAA. The relationship between these federal institutions and HEIs is more horizontal or functional than direct accountability.

Finally, the domains of accountability that HEIs are expected to render an account include: (a) *academic* (teaching/learning, research and community engagement), (b) *administration* (finance, property, human resource, etc.), and (c) *cross cutting issues* (equity related issues such as gender, ethnic, region, disability, environment, epidemic diseases, implementation of reform programs, etc.). Table 9.3 demonstrates some of the major external institutions involved and some of the common elements observed in the accountability of HEIs. Assuming that the issues related to domain, relationships (spatial direction) and consequences of accountability could be understood from Table 9.3, we proceed to purpose, focus, types, and mechanisms, and challenges of accountability.

With regard to the *purpose* of accountability, all informants commonly argued that augmenting performance is the ultimate goal in making HEIs accountable. The common stand observed was that controlling and punishing failure is not the main intention of their institution behind making HEIs accountable. For example, the informant at MoSHE said, "Supporting and building the capacity of HEIs is the primary goal when we monitor and evaluate them. However, unwarranted failures are not acceptable" (interview, 11 April 2019). Similarly, the informant from the OFAG said, "Although our explicit focus could be on ensuring compliance, the ultimate goal is to help HEIs use their resources properly in line with their mission so that they can achieve their stated objectives" (interview, 5 April 2019). However, the informant from MoSHE had a different opinion on this. He said, "Controlling institutions like the OFAG focuses too much on obedience and this has been putting unnecessary pressure on HEIs in balancing compliance and performance." In relation to this, the informant from the Parliament Standing Committee (HRTSC) stated, "We understand that the situation in HEIs is highly complex and demands a special treatment. However, this should not be a pretext for abuse nor should it be a reason for failure" (interview, 5 April 2019).

# EXTERNAL ACCOUNTABILITY IN ETHIOPIAN PUBLIC HIGHER EDUCATION    173

TABLE 9.3    External accountability relationships (based on interview results)

| Elements of accountability | Institutions (forums) | | | | |
|---|---|---|---|---|---|
| | MoSHE | HERQA | CSC | MoFEC | OFAG |
| Domain | Academic, administration & cross-cutting issues | Quality of education | Administrative structure & staff | Finance | Finance & property |
| Main purpose | Improving performance & ensuring compliance | Ensuring compliance | | | |
| Main focus | Input, activity, process, result | Input & process | Procedure | | |
| Mechanism | Directives, guidelines, strategic plan, annual plan, reporting checklist, reports, sit visit appointment of board members and the President, peer evaluation, ranking, etc. | Quality audit | Directives' guidelines, reviewing administrative organizational structure and staff complaint hearing | Directives and guidelines, reviewing reports | Auditing |
| Relationship | Vertical | Horizontal | | | |
| Potential consequences | Removal of Presidents, boards members for failure & recognition for achievement | Closing academic programs or HEIS via MoSHE | Rejecting/ modifying administrative structures, Reversing decision made on staff | Withholding Budget | Reporting to the parliament, consulting the EACC to start investigation |

## 4.2    *Focus/Orientation of Accountability*

According to the pertinent literature, the orientation of accountability has shifted from the input side to the result side (output, outcome and impact) (Yorke & Vidovich, 2016; Mulgan, 2000). In Ethiopia too, there is a similar trend. In relation to this, the informant from MoSHE said the following:

> Over the recent years, our focus of accountability has been shifting towards outputs, outcomes and impacts, although sufficient attention has still been given to inputs, activities, and processes, owing to the nature of the sector. You can observe this in our strategic plans, annual plans and reporting checklists of the last five years or so. They include indicators such as degree completion rate, employability of graduates, number of publications and impacts of research and engagement activities, etc. Although we are still in the making, we have already started tracer studies about graduates' employability. We are also preparing to organize national exit exams that will be taken by all new graduates. The problem we have concerning accountability is that we have not yet established predictable consequences. (Interview, 11 April 2019)

A review of the education sector development program (ESDP-V)[2] (MoE, 2015b), the higher education Growth and Transformation Plan-II[3] (MoE, 2015a) as well as MoSHE's 2019 annual plan (MoSHE, 2019b) and reporting checklist (MoSHE, 2019c) demonstrate that indeed elements of output and outcome indicators are envisioned and quantification has become a norm. However, the reporting checklist shows that high emphasis is still given to activities and inputs, particularly in relation to service provision to students (cafeteria, dormitories, etc.), campus security, course delivery, etc.

The informants from HERQA and HRTSC conveyed the following similar message with regard to student services. Since HEIs still provide cafeteria and dormitory services to students, the government has a huge concern over the provision of these services because mishandling them serves as an immediate cause of campus conflicts. Managing student service provision remains a huge burden to HEIs, detracting them from their result-oriented tasks (interviews, 5 and 8 April 2019).

### 4.3    Types and Mechanisms of Accountability

Based on the conceptual framework developed above, in this section we evaluate Ethiopia's public HE sector against the conceptions of political, administrative and academic accountability. Rather than detaching them from the typologies, we decided to address the mechanisms of accountability in an integrated way.

"Political accountability is apparent when university representatives explain to governments and parliaments – either by invitation or proactively– what their institutions do and why …" (Huisman, 2018, p. 2). In this regard, Ethiopia's parliament is involved in accounting for HEIs in three ways. HRTSC reviews and provides feedback to the strategic and annual plans, specifically the quarterly and annual reports of each public HEI. The feedback contains detailed reflections (including strengths and weaknesses) about the plans and reports (see for example HPR, 2017, 2018). HRTSC also requires university presidents or their representatives to explain before the parliament if OFAG reports to the parliament grave findings about the university. Finally, HRTSC conducts site visits to evaluate whether what was reported is actually on the ground and to gather information from the leadership, staff and students, and forwards recommendations on issues that need attention from HEIS and/or MoSHE or the government (interview, 3 April 2019). As a political body, in its review of plans, reports, and site visits, the HRTSC focuses on politically salient issues such as gender, implementation of reform programs, the opening of new master and doctorate programs, campus security, student drop out, participation of stakeholders, engagement (with community and industry), and good governance in general (see HPR, 2017, 2018).

The above politically salient issues have also received high attention from the government and hence an HEI that failed to respond would face severe consequences. For example, owing to ethnic or religious based political tensions in the country, campus security has been highly politicized. Any incident on campus results in fierce criticisms (and other consequences) from the government. For instance, during the beginning of the 2019/20 academic year, ethnic based violence occurred in some universities. Following this, Ethiopia's Prime Minister, Abiy Ahmed, called university board members and presidents for a meeting where he "... urged [them] to take action on violent students and warned the government will shut down universities if they continue to be grounds for ethnic-based clashes" (Ezega News, 2019).

Reducing the gender gap in the HE sector is another salient political issue. So far, this mainly concerns supporting female staff and students through various means. For example, HEIS are expected to support female students through tutorial programs (for selected courses), and provision of training on life skill and reproductive issues. They have also been required to hire female candidates to the academic wing, including through affirmative action and to include female staff in the top (including board), middle and lower leadership. To facilitate this, all HEIS have established a gender office. The system also requires all public HEIS to align their strategic and annual plans with national priorities (interview, 11 April 2019).

The other element of political accountability is the appointment of the board and the president. According to the HEP, all public HEIS have a board composed of seven members who are all external. The board is the supreme governing body, with plethora responsibilities extending from supervising to monitoring the overall operation of HEIS. MoSHE appoints the chairperson and three of the board members directly and the remaining three in consultation with universities. The board is directly accountable to MoSHE and the latter has the power to reform it completely or in part. Members of the board are expected to come from past or present position holders or notable personalities or representatives of the customers of the products and services of HEIS (HPR, 2019).

Practically, however, board members have so far been drawn mainly from top high ranking members of the ruling party who are also top government officials (including Ministers, deputy ministers, federal agency heads, regional presidents/governors, zonal governors, etc.), and ruling party affiliated notable personalities, particularly from the area where the HEI is located (interview, 11 April 2019). Generally, therefore, the board appears to be part of the external governance (or at least in between MoSHE and HEIs) rather than internal, and its practical composition implies it is mainly meant to safeguard government's political interest.

MoSHE also appoints presidents of public HEIS, although the board, based on merit, nominates them (HPR, 2019). According to the HEP, the president is designated as a 'chief executive officer', which implies the country's desire to corporatize HEIS. The president, whose term of office is six years, takes ultimate responsibility for both academic and administrative matters. Unlike the board, the line of accountability of the president is not clearly stated by the HEP. However, the board is authorized to make monitoring reviews biannually and comprehensive in-depth reviews every three years on the performance of the president (HPR, 2019). Moreover, the board has the power to "cause the removal or remove the president ..., if it determines through three consecutive monitoring review or one in-depth review, his continuity in office would be injurious to the institution" (p. 11494). The same proclamation also gives power to the Minister of MoSHE to relieve the president (with or without the advice of the board) if the Minster "... is convinced that it is the right action to take" (p. 11494). Thus, though supposedly appointed on a merit basis, the president is a politically appointed official.

Among other requirements, public HEIS are required to submit a five year strategic plan agreement and get permission for all academic programs from MoSHE, return their unspent budget annually, report any income generated and submit a financial report quarterly to MoFEC, get approval for their administrative wing's organizational structure from the CSC, and submit their annual purchase request of 'common user items' to PPAA. HEIS are legally subject to an external financial and property audit (by OFAG) and academic quality audit (by HERQA). For the purpose of transparency, both OFGA and HERQA publish their audit report and make it publicly accessible. HEIS are also required to establish internal audit (accountable to MoFEC) and internal quality assurance units (accountable to the president) (HPR, 2019). They also are obliged to respect university entry requirements set by the HEP and the cutting points and other criteria set by MoSHE annually when enrolling undergraduate students, and to adhere to the civil service laws and MoSHE's academic staff recruitment directive during the recruitment of administrative and academic staff, respectively (HPR, 2017; MoE, 2018). Their tenured administrative staff has the right to appeal to the CSC if they feel that they are mistreated and thus, HEIs are subject to external grievance review (HPR, 2019). According to the informant from OFAG, HEIs are among the top institutions accused of violating financial, procurement and property administration and civil service laws and utilizing resources inefficiently (interview, 5 April 2019). The Reporter Newspaper also confirms this (The Reporter, 2016).

Academic accountability involves proactive and retrospective mechanisms of accountability. Among others, the proactive mechanisms include the following: requiring HEIs to get permission for opening new academic programs; align their research and engagement plan with the country's priority needs; enter into contract agreements with their academic staff who won project grants from state funds to ensure that projects are accomplished as planned and with the desired output/outcome; and conduct course delivery evaluations regularly (interview, 11 April 2019). The retrospective aspect involves different components. First, although public HEIs are not subject to accreditation, they are subject to external academic program quality audit (HPR, 2019). Second, the new public universities that have been established over the last two decades began with mainly bachelor degree holding academic staff, who, in principle, are not allowed to run courses independently (interview, 11 April 2019). Thus, on the one hand HEIs (particularly the relatively well-established ones) have been encouraged to open master and doctoral degree programs. They have also been required to build the capacity of their academic staff by sending them for further education, providing them training on pedagogy, research undertaking and publication, and English language improvement (MoSHE, 2019b). Third, HEIs are required to let students evaluate their professors (on course delivery, assessment, etc.), within which, in principle, obtaining below 50% of the value allocated to this evaluation would result in denying promotion to the next academic rank (interview, 11 April 2019). Fourth, recently, MoSHE directed HEIs to establish incubation centers and to provide training on entrepreneurship to potential graduates. As a means of *ex post facto* accountability, MoSHE has started conducting graduate satisfaction surveys and tracer studies about the employability of new graduates, although these are not yet institutionalized. MoSHE's report shows that in the 2018/19 academic year, the graduate employability rate was 58.5%. MoSHE is also preparing to organize a national exit exam for all new graduates (MoSHE, 2019b). So far, national exit exams have been given to Law graduates. Fifth, Moshe uses the *forum of institutions* (or the institutional transformation council) to bring all public universities' presidents or their representatives to present their performance, at least annually, in the presence of representatives from MoSHE, HRTSC, and federal level student union representatives and other concerned bodies. After the presentation, universities are ranked and best performing ones are recognized (interviews, 3 and 11 April 2019). Finally, public HEIS are required to ensure that only publications by reputable publishers are considered for promotion. To this end, a draft directive produced by MoSHE concerning the reputation of publications and other requirements for promotion is under discussion (MoSHE, 2019a).

### 4.4    *Challenges of External Accountability*

Generally, measuring and promoting performance, ensuring compliance with applicable laws, standards and norms, and enhancing transparency and responsiveness, are among the major goals of accountability, notwithstanding the restriction and burdens it imposes on individuals or institutions (Trow, 1996; Hazelkorn, 2018; Romzek, 2000). However, there are various challenges that prevent realizing this. In this section, we shall see the challenges associated with the three types of accountabilities discussed above, in the context of Ethiopia. The challenges presented are a summary from interview results and document analysis.

Among others, eight challenges stand out in relation to political accountability. First, according to the informants from HERQA, politically loaded various reform programs such as business process reengineering, balanced scorecard, citizens' charter, developmental/change army, Kaizen, deliverology, etc., have been imported from abroad and externally imposed on HEIs. Here, HEIs have been either resisting or simply conforming (interview, 8 April 2019). Second, achieving some of the politically sensitive issues such as ensuring gender balance and campus security are highly influenced by the external political culture and thus they remain a huge challenge for HEIs (interview, 5 April 2019). Third, board members are criticized for not properly directing HEIs due to either lack of time or lack of knowledge or both. Fourth, according to the HEP (HPR, 2019), the board is expected to conduct self-performance evaluation quarterly. However, the results of such evaluations are never publicly communicated and thus external stakeholders do not have the required information to hold the board accountable (interview, 5 April 2019). Fifth, the fact that all board members are drawn externally and are only seven in number may prevent including various internal and external stakeholders who could help HEIs to deliver what is expected from them. Sixth, it is repeatedly observed that board members have the temptation to channel resources from the HEI to their constituency in different ways. A typical example here is sponsorship of different events (interview, 3 April 2019). Cognizant of this, MoFEC has recently produced a circular letter restricting public HEIs from providing sponsorship (MoFEC, 2018). Seventh, holding the board accountable has been very challenging. Most members of the board are position holders of equal status with the Minister of MoSHE at the federal level or high ranking officials in the region where the university is located, and thus removing such members requires political negotiation, albeit their position enabled them to create smooth state-university relationships (interview, 11 April 2019).

Finally, similar to the board members, holding accountable university presidents has been challenging. A senior official at MoSHE had to say this in relation to the challenges of holding accountable or dismissing university presidents from power:

> As far as the president is in a good mood with the board, particularly the chairperson, it has been difficult to account or remove him whatever malpractice is reported. Since most board members are top government officials at the region where the university is located or at the federal government, they are able to give immunity to the president so long as their interest is respected. Recognizing this, we have recently reformed board members of several public universities. Whether this will bring any change is yet to be seen. (Interview, 11 April 2019)

In relation to administrative accountability, the following are among the major factors challenging HEIs from achieving what is expected of them. First is the fact that the general financial, procurement and property administration laws that govern HEIs do not consider their unique context. For example, they do not adjust salaries and other payment rates as well as student allowances regularly based on market price. Delays are common, owing to the fact that the procurement of federal institutions' (including HEIs) 'common user' items are facilitated by PPAA. HEIs also lack sufficient autonomy in determining the recruitment, promotion and dismissal procedures and criteria of their administrative staff. They also lack autonomy to award state funded research grants to researchers based on contract (except for materials and sub-contracts, researchers get only per diem), which is negatively affecting the quality of research output and creating an unnecessary burden on researchers (interviews, 11 and 12 April 2019).

The following are some of the challenges and limitations observed in relation to academic accountability. First, according to the informant from HERQA, MoSHE has not been capable enough in blocking curricula that has low demand in the market. In some universities, there were experiences where curricula were started simply because of the interest of academic staff wanted to teach them (interview, 8 April 2019). Second, HERQA, the agency authorized to conduct external audit, has not been in a position to handle the rapid expansion of HEIs (from two public and no private HEIs before the end of the 1990s, to 46 public and 127 private HEIs now). Moreover, HERQA is accountable to MoSHE and it does not see itself as an independent entity capable of regulating HEIs. So far, its main function is limited to providing recommendations based on its quality audit findings to MoSHE but it cannot do anything if the latter fails to act accordingly. Third, since public HEIs are not subject to accreditation, almost all the recently established ones have been opening new academic programs (including medicine and engineering) without having laboratories, workshops and other necessary resources, which, needless to say, seriously compromises quality (interview, 8 April 2019). Fourth, there is no independent institution that evaluates HEIs' academic performance, collecting data and producing reliable reports (interview, 5 April 2019). Fifth, except when they seek promotion, academic staff has not been subject to evaluation biannually or annually against research and engagement although 25% of their workload is allotted to these areas. Sixth, despite their good intentions, both students and academic units have not taken seriously the involvement of students in evaluating academic staff, which could have been helpful in holding accountable the latter (interview, 11 April 2029).

## 5    Conclusion

This chapter contributes to the scholarship on accountability in HE in general and on external accountability in Ethiopian public HE in particular. It addressed the five fundamental questions related to accountability in the context of HE. It also identified the domains and types of external accountability commonly observed in HE. Finally, this chapter brought to the fore that cross cutting issues are not commonly addressed as one of the important domains of accountability in HE in the literature.

With regard to Ethiopia, the chapter examined the actors involved, the purpose, orientation, types and mechanisms, consequences and challenges of external accountability in public HE. About 13 federal agencies are involved in ensuring accountability in this sector. Improving performance and ensuring compliance are seen as the ultimate goals of external accountability. The sector shows trends towards result orientated accountability, albeit much focus is still given to inputs, activities and process. The move towards result-oriented accountability is in line with the international trend (Alach, 2016; Yamamoto, 2011; Yorke & Vidovich, 2016) but this warrants close attention to minimize the risk of 'playing with numbers'. Following the introduction of the New Public Management in the HE sector, there is a danger of counting what is measured rather than measuring what counts, which usually leads to fabrications (see Yorke & Vidovich, 2016). Thus, in HE, focusing on quantifiable indicators could be misleading. For example, a reduced dropout rate may imply efficiency but this may happen at the expense of quality. According to one of the informants from HERQA, in Ethiopia, since high attrition rates result in severe criticism from the government, in some cases professors were asked to justify low grades given to students (interview, 8 April 2019). In the context of Ethiopia, questioning HEIS regarding student dropout is problematic since neither students have the right to determine the discipline they wish to study nor HEIs have the right to select their undergraduate students. Finally, although conducting a tracer study could be helpful for policy input, imposing any consequences on HEIS based on graduate employability rate would be unfair since this is mostly determined by the prior capabilities of the students, the national macro-economy, and political stability of the country.

The study also found that public HEIS in Ethiopia are accountable to multiple external stakeholders, particularly through political, administrative and academic types of accountability. The external accountability system also imposes consequences on HEIS although they have not been effective or predictable. The mechanisms of accountability of HEs in Ethiopia include: alignment of strategic and annual plans with national priorities, appointing external board members, setting key performance indicators and various standards, setting reporting checklist, reviewing and providing feedback on plans and reports, conducting customer satisfaction survey and tracer studies, organizing forum of institutions, and conducting financial and academic program audits. Despite the extensiveness of this list, the system of external accountability is characterized by several challenges, which demand the attention of various stakeholders. Subjecting public HEIS and their academic programs to accreditation, introducing performance-linked funding and predictable consequences, supporting HEIS to automate their administrative services, outsourcing student services, updating salaries and incentives regularly and depoliticizing the sector are recommended to minimize the challenges and to enable HEIS to focus on their mission.

Finally, we expect the study, particularly the challenges identified in relation to external accountability and the recommendations forwarded, to serve as policy input. Further, as studies on HE accountability in Ethiopia remain rare, the study may serve as impetus for other researchers to do further research on the area.

## Notes

1  Before it was established as MoSHE in 2018, while *higher education* as a sector was under the Ministry of Education, *Science* was under the Ministry of Science and Technology.
2  The education sector development program (ESDP) was introduced in 1998 and has been revised five times the fifth being the ongoing ESDP-V.
3  In 2010, Ethiopia adopted a strategic development plan called Growth and Transformation Plan (GTP-1). By 2015, GTP-1 was updated to GTP-2. All Ministries and other government agencies are expected to cascade their five year strategic plans based on the national GTP, which involves higher education.

## References

Akalu, G. A. (2016). Higher education 'massification' and challenges to the professoriate: Do academics' conceptions of quality matter? *Quality in Higher Education, 22*(3), 260–276.

Alach, Z. (2016). Performance measurement and accountability in higher education: The puzzle of qualification completions. *Tertiary Education and Management, 22*(1), 36–48.

Asgedom, A., & Hagos, T. (2015). Governance reforms in higher education of Ethiopia : The case of autonomy and accountability in. *Ethiopian Journal of Development Research, 37*(1), 1–40.

Bovens, M. (2007). Analyzing and assessing accountability: A conceptual framework. *European Law Journal, 13*(4), 447–468.

Chineze, U., & Olele, C. O. (2011). Academic accountability, quality and assessment of higher education in Nigeria. *Makerere Journal of Higher Education, 3*(2).

Daigle, S. L., & Cuocco, P. (2002). *Public accountability and higher education: Soul mates or strange bedfellows*. EDUCAUSE Center for Applied Research. http://www.educause.edu/ir/library/pdf/ERB0209.pdf

Dea, M., & Zeleke, B. (2017). Governance of Ethiopia public universities in Southern region: Professional & administrative accountability perspective. *OSR Journal of Humanities and Social Science (IOSR-JHSS)*, 22(5), 86–98.

Ezega News. (2019, November 15). PM-Abiy Urges Universities to take action, warns closure if violence persists. Retrieved from https://www.ezega.com/News/ News Details/7444/PM-Abiy-Urges-Universities-to-Take-Action-Warns-Closure-if-Violence-Persists

Graycar, A. (2016). Accountability mechanisms. In A. Farazmand (Ed.), *Global encyclopedia of public administration, public policy, and governance* (pp. 1–5) Springer International Publishing.

Han, Y., & Demircioglu, M. A. (2016). Accountability, politics, and power. In A. Farazmand (Ed.), *Global encyclopedia of public administration, public policy, and governance*. Springer International.

Hazelkorn, E. (2018). The accountability and transparency agenda: Emerging issues in the global era. In A. Curaj et al. (Eds.), *European higher education area: The impact of past and future policies* (pp. 423–439). Springer.

HPR. (2003). Higher Education Proclamation No. 351/2003. *Federal Negarit Gezeta*. Addis Ababa.

HPR. (2017). Federal Civil Service Proclamation, No. 1064/2017. *Federal Negarit Gezeta*. Addis Ababa.

HPR (House of Peoples Representatives, FDRE). (2019). Higher Education Proclamation No. 1152/2019. *Federal Ngarit Gazeta*. Addis Ababa.

Huisman, J. (2018). Accountability in higher education. In J. C. Shin & P. Teixeira (Eds.), *Encyclopedia of international higher education systems and institutions* (pp. 484–488). Springer Science Business Media.

Kahsay, M. N. (2017). The links between academic research and economic development in Ethiopia: The case of Addis Ababa University. *European Journal of STEM Education*, 2(22), 5.

Kearns, K. P. (1998). Institutional accountability in higher education : A strategic approach. *Public Productivity & Management Review*, 22(2), 140–156.

Kivistö, J., Pekkola, E., & Berg, L. N. (2019). Performance in higher education institutions and its variations in nordic policy. In R. Pinheiro et al. (Eds.), *Reforms, organizational change and performance in higher education* (pp. 37–67). Plagrave Macmillan.

Leveille, D. E. (2006). Accountability in higher education : A public agenda for trust and cultural change. *Research & Occasional Paper Series*, (December), 1–201.

Lindberg, S. I. (2013). Mapping accountability: Core concept and subtypes. *International Review of Administrative Sciences*, 79(2), 202–226.

MoE. (2015a). *Education and training: Growth and transformation plan II*. MoE.

MoE (2015b). *Education Sector Development Program V (ESDP-V) 2015/16–2019/20*. MoE.

MoE (Ministry of Education, FDRE). (2018). *Academic staff recruitment and development in public higher education institutions.* Directive 03/2010.

MoSHE (Ministry of Science and Higher Education, FDRE). (2019a). *Guideline for academic publishing and promotion.* Unpublished.

MoSHE. (2019b). *Higher education sector 2019–2020 indicative annual plan* (Amharic version). Unpublished.

MoSHE. (2019c). *Higher education supervision checklist.*

Mulgan, R. (2000). 'Accountability': An ever-expanding concept? *Public Administration, 78*(3), 555–573.

Romzek, B. S. (2000). Dynamics of public sector accountability in an era of reform. *International Review of Administrative Sciences, 66*(1), 21–44.

Romzek, B. S., & Ingraham, P. W. (2000). Cross pressures of accountability: Initiative, command, and failure in the Ron Brown plane crash. *Public Administration Review, 60*(3), 240–253.

Salmi, J. (2009). *The growing accountability agenda in tertiary education: Progress or mixed blessing?* (World Bank Education Working Paper Series, No. 16). The World Bank.

Salmi, J, Sursock, A., & Olefir, A. (2017). *Improving the performance of Ethiopian universities in science and technology: A policy note.* Retrieved from https://papers.ssrn.com/sol3/papers.cfm?abstract_id=3074802

Tamrat, W. (2012). University governance in Ethiopia: Trends, challenges and options. *The Teacher, 5*(10), 1–12.

The Reporter. (2016, May 21). *Catch 22: The audit report vs. the static predicament.* Retrieved from https://www.thereporterethiopia.com/content/catch-22-audit-report-vs-static-predicament

Trow, M. (1996). Trust, markets and accountability in higher education: A comparative perspective. *Higher Education Policy, 9*(4), 309–324.

Vidovich, L. (2018). Institutional accountability in higher. In P. T. J. C. Shin (Ed.), *Encyclopedia of international higher education systems and institutions* (pp. 1–8). Springer Science+Business Media.

Vidovich, L., & Slee, R. (2001). Bringing universities to account? Exploring some global and local policy tensions. *Journal of Education Policy, 16*(5), 431–453.

Yamamoto, K. (2011). Educational and public accountability of higher education institutions in case of National Universities in Japan. *The Journal of Management and Policy in Higher Education,* 1–19.

Yorke, J., & Vidovich, L. (2016). *Learning standards and the assessment of quality in higher education: Contested policy trajectories.* Springer Nature.

Zumeta, W. M. (2011). What does it mean to be accountable? Dimensions and implications of higher education's public accountability. *Review of Higher Education, 35*(1), 131–148.

CHAPTER 10

# Finnish-Russian Double Degree Programs: When Partners' Responsibilities Become a Challenge for Internationalization

*Svetlana Shenderova*

### Abstract

Finnish and Russian universities have developed internationalization activities including double degree programs (double degrees), taking advantage of such benefits as their common border, membership of the Bologna Process and support from the governments of both countries. This chapter discusses how the division of responsibilities influences the implementation of master's double degrees in Finnish-Russian partnerships. The research concentrates on cases of the internal allocation of responsibilities in double degrees within each partner university, including the role of central/faculty and administrative/ academic departments. In addition, it investigates how Finnish and Russian universities allocate responsibilities for double degrees between one another. In conclusion, the chapter demonstrates the role of transaction costs challenging double degree implementation and university internationalization.

### Keywords

internationalization of higher education – double degrees – transaction costs – responsibilities

## 1 Introduction

Double degree programs are considered by the Government of the Russian Federation (RF Government) to be important tools for enhancing the competitiveness of Russian higher education institutions (HEIs) in the global higher education market. Double degrees have developed with funding from the EU and its member states since Russia joined the Bologna Process in 2003. The RF Government started funding double degrees in leading Russian HEIs from

© KONINKLIJKE BRILL NV, LEIDEN, 2020 | DOI: 10.1163/9789004436558_011

2006 onwards, and has expanded funding programs aimed at strengthening the international dimension of selected Russian HEIs and the export of education from 2013 onwards.

Previous research studied partnerships providing the opportunity to earn at least two degrees in different countries. For example, two research projects looked at partnerships providing the option to earn two degrees in Russian and European HEIs (Sinyatkin, Mishin, & Karpukhina, 2010; Burquel, Shenderova, & Tvorogova, 2014a, 2014b). The total number of such degrees increased from 2010 to 2013; but by 2013, 44% of the programs that existed in 2010 had disappeared.

It drew attention to the challenges for collaborative degree programs including joint and double degrees. The literature mainly concentrated on the external challenges for double degrees such as funding, quality assurance, and differences in the national legislation of the countries where the partner HEIs were located (Zheng, Cai, & Ma, 2017; JDAZ, 2015; Kuder, 2013; REDEEM, 2016; JOIMAN, 2011, 2012). It has been noted (Shenderova, 2018a) that the incoherence of the Bologna reforms and unclear areas of responsibilities for the administration of Russian internationalization policy impeded its implementation at an institutional level. Karpukhina (2013) found that the non-harmonized legislation framework seriously impacted on the perspectives for double degrees in Russian and European HEIs.

Amongst the other EU member states, Finland has sustainably supported higher education cooperation with the HEIs of its Eastern neighbour (Ministry of Education, Finland, 2009; Jänis-Isokangas, 2017; Better Together to a Better World, 2017), despite the complicated historical heritage and recent EU-Russian tensions. In addition, Finland shares its largest border with Russia; the largest Finnish and Russian cities have reliable transport connection, convenient for academic and student mobility. Finnish HEIs ranked third among European HEIs implementing double degrees in collaboration with Russian partners (Burquel, Shenderova, & Tvorogova, 2014a, p. 66). It is noteworthy that Finnish-Russian double degree partnerships successfully combined funding provided by the governments of both countries (Shenderova, 2018b). Khudoley, Novikova, and Lanko (2010) analyzed experience in launching a Finnish-Russian master's double degree in International Relations in partnership between one Finnish and two Russian universities since 2005. The rigorous government alignment of the higher education sector in Russia, which prescribed the structure and content for any degree program for all HEIs, was considered a challenge for the development of double degrees.

This chapter focuses on the experience of all Finnish HEIs where the EDU-neighbours project (2020) revealed master's degree programs with the option of the second degree being issued by the Russian partner HEI in 2017. In particular, the chapter explores internal challenges for internationalization and identifies where they may appear within each partner HEI and their partnerships as exemplified by Finnish-Russian double degree programs. In discussing responsibilities for double degrees, the chapter investigates how Finnish and Russian HEIs allocate decision making in relation to administrative and academic issues, and when allocation of these responsibilities becomes a challenge for internationalization. How does each partner university allocate responsibilities for a double degree within itself? How does the role of central/faculty and administrative/academic departments vary? How do Finnish and Russian HEIs allocate responsibilities for double degrees between one another? How and when does the division of responsibilities produce transaction costs? The chapter answers these questions using an opportunity to compare how differently a particular Russian partner has implemented the same degree with the same Finnish partner.

Narrow definitions are inapplicable to the study programs developed by international partners in cooperation with Russian HEIs. That is why a broad definition was chosen for this study: "a double degree program awards two individual qualifications at equivalent levels upon completion of the collaborative program requirements established by two partner institutions" (Knight, 2011). This definition, combined with the transaction costs approach, provides an understanding of how the allocation of responsibilities impacts on the implementation of double degrees. Double degree transaction costs could be defined here as all hidden efforts, time and expenditures of stakeholders both inside any partner university and between each of them, which may be unexpectedly incurred when HEIs cooperate in providing a double degree program. The chapter considers as an internal challenge any issue of double degree development, where vaguely allocated responsibilities produce transaction costs. The study concentrates on the allocation of responsibilities for such issues as partner selection, curriculum design, recognition to study abroad and quality assurance.

In conclusion, the chapter demonstrates the role of transaction costs challenging double degree implementation and university internationalization.


## 2      Methodology

This study was implemented within the framework of the Finnish-Russian research project "Towards good neighbourliness with higher education cooperation" (EDUneighbours) in 2017–2020. The EDUneighbours team included

Finnish and Russian academics experienced in double degree implementation and studies in the internationalization of higher education (EDUneighbours, 2020). The methodology of the project has been introduced in detail elsewhere (Shenderova, 2018b); in this chapter the methodology is considered in relation to the allocation of responsibilities within and between partner HEIS.

The EDUneighbours project concentrated on master's degrees 120 ECTS (ECTS User's Guide, 2015), which Finnish HEIS announced as providing an option to earn a second degree in Russia in 2014–2017. Master's degrees were chosen as the most prevalent among the EU-Russian and Finnish-Russian collaborative study programs. To identify these degrees, the websites of all Finnish HEIS (38) listed in 2017 on the website of the Finnish Ministry of Education and Culture, were surveyed, as well as the websites of all the Russian HEIS named as their partners. Following the criteria of selection, the EDUneighbours team found 18 master's double degrees implemented in five Finnish HEIS; the latter represented the universities, but not universities of applied sciences. The geographical scope comprised 23 Russian partners located from the North-West of Russia to Siberia.

The Finnish universities represented such cities and regions as Rovaniemi in the North (University of Lapland), Tampere University (West), University of Eastern Finland in Joensuu, Lappeenranta University of Technology (South) and Helsinki as the capital of Finland (Aalto University). Usually one Finnish university established partnerships with several Russian universities. The EDUneighbours team then selected ten Russian HEIS which had 13 double degree partnerships in different fields of studies. The cases were concentrated in the regions of Russia providing the easiest transport connections with Finland for cross-border cooperation. Two cases are located in Arkhangelsk, one in Petrozavodsk (Northwestern federal district); four in St. Petersburg, and three in Moscow, the two largest federal cities of Russia. All the selected HEIS are state universities, six of them had an institutional background oriented on the needs of certain industries, two of them were established as universities with a wide range of undergraduate, graduate and doctoral studies.

After selecting the cases, the EDUneighbours team conducted interviews at five Finnish universities and their ten Russian partner HEIS with 35 internal university stakeholders in 2017 such as: academic heads and/or academic coordinators of double degrees; academics involved in curriculum development; administrators in international and/or academic offices at central and faculty levels. 15 persons in Finland and 20 in Russia were asked similar questions including regarding their responsibilities relating to double degree implementation. The language of the interviews was English in Finland and Russian in Russia. 45 graduates of Finnish-Russian double degree programs were enrolled for interview in groups in English in St. Petersburg, Russia, in

2018. The graduates represented different countries; they were asked about the administrative barriers, unexpected costs and efforts, arising during the process of application and study.

The interviews with stakeholders included such issues of double degree implementation as personal responsibilities within the program, its management and finance in the context of university governance. In relation to internal responsibilities and their allocation within a certain program and partnership, the EDUneighbours team considered such issues as: partner selection and its practices, harmonization of the curriculum, quality assurance, and procedures for the recognition of periods of study abroad. The interviews were coded and analyzed with the help of qualitative content analysis. Due to the guaranteed anonymity, there are no links in any publication that would allow any particular program studied or person interviewed to be identified.

## 3 Double Degree: Who Chooses a Partner?

The EDUneighbours study demonstrated that most sustainable partnerships were based on previous research cooperation started in the late 1990s, and turned into internationalization activities in higher education after 2003. However, recent priorities of national policies (Better Together to a Better World, 2017; Russian Academic Excellence Project 5-100, 2020) have pressured *partner selection* in both Finnish and Russian universities.

Finnish universities often judged the potential of a Russian partner as a source of international students to increase the numbers of incoming mobility, and the development of double degree partnerships is considered as one but not the only option for providing this. However, simultaneously this approach increased uncertainty for a partnership. Some double degree students had not been motivated to study, which led to the end of cooperation. Therefore, the efforts and time spent on organizing a double degree were in vain. An interviewee described the case, when a partner HEI in Russia

> sent us students, but they were not top-level students, and there were huge difficulties to get them engaged, and they were more interested in spending time in Finland than studying, and this is not what we are expecting from our partners. That's why we dropped them. (IntervieweeFI10)

Meanwhile Russian universities had to select a partner under the pressure of ranking-oriented Key Performance Indicators (KPIS) dictated by national internationalization policy (Shenderova, 2018a). One of these KPIS is the number of double degrees implemented with highly ranked universities. The author of this chapter had negative personal experience during previous work in a Russian HEI trying to develop internationalization activities with a Finnish university. A vice-rector rejected a suggestion identifying a foreign university as 'not included in top-300' in a certain world university ranking (WUR). The fact that the same university occupied a top-200 ranking in another WUR was not taken into account.

The EDUneighbours study confirmed the impact of ranking-oriented policy on partner selection in Russian universities. For example, a Russian administrator explained why a certain Finnish partner was chosen, by naming a certain RF Government funding program, and the position of a Finnish partner in a certain ranking. A Russian academic head echoed the KPI approach clarifying the expectations from double degree cooperation:

> A manager told me that [name of Finland HEI] appeared, expressed interest in the [name the field of study] and the initiative to develop a double degree. We, like any Russian HEI, are interested in KPIs. (IntervieweeRU13)

However, Table 10.1 demonstrates that in 2014–2017, Finnish-Russian double degrees were implemented by partners which relied more on the positive

TABLE 10.1    Finnish universities: Reasons to cooperate

| University | Main reason to select Russian partner | THE overall 2017 | THE overall 2018 | QS overall 2017 | QS overall 2018 |
| --- | --- | --- | --- | --- | --- |
| University of Lapland | Common area of study | - | - | - | - |
| Tampere University | Common area of study | 251–300 | 201–250 | 501–550 | 551–600 |
| University of Eastern Finland | Common area of study | 351–400 | 301–350 | 382 | 451–460 |
| Lappeenranta University of Technology | Internationalization strategy | 501–600 | 501–600 | 471–480 | 501–550 |
| Aalto University | Internationalization strategy | 201–250 | 190 | 133 | 137 |

SOURCE: INTERVIEWS FOR EDUNEIGHBOURS PROJECT (UNPUBLISHED), QS, THE

FINNISH-RUSSIAN DOUBLE DEGREE PROGRAMS

experience of previous cooperation and common area of studies than on such influential WURs as Quacquarelli Symonds (QS) and Times Higher Education (THE).

Table 10.2 comprizes Russian universities selected as case studies and their positions in WURs. Five of these Russian universities were not ranked in QS and THE al all; the others were ranked in the segment from 351 to 800 in 2017.

Meanwhile, four Finnish universities were ranked between 201 and 600, but only two of them were over top-300. Therefore, instead of the indicators prescribed, a partner's positions in the WURs are not crucial criteria to select; and it is not a guarantee that the partnership established could be successful.

Thus, academics at faculties are not entirely responsible for deciding with which foreign HEI to collaborate. From the transaction costs perspective, this means that giving the responsibilities to the academics and more trust to the faculties may be more productive than concentrating budgets on expensive travels of university administrators to different corners of the world with very uncertain results for double degree development and internationalization in general. In addition, previous cooperation at the bottom level provided academic heads with confidence in a partner's reliability and competency in the area of study, and thus in their ability to provide high added value of the double degree from the perspective of research and expertize. At the same time, the ranking-oriented approach multiplies internal transaction costs, first of all, the time spent by academics on explanations of why the old partner might be better than a little-known high-ranked university not necessarily interested in cooperation.

Therefore, the pressure of national internationalization policies can be considered as an internal challenge for double degree development, when a HEI administration blindly pursues quantitative KPIs and does not rely on the practices of academic cooperation developed at the faculty level. However, the top-bottom approach has prevailed in Russian universities specially supported by the RF Government to develop internationalization; the roles of academics is passive. An academic head of a double degree explained the motivation for cooperating with a Finnish university:

> The motivation is understandable, [...], the rector personally oversees everything. It's fair, he's made sufficient efforts, we are ranked in [names of WURs] decent positions. [Name of the rector] has already worked hard, but he needs backup, that's why there is enforcement within the university. [Name of the rector] supports international activities, and I feel it. We get called and told that there is a certain event, so it is necessary to

TABLE 10.2    Russian universities: Reasons to cooperate

| University | Main reason to select Finnish partner | THE overall 2017 | THE overall 2018 | QS overall 2017 | QS overall 2018 |
|---|---|---|---|---|---|
| Bauman Moscow State Technical University (Mytischi Branch), former Moscow State Forest University | Common area of study | 601–800 | 801–1000 | 306 | 240 |
| National Research University Higher School of Economics (Moscow) | Internationalization strategy | 401–500 | 351–400 | 411–420 | 382 |
| Saint Petersburg National Research University of Information Technologies, Mechanics and Optics (ITMO University) | Internationalization strategy | 351–400 | 501–600 | – | 601–650 |
| Northern Arctic Federal University | Common area of study | – | – | – | – |
| Northern State Medical University | Common area of study | – | – | – | – |
| Peter the Great St. Petersburg Polytechnic University | Internationalization strategy | 601–800 | 601–800 | 411–420 | 401–410 |
| Petrozavodsk State University | Common area of study | – | – | – | – |
| Russian University of Transport (MIIT) | Common area of study | – | – | – | – |
| St. Petersburg State Forest University | Common area of study | – | – | – | – |
| St. Petersburg State University | Common area of study | 401–500 | 401–500 | 258 | 240 |

SOURCE: INTERVIEWS FOR EDUNEIGHBOURS PROJECT (UNPUBLISHED), QS, THE

FINNISH-RUSSIAN DOUBLE DEGREE PROGRAMS 193

participate in it. [...] The university establishes the contacts. (Interviewee RU10)

However, even positive experience in research did not mean fruitful cooperation in higher education because of the many new stakeholders involved, and new challenges appeared.

## 4  Double Degrees on Finnish and Russian Grounds

The internal design of double degree curricula faced barriers both in Finnish and in Russian HEIs. However, the reasons and costs of *curricula revisions* have been different. For example, a Finnish academic named a school (faculty) decision to change the average number of credits within each course as a problem. That is why, instead of academic freedom flourishing in Finnish HEIs, curricula design and revision could be considered an internal challenge, which produced unpredictable transaction costs of double degree implementation, e.g. the time spent on internal negotiations.

> ... A couple of years ago we had courses that were from 3 to 7 credits, [...], then at some point all the courses were 5 credits, and then the school decided: okay, now everything needs to be 6. So, kind of if we need to give 30 credits, it's 6 times 5-credit courses, and then moving to 5 times 6-credit courses kind of changes the content. So, that is the difficulty. (InteriveweeFI11)

However, Finnish interviewees confirmed: administrators did not intervene in these issues at all, while academic heads at the faculty level played a more significant role in the double degree track control, approval and implementation than central offices. That definitely diminished the transaction costs of internal negotiation related to curricula design in Finland, while Russian universities could not avoid them.

> The academic director [of a degree] is the person responsible for academic issues such as curriculum, study-related issues, then the selection process, curricula design, selection, what else, student feedback, quality assurance. (IntervieweeFI13)

Finnish interviewees emphasized the decentralization of administrative responsibilities including the physical relocation of coordinators from the central offices to the faculties which happened a few years ago.

> We don't have any more university level centralized international office. [...] There are certain admission service units. There are certain admissions working at university level, and then at schools there are certain officers. But no international relations office as such exists anymore at [the university name]. There are a couple of people working at the university level. Most of the staff related to the international relations are at the school level. (IntervieweeFI14)

In Finland, universities seemed to integrate academic and international affairs successfully. Meanwhile in Russia, the internal alignment of curricula design has been pressured by the demands of the Federal Education Standards, and the changing views of internal administrative officers on their implementation.

> When we opened our programme, we [academics in a programme committee] were given a limited amount of freedom, because it was international, a double degree after all. We were given a path of freedom that did not strictly meet the [Federal Education] standards, did not customize the curricula to them. But a year later when the merger [of several departments] happened, and new people were appointed, we were told: that's it. We had to change all the courses for the first year of study [on the master's double degree] and to shove in the obligatory courses [prescribed by the Federal State Standards for all master's degrees in Russia], which no one needed. (IntervieweeRU9)

Russian academics at faculties have been overburdened by ongoing negotiations with officers at different central administrative departments, who often did not want to adapt traditional domestic program rules for the purposes of the double degree. Historically, Russian universities have had multiple places for decision-making even in relation to domestic degrees. For example, academics have usually been responsible for (double) degree learning outcomes, the content of courses and their delivery to students. Notwithstanding the fact that these parts of the double degree should also be approved by the central administration before their launch, and during the implementation.

In addition, the central administration had separate sections for academic and for international affairs. Their officers controlled double degrees without any specific knowledge of their fields, and had no responsibility as to students and academics. One person may combine administrative and academic duties officially, or be involved in related decision-making informally. For example, many Russian academics involved in curricula design simultaneously shared their experience in renting a bus for travelling students, or negotiations to provide international students with accommodation etc.

On the other hand, there are cases in Russia when a clerk from an administrative department has responsibility for deciding whether a double degree will be launched or not. A Russian academic described the situation as follows:

> It is hard for us – this organisation. But it doesn't matter. Well, certain decisions are made. There's a vice-rector for international affairs, there's a vice-rector for educational affairs. I don't know but I think they have normal contact and find a consensus fast. [...] The organisational support of enrolment is divided. International offices support the enrolment of international students, administrative offices are responsible for education support for the enrolment [of domestic students] from their side. (IntervieweeRU10)

Some Russian universities hired special managers to combine the demands of the international partner, academic head and different administrative offices regarding double degrees. Therefore, top-managers in these HEIS have not been able to organize a system of decision-making which would be able to harmonize internal regulations for international (double) and domestic degrees.

Meanwhile, other Russian universities did not need to use their resources so counterproductively, and have been able to organize a double degree implementation more smoothly. However, these academic heads have been overburdened with administrative issues; their ability to solve problems has been based more on their personal credibility and charisma than on the system solutions within the HEI. Where administrative and academic offices have not been sufficiently effective, their students have carried the burden of reimbursement of mobility costs and recognition of the period of study abroad.

*Recognition of the period of studies abroad* in Finland did not demand significant participation by students. Their administrative offices dealing with student records were located at the faculties, which provided fast integration of the results of previous studies into the university credit system:

> "students who have done some courses in Russia, have to provide, of course, a transcript of records, mainly certificates signed by our coordinator stating that this student has taken this course and the number of credits in ECTS is this and the grade is this. And based on that information we will include credits in our system." (IntervieweeFI8)

In contrast, some Russian universities considered double degree students as absent. Therefore, the students had to spend their time retaking their exams in their home university, or attending an additional semester, or preparing two different master's theses – one according to Finnish regulation, and the second in accordance with Russian alignment.

*Quality assurance* has been so different that the partners had not attempted to harmonize their approaches. Instead of exhaustive procedures of obligatory state accreditation every five years, and a lot of required KPIs, Russian academics and administrators on the ground have relied on informal exchanges of opinion with double degree students in relation to their study abroad. Likewise, Finnish stakeholders are not interested in knowing how quality assurance has been organized in Russia. However, some other issues have been agreed by the partners to a different extent.

## 5 Double Degrees: Putting the Puzzle Together

Finnish and Russian HEIs have often allocated double degree responsibilities based on a general cooperation agreement without any amendments in relation to certain programs. Some academic heads trusted in their partners and their ability to organize everything in the best way. For example, one of them explained:

> Why don't our students pay for the dormitory in Finland? [Name of Finnish head] and I just had a handshake and agreed it! Are the other universities paid for their students? (IntervieweeRU16)

These interviewees indicated positive experiences of previous collaboration between the heads, mainly in research, which had led to a good personal relationship. These partners, as old friends, did not need any specific regulations in the agreement regarding the practical arrangement of cooperation. However, the challenge appeared from the other side: if an HEI has not had any formal regulation of such agreements, the academic coordinator becomes overburdened by internal negotiations. The same Russian interviewee indicated: "I am responsible for everything!" (Interviewee RU16).

In addition, different Russian partners have been able to organize reimbursement of travel and living costs for their students and academics to a different extent, even collaborating with one Finnish university within the framework of the same degree. The extent of personal commitment of Russian academics and administrators has depended on their understanding of responsibilities in relation to domestic colleagues, international partners and students. Several coordinators in Russia had difficulty explaining how (if any) student expenses were reimbursed, but clearly indicated the procedures and sources of reimbursement of their own costs.

This kind of attitude makes it clear why the very few graduates of such programs had not been inspired by their experience: "I paid for everything!" (GraduateRUI).

Therefore, the lack of detail in formal agreements and the lack of personal accountability of coordinators created conditions for shifting the burden of travel and accommodation costs onto the student. Only a couple of programs found internal opportunities to rent buses and book hostels for Russian students travelling abroad. The academic heads were able to overcome the curricula challenge and simultaneously increase the numbers of mutual mobility, organizing seasonal schools.

However, in these cases the academic heads and/or coordinators have been overburdened by internal administrative issues including searches for the bus company/hostel, provision of all necessary documents as requested by the central university offices, and ongoing negotiations with numerous administrative departments within their own universities. In addition, these academics have been responsible for the invitation of international students and visa document preparations.

The study revealed that partner universities may agree the allocation of travel and accommodation costs, but may not take these costs into consideration. As a result, while the students of some programs paid for everything out of their own budget, the others enjoyed travel and accommodation for free. The challenge for double degrees appeared from transferring the responsibility from reckless university administrators to those students and/or academics who simply could not avoid the costs.

The interviewees in both countries described the curricula development as the toughest challenge for program implementation which demanded not only internal, but a lot of mutual negotiations. The partners have often chosen to build a double degree as part of an existing master's program either offered in English, or in Finnish and Russian. The curricula of both programs (double degree and single domestic degree) seemed partly similar, and this similarity became one of the reasons to choose the given partner and its domestic program.

At the same time, that has called into doubt the added value of a double degree organized as a trivial combination of first year of study at home university plus second year abroad, or vice versa. In summary, a double degree combining two 'twin' programs has offered new experiences such as living and studying abroad more than to acquire new knowledge beyond the domestic curriculum.

A special agreement between partner HEIS may become another option for regulating the allocation of responsibilities for double degrees. It might include a description of how the partners internally and mutually allocate responsibilities regarding funding, travelling and quality assurance. However, partners have often agreed to manage these issues independently from each other.

For example, students studied the first year of the master's program as specified in a Russian university for a domestic degree. But Russian HEIS rarely collected feedback from students and academics, did not use anonymized examinations and prohibited foreign students from working in industry even as interns because of migration laws. Meanwhile, the second year of the double degree complied with the Finnish university's rules, and included, for example, the opportunity to work for the thesis in a company, written anonymized exams, and a small number of contact hours for teachers and students. Therefore, while Finnish universities provide international students with internships, as a rule most Russian universities simply do not provide any internship for double degree students, being eager to avoid any problems with the migration services.

Most Finnish universities recently introduced IELTS or TOEFL and define their own threshold as an obligatory requirement for admission. However, few Finnish universities completely rely on student selection made by their Russian partners, e.g., Russian universities do not require English language certificates. It is noteworthy that some Russian universities are able to use new legislative developments, and organize the supervision and defending of the thesis in English, therefore avoiding the duplication of the master's theses. Therefore, language has not been a serious challenge for double degree implementation. To return the definition given by Knight (2011) and cited in the Introduction, Finnish and Russian universities have demonstrated the ability to establish collaborative program requirements. However, often these requirements have continued to be isolated from each other.

## 6 Conclusion

Kompanets and Väätänen (2018) investigated the experience of one Finnish university which shaped the network of Russian partners to run double degree programs in Engineering and Management. Concentrating on the motivation for developing a set of master's double degrees for internal and external university stakeholders, these authors specified such challenges as the defence of the master's thesis and recognition of the period of studies. Yefanova (2013) noted the importance of institutional support and clarifications of double degree goals and benefits to the internal stakeholders involved. That could be helpful for overcoming the challenges for partnerships caused by a lack of information. Meanwhile, Tarazona (2013) mentioned the positive role of formal regulations developed within each partner to align a double degree.

The increase in transaction costs has been considered as an implicit threat to any double degree (Shenderova, 2018b). Being a 'by-product' of a domestic degree, a double degree and its internal regulations have been developed residually, because the internal stakeholders have not considered them as their priorities. Therefore, the volume of transaction costs has become the crucial criterion to developing a double degree both within a university, and between them in partnership. Initially any HEI has allocated the responsibilities of internal stakeholders based on the needs of a domestic degree. In addition, no activity could avoid transaction costs (Coase, 1988; Williamson, 1985; Pesch & Ishmaev, 2019). But if an HEI and its stakeholders have the willingness and ability to reallocate, adapt and document their responsibilities clearly both for domestic and for international double degrees, that means an opportunity to overcome challenges and minimize transaction costs at any stage of double degree development.

When responsibilities for partner selection, curricula design, recognition of the study abroad period and quality assurance have been detailed, agreed, allocated and monitored within and between double degree partners, the program requirements become clear for the internal university stakeholders, which enhances the quality of a double degree. However, the extent of university autonomy and academic freedoms in the countries where partner HEIS operate should be taken into consideration (Shenderova, 2020).

Both countries have recently pushed their universities to achieve the quantitative objectives of national internationalization policies. This pressure could be considered as a serious challenge to double degree development, especially when university top-managers insist on KPIs and a ranking-oriented approach, without taking into account the opinion of academics cooperating on the ground. When cooperation in research has preceded a double degree partnership, it has minimized transaction costs recognizing the paths of cooperation with a certain partner, and understanding its institutional reliability. The oldest double degree partnerships have been based on previous academic cooperation.

The other internal challenge for double degree development is the multiplication of decision-making centres within Russian universities. This has consequently increased the number of required internal university reports, meetings and additional requests not necessarily understandable for an international partner. On the one hand, administrators have intervened in such academic issues as curricula development, revision and content. On the other hand, Russian academics have been overburdened with administrative issues. The most typical internal conflict is 'academic affairs department vs international affairs department' caused by the traditional isolation of these offices from each other both in Russian HEIs, and within the Ministry. Academics play the role of the 'civilian population' between these administrative armies, turning to bureaucratic legislation to justify their own actions (or the absence thereof).

Curricula design and credit transfer have been mostly challenged for double degree implementation both at institutional level and at the level of partnership. Curricula challenges have been overcome by intensive courses during seasonal schools. However, at the same time the heads of double degrees have been overburdened not only with their direct academic responsibilities, but with numerous administrative issues as well.

Academics and administrators of double degree programs have come into continual conflict regarding the recognition of the period of study abroad with many central offices in their own universities. Some Russian HEIs have preferred not to change the system of confused internal responsibilities, but to hire special managers responsible for combining the demands of an international partner, domestic academic head and different administrative offices regarding double degrees. This is the most telling illustration of transaction costs caused by the multiplication of decision-making centres. As a result, there has been a trend of isolating the responsibility of partners relating to the curriculum, quality assurance and student assessment.

Many double degree graduates had to take their exams or even attend an additional semester in their Russian home university. These transaction costs directly influenced double degree sustainability: annual intake or symmetrical mobility was not found in any program. Moreover, 4 from 13 partnerships had ended by 2019, and some continuing programs have had uncertain prospects.

To conclude, if the implementation of a double degree program requires too many efforts for responsibilities to be divided clearly and for this division to be adhered to, the partners prefer to return to the mobility programs as the only appropriate approach for attracting international students. The isolation of curricula design, recognition of the period of study and quality assurance hamper opportunities for making a double degree an entire study program. However, isolation is the way to minimize the transaction costs of double degree and the challenges brought about by the differences in university governance and degree program management.

## Acknowledgements

The author expresses her deep gratitude to the reviewers, Dr. Sirke Mäkinen, University of Helsinki, and Tania Northorpe (Shevchenko), MA, University of Cambridge, for their positive encouragement and inspiring comments during this chapter's preparations. The author would also like to thank all the interviewees who shared their experiences for the study.

## References

5-100-2020 Russian Academic Excellence Project. (2020). Retrieved January 4, 2020, from http://5top100.com/documents/

Better Together to a Better World. (2017). *To promote internationalisation in Finnish higher education and research 2017–2025.* Retrieved January 4, 2020, from http://minedu.fi/documents/1410845/4154572/YMP-en-net.pdf/ab74d6b2-a48f-49ee-9563-6313f87198aehttp://minedu.fi/documents/1410845/4154572/YMP-en-net.pdf/ab74d6b2-a48f-49ee-9563-6313f87198ae

Burquel, N., Shenderova, S., & Tvorogova, S. (2014a). *Innovation and transformation in transnational education. Joint education programmes between higher education institutions of the European Union and Russian Federation.* Final Report. European Union. Retrieved January 4, 2020, from https://publications.europa.eu/en/publication-detail/-/publication/6bb2175a-75f9-11e8-ac6a-01aa75ed71a1/language-en/format-PDF/source-78326987

Burquel, N., Shenderova, S., & Tvorogova, S. (2014b). *Catalogue 'sampled joint programmes between European and Russian higher education institutions. Innovations and transformation in transnational education'.* European Union. Retrieved January 4, 2020, from https://publications.europa.eu/en/publication-detail/-/publication/b01303b3-fba4-415b-8d36-b8e10663f9dd/language-en

Coase, R. (1988). *The firm, the marker and the law.* University of Chicago Press.

Deriglazova, L., & Mäkinen, S. (2019). Still looking for a partnership? EU-Russia cooperation in the field of higher education. *Journal of Contemporary European Studies, 1–12.* https://doi.org/10.1080/14782804.2019.1593113

de Wit, H., Hunter, F., & Coelen, R. (2015). Internationalisation of higher education in Europe: Future directions. In H. de Wit, F. Hunter, L. Howard, & E. Egron-Polak (Eds.), *Internationalisation of higher education. Study* (pp. 273–280). European Union. Retrieved January 4, 2020, from https://www.europarl.europa.eu/RegData/etudes/STUD/2015/540370/IPOL_STU(2015)540370_EN.pdf

ECTS User's Guide. (2015). *European Union*. Publications Office of the European Union, 2015. Retrieved January 4, 2020, from http://www.ehea.info/media.ehea.info/file/ECTS_Guide/00/0/ects-users-guide-2015_614000.pdf

EDUneighbours. (2020). *Finnish-Russian research and action project*. Retrieved January 4, 2020, from https://research.uta.fi/eduneighbours/about/

Jänis-Isokangas, I. (2017). *Higher education cooperation with Russia. Finnish National Agency for Education*. Assessment of CIMO's Russia Operations.

JDAZ. (2015). *Joint degrees from A to Z. Guide*. Retrieved January 4, 2020, from http://ecahe.eu/w/index.php/Portal:Joint_degrees_from_A_to_Z

JOIMAN. (2011). *Guide to developing and running joint programmes at bachelor and master's level*. Retrieved January 4, 2020, from https://www.joiman.eu/ProjectResults/PublicDeliverables/JOIMAN%20template_JP_final.pdf

JOIMAN. (2012). *Joint degree management and administration network. How to manage joint study programmes*. Retrieved January 4, 2020, from http://ecahe.eu/w/images/f/f3/How_to_Manage_Joint_Study_Programmes_-_Guidelines_and_Good_Practices_from_the_JOIMAN_Network.pdf

Karpukhina, E. (2013). Russian-European double degree programs: Key factors of success. In M. Kuder, N. Lemmens, & D. Obst (Eds.), *Global perspectives on international joint and double degree programs* (pp. 139–149). Institute of International Education.

Khudoley, K., Novikova, I., & Lanko, D. (2010). Innovative education for the Baltic region: The experience of the Finnish-Russian Cross-Border University. *Baltic Region, 2*(3), 15–20. doi:10.5922/2079-8555-2010-3-2

Knight, J. (2011). Doubts and Dilemmas with double degree programs. In *Globalisation and internationalisation of higher education* [Online monograph]. *Revista de Universidad y Sociedad del Conocimiento (RUSC), 8*(2), 297–312. Retrieved from http://ecahe.eu/w/images/e/e6/Doubts_and_Dilemmas_with_Double_Degree_Programs.pdf

Kompanets, V., & Väätänen, J. (2018): Different, yet similar: Factors motivating international degree collaboration in higher education. The case of Finnish-Russian double degree programmes. *European Journal of Engineering Education*. https://doi.org/10.1080/03043797.2018.1520811

Kuder, M., Lemmens, N., & Obst, D. (Eds.). (2013). *Global perspectives on international joint and double degree programs*. Institute of International Education.

Ministry of Education, Finland. (2009). *Strategy for the internationalisation of higher education institutions in Finland 2009–2015*. wHelsinki University.

REDEEM I. (2016). *Reforming dual degree programmes for employability and enhanced academic cooperation*. Retrieved January 4, 2020, from https://www.redeemproject.eu/wp-content/uploads/sites/26/2018/04/REDEEM-Full-Final-Activity-Report.pdf

REDEEM II. (2019, September 24–27). *The impact of joint programmes on HEIs and their graduates: A comparative analysis.* Paper presented at 31st EAIE Annual Conference.

Shenderova, S. (2018a). Internationalisation of higher education in Russia: National policy and results at institutional level. In V. Korhonen & P. Alenius (Eds.), *Internationalisation and transnationalisation in higher education* (pp. 69–100). Peter Lang AG. https://doi.org/10.3726/b11212 https://www.peterlang.com/view/9783034329675/chapter03.xhtml

Shenderova, S. (2018b). Permanent uncertainty as normality? Finnish-Russian double degrees in the post-Crimea world. *Journal of Higher Education Policy and Management, 40*(6), 611–628. https://doi.org/10.1080/1360080X.2018.1529134

Shenderova, S. (2020). *Russian-European internationalisation of higher education: Cooperation vs competition?* Manuscript submitted for publication.

Sinyatkin, I., Mishin, A., & Karpukhina, E. (2010). *Analysis of double degree programmes between EU and Russian HEIs.* Final report.

Tarazona, M. (2013). Influences on the sustainability of joint and double degree programs: Empirical findings from programs with German participation. In M. Kuder, N. Lemmens, & D. Obst (Eds.), *Global perspectives on international joint and double degree programs* (pp. 37–43). Institute of International Education.

Williamson, O. E. (1985). *The economic institutions of capitalism.* The Free Press.

Yefanova, D. (2013). Cross-border graduate double degree program implementation: Two case studies in Japan of faculty and administrator views and involvement. In M. Kuder, N. Lemmens, & D. Obst (Eds.), *Global perspectives on international joint and double degree programs* (pp. 45–52). Institute of International Education.

Zheng, G., Cai, Y., & Ma, S. (2017). Towards an analytical framework for understanding the development of a quality assurance system in an international joint programme. *European Journal of Higher Education, 7*(3), 243–260. doi:10.1080/21568235.2017.1290877

# PART 3

## *Higher Education Impact*

∴

CHAPTER 11

# High-Impact Practices, Degree Completion, and Academic Quality: A Study of Student Participation in Practices That Promote Success

*Kathi A. Ketcheson*

### Abstract

A collaboration among faculty and institutional researchers explored the relationship between High-Impact Practices and graduation outcomes at an urban university in the US. The study included examination of survey data and actual enrollment, mapping of courses to a list of practices, and a survey of degree programs to determine students' exposure to High-Impact Practices and their effect on six-year graduation rates. Results indicated that student self-reports may be different from their actual exposure to these practices, and suggested a method for identifying high-impact practices in the curriculum, combining enrollment data with qualitative data gathered from faculty.

### Keywords

High-Impact Practices – academic quality – degree completion

## 1 Introduction

The Association of American Colleges and Universities (AAC&U) identified a set of research-informed teaching and learning practices that have a positive effect on student learning, as well as on retention and degree completion. These practices are known as *High-Impact Practices* (HIPS). They represent broad categories of instructional and co-curricular practices that may vary across institutions, according to student characteristics and organizational structures.

In research on the National Survey of Student Engagement (NSSE), Kuh (2008) indicated that participation in at least two HIPS was associated with higher graduation outcomes. His research also suggested that completion of

© KONINKLIJKE BRILL NV, LEIDEN, 2020 | DOI: 10.1163/9789004436558_012

one HIP at the beginning of undergraduate study and one toward the end contributes positively to degree completion. Other studies also have indicated that traditionally underrepresented students, including African-American, Hispanic/Latinx, and Native American students, may benefit the most from these experiences (Kinzie, 2018).

## 2    Research Questions

In 1994, Portland State University launched an innovative four-year general education program for undergraduates called University Studies (UNST). At many US universities, students are required to choose from a list of general education courses in addition to the courses required for their major programs of study. Portland State's general education program, however, offered a specific set of courses integrated across four years of undergraduate study that included what we now know as HIPS, although they predated the AAC&U set of HIPS by at least a decade.

Portland State undergraduate students are required to participate in these courses in order to graduate. Over the years, the institution has won recognition and awards for the program, as well as its assessment of learning outcomes. However, it has struggled with sustaining gains in retention (enrollment from the first to the second year), persistence (continuous enrollment until graduation), and degree completion rates, despite requiring their participation in HIPS through UNST and other areas of the curriculum. According to Kuh's research, this participation would have been expected to have a more positive impact on degree completion.

In 2017, the Portland State Faculty Senate created the Academic Quality Committee (AQC) to study aspects of academic quality at the university and to make recommendations for policies or actions. The AQC defined 'quality' as instructional or co-curricular practices that lead to student success, which is defined as degree completion. Prior to this study, the only information available on student participation in HIPS beyond required courses was self-reported in the NSSE, in which the university had participated from 1999 through 2013. In order to gain a better understanding of how Portland State's use of HIPS in the undergraduate curriculum was related to degree completion, the AQC collaborated with the Office of Institutional Research and Planning (IR) on a project to address the following questions:

1.    Does enrollment in courses that include HIPS have an effect on degree completion at Portland State?
2.    How does student self-reported participation in HIPS correspond to actual enrollment in classes that include HIPS?

HIGH-IMPACT PRACTICES, DEGREE COMPLETION                    209

The AQC also hoped to find out where HIPS could be found in other parts of the curriculum, outside of general education, and to use results from the study to stimulate conversation among faculty across the university about teaching and learning practices that support student success.

## 3      HIPS at Portland State University

UNST integrates broad learning goals across four years of the program: critical thinking; communication; ethics, agency, and community; and, diversity, equity, and social justice. Students entering the university as freshmen began with a year-long set of classes, while transfer students enroll in second or third-year courses (known as 'Cluster Courses') that introduce them to the inquiry approach. Students follow inquiry-based courses on each subsequent student level: Freshman Inquiry (FRINQ), Sophomore Inquiry (SINQ), Junior Clusters, and the Senior Capstone. The general education program also includes the University Honors College, which prepares students for graduate study.

As mentioned earlier, the AAC&U list (below) includes HIPS that have been embedded in UNST from its earliest days:
– First-Year Experiences
– Common Intellectual Experiences
– Learning Communities
– Writing-Intensive Courses
– Collaborative Assignments and Projects
– Undergraduate Research
– Diversity/Global Learning
– ePortfolios
– Service Learning, Community-Based Learning
– Internships
– Capstone Courses and Projects
FRINQ is organized as a first-year experience and also as a learning community. In other levels of the program, Common Intellectual Experiences, Collaborative Assignments and Projects, and Service Learning/Community-Based Learning are embedded as teaching and learning practices. Students also prepare e-portfolios, another HIP, that help students document and reflect on their learning under each of the program's goals.

All undergraduates also experience Diversity/Global Learning, Writing Intensive Courses, Service Learning/Community-Based Learning, and Internships through their degree programs, or in elective courses. These courses are identified through course descriptions or titles, or are flagged in the course registration schedule with specific icons. Completion of two college-level composition courses or approved equivalents are required for the baccalaureate, which can be fulfilled through UNST for students who enter as freshmen, or from an approved list that includes Writing Intensive Courses for those who transfer from another institution.

Community engagement and community-based learning are hallmarks of the university. In the early 1990's President Judith Ramaley led Portland State to embrace its identity as an urban university, adopting the motto, "Let Knowledge Serve the City". Faculty had been engaged in work with the external community throughout the institution's history, offering learning experiences for students or conducting research with partners in government, business, or non-profit organizations. However, with leadership from President Ramaley, the university built its reputation as a model for engagement and formally embedded it in the curriculum through the development of community-based learning courses. Students in community-based learning courses either work on a project with a community partner, or study community issues in the classroom. These are distinct from internships, where students perform paid or unpaid work in an organization, and also from volunteer opportunities, because of the connection of community-based learning to the curriculum.

Apart from UNST and baccalaureate writing requirements, not much is known about how HIPS are used in departmental majors or programs. Anecdotal evidence suggests that many departments or individual faculty include practices in their courses that could be classified as HIPS, but no systematic investigation has been conducted to determine how widespread these practices are across the curriculum, nor on their impact on student success. The collaborative project launched by AQC and IR was a first step in this inquiry. Lessons learned from this project will inform continuing research at the institution, and may provide guidance to other institutions that wish to understand more about the effect of HIPS on student learning. The project revealed challenges to quantitative analysis of this question, and supported findings from previous studies regarding the effect of HIPS on degree completion.

## 4 Research on the Effect of HIPS on Student Success

In a presentation to the 2019 European Association for Institutional Research Forum in Leiden, Netherlands, entitled "Empirically Substantiating Claims about 'High-Impact' Practices on Teaching and Learning", Gregory Wolniak and Mathew Mayhew summarized a number of published works that examined the effect of HIPS on student learning and student success, i.e. retention and graduation rates. They determined that many of the studies were inconclusive, or showed little relationship between HIPS and degree completion.

In one study, Johnson and Stage (2018) concluded that direct links between participation in HIPS and graduation outcomes were difficult to make. Their study combined data on graduation rates reported to the US Department of Education's Integrated Postsecondary Education Data System (IPEDS) with data from a survey sent to academic officers on the availability of HIPS at their institutions. It should be noted that the survey represented self-reports of what constituted HIPS in the curriculum. Modeling to test for the relationship between graduation and HIPS included institutional characteristics and student data, such as financial aid received and the proportion of the student body that identified as 'White'. Findings showed that eight of the 10 HIPS tested in the model had no significant relationship to graduation rates.

The effect of the entering characteristics of the students on persistence and graduation, such as grade point averages at admission or demographics, is widely documented in higher education literature. Pascarella and Blaich (2013), in a longitudinal study of academic and non-academic experiences that further liberal learning, indicated differences among entering student characteristics were the strongest predictors of success, regardless of what happened during college. Some of these characteristics were found to moderate the effect of practices, such as organized instruction, deep learning, and interactional diversity. While effective teaching and learning practices play an important role in furthering academic success, the study concluded that student support services, including advising, financial support, and other activities outside the classroom, are needed to ensure student success.

## 5 Characteristics of Undergraduates at Portland State

Given the importance of entering student characteristics on success, the AQC and IR set their work in the context of Portland State's student population. Student characteristics at Portland State are similar to those of other urban universities in the US, including large numbers of students from the local area, lower-income students, and many who transfer from other higher education institutions. Drawing largely from Portland and the surrounding metropolitan area, the university enrolls more than 4,000 new undergraduates every Fall Term, including those enrolled full or part time. More than 60% of new students transfer to the university from local area community colleges, or other four-year institutions, after a year or more of study. Many represent the first-generation in their families to attend college, and a large number come from low-income households. According to US News rankings for 2019, Portland State ranked first among four-year universities in Oregon for enrolling and graduating students eligible for federally-funded, need-based Pell Grants.

TABLE 11.1    Portland State new undergraduates, fall term 2018

| | |
|---|---|
| Total new undergraduates: 4,757 | |
| New freshman | 36% |
| New transfers from other institutions | 64% |
| Minority students | 42% |
| Oregon residents | 76% |
| International students | 3% |
| Other states | 21% |
| Pell Grants | 50% |

SOURCE: STUDENT CENTRALIZED ADMINISTRATIVE REPORTING FILE,
FALL TERM 2018 4TH WEEK.

First-year retention and six-year graduation rates have remained somewhat lower than similar institutions. Beginning in 2012, the university implemented a number of student success initiatives, consolidating them in fall 2019 under the name 'Students First.' Many universities have been able to achieve dramatic increases in retention and graduation rates after launching similar student success initiatives. UNST originally was envisioned as a way to increase student retention and shorten the time it takes for undergraduates to complete the baccalaureate by reducing the number of required general education courses. Retention and graduation rates were expected to increase after implementation of the program, based on what was known from research on effective teaching and learning practices and their effect on successful degree completion.

After the adoption of UNST, retention of full-time enrolled freshmen increased over a six-year period, from 63% to 69%. But after 2000, as shown in Figure 11.1, there were no increases in retention, and the rate hovered around this level until it reached 72% for the 2010 cohort. Between 2010 and 2017, the annual rate for entering cohorts of freshmen hovered below 74%, with only slight increases, and even some decreases, for each new cohort. Graduation rates, however, improved more dramatically since 1994, from 31% to 47% for the 2012 cohort of entering freshmen (Figure 11.2). Retention and graduation of transfer students remained higher than for entering freshmen. First-year retention increased from 69% in 1994 to 80% in 2018; during this period, the six-year graduation rate, which is used to compare against that for freshmen, increased from 63% to 73%.

FIGURE 11.1   Retention rates for first-time, full-time enrolled freshmen and transfer students (Source: Portland State University Student Information System)

FIGURE 11.2   Six-year graduation rates first-time, full-time enrolled freshmen and transfer students (Source: Portland State University Student Information System)

## 6   Research Design

The AQC and IR recognized the importance of instructional practices to academic quality and success, and noted that research on this was missing from earlier initiatives. Their first step was to survey faculty to find out how they define 'academic quality,' and also to identify teaching and learning practices that faculty felt contributed to quality. Surveys were sent to 553 tenured faculty, 183 or 33% of whom responded. Four broad areas of practice emerged, two of which reflect HIPS: writing, undergraduate research, interdisciplinary teaching and research, and the graduate student experience. This was followed by an examination of the literature on HIPS and development of a research focus on these practices as they relate to academic quality.

As mentioned earlier, the AQC and IR were interested in understanding why embedding HIPS in the general education curriculum apparently had not had more of an effect on persistence and graduation rates. The committee hoped to use enrollment data to examine student exposure to HIPS and the relationship of participation in HIPS to graduation. Once an understanding of the relationship between participation in HIPS and graduation could be established for undergraduates as a whole, further analysis could be conducted for subpopulations, such as by race and ethnicity, gender, or low-income status.

They also were interested in understanding how student self-reports of participation in HIPS reflected their actual participation through enrollment in HIPS-designated courses. The AQC, from its faculty perspective, felt that students' understanding and knowing participation in HIPS could contribute positively to learning and their eventual success in achieving academic goals. Sharing results of the study with faculty could stimulate further conversations about what constitute effective teaching and learning practices, as well as ways to engage students in their own learning.

The research design included examination of data drawn from three different sources: student responses to the 2013 administration of the NSSE; mapping of courses to HIPS categories and examination of enrollment in these courses; and results of a survey of program directors and department chairs regarding the availability of HIPS among courses required for the degree. The design built on approaches used in previous research on the topic, and sought to combine quantitative information with self-reports from faculty.

For the purposes of this study, 'student success' was defined as graduation within six-years of initial enrollment at the university. This aligns with measures used by IPEDS, which is a commonly used source of data on higher education institutions in the US.

## 7 The National Survey of Student Engagement

NSSE was first launched in 1998 to collect information about student experiences and collegiate quality. The Center for Postsecondary Research at Indiana University Bloomington, College of Education, regularly publishes and presents research using national findings from the NSSE. Portland State participated in

HIGH-IMPACT PRACTICES, DEGREE COMPLETION                                    215

the survey yearly from 1999 to 2013. The survey includes six items regarding HIPS, as shown in Table 11.2.

TABLE 11.2    NSSE high-impact practices

Which have you *done* or *plan to do* before graduation?

- Learning community or formal program where groups of students take two or more classes together
- Courses that included a community-based project (service learning)
- Work with a faculty member on research
- Internship, co-op, field experience, student teaching, clinical placement
- Study abroad
- Complete a culminating senior experience (capstone, senior project or thesis, comprehensive exam, portfolio, etc.)

SOURCE: NSSE INSTITUTIONAL REPORT (2013)

As mentioned earlier, the NSSE research findings indicate that students who complete at least two courses that include HIPS are more likely to complete degrees, and that traditionally underserved students (defined by race or ethnicity) benefit the most from participating in these courses. In responding to the question, students answer to the best of their knowledge whether or not they have participated or plan to participate in any of these experiences. It should be noted that while the question itself combines actual participation with planned participation, students were given the following response options: "Done or in Progress", "Plan to Do", "Have Not Decided", or "Do Not Plan to Do."

## 8    Course Mapping

The course mapping portion of the study involved assigning courses to each of the broad categories of HIPS. At Portland State, each course is assigned a course prefix, which designates the subject area or department (e.g. CHEM is the course prefix for Chemistry courses), a course number that corresponds to the course level (e.g. 100–200 for lower division undergraduate, 300–400 for upper division undergraduate, and 500 for graduate level), and a course title. IR undertook a general assignment of courses to HIPS using this system.

For example, internships and practicum courses are identified by specific course numbers and titles, and these courses were assigned to the 'Internship' HIP. The same process was used for all courses that could be assigned to HIPS using the course prefix, number, or title (i.e., Writing Intensive Courses, Diversity/Global Learning, Service Learning/Community-Based Learning, etc.). When the purpose or content of the course was known because it was part of UNST or University Honors, these courses were assigned to the appropriate HIP (i.e., First-Year Experience, Learning Community, Undergraduate Research, Collaborative Assignments or Common Intellectual Experiences).

Table 11.3 reports the number of courses assigned to each of the HIPS; in total, 1,642 courses were mapped to at least one HIP. Table 11.4 provides examples of individual course assignments to HIPS.

TABLE 11.3     Portland State University courses mapped to HIPS[a]

| | |
|---|---|
| First-year experience | 283 |
| Common intellectual experiences | 479 |
| Learning communities | 463 |
| Collaborative assignments and projects | 633 |
| Writing intensive courses | 196 |
| Diversity/global learning | 566 |
| Service learning/community based learning/internships | 91 |
| Capstones | 23 |

a  Identification of courses associated with undergraduate research could not be made
   definitively from course numbers or titles, so no mapping was conducted for this HIP

TABLE 11.4     Example courses assigned to HIPS

First-year experience: UNST 133M Mentored inquiry
Common intellectual experiences: UNST 242G Leading social change
Learning community: HON 101A The global city
Writing intensive course: WR 222 Writing research papers
Collaborative assignments and projects: ANTH 363U Egyptian archaeology (UNST cluster course)
Diversity/global learning: BST 207 Race, class, and gender
Internships: BI 404 Internship: Marine mammal study
Capstone: BA 495 Business strategy

HIGH-IMPACT PRACTICES, DEGREE COMPLETION 217

A limitation to this approach was that course numbers or titles were assigned to HIPS without clear evidence that HIPS were actually carried out in the courses. Many departmental courses – those specific to degree programs – may include HIPS, but do not clearly indicate this in the course titles. Most of these were not included in the analysis. Also, because all first-time students (excluding transfers) and all seniors are required to enroll in the first and fourth year of UNST, they experience at least one HIP by default. To mitigate these limitations, IR worked with the AQC to confirm that the mapping made sense from a curricular standpoint, as well as from the perspective of faculty. This step was a key step organizing the data that was planned to be expanded or amended at a later date, in part using results from the survey of programs that is described below.

## 9    Survey of Programs

In order to address limitations inherent in the course mapping, the AQC conducted a survey of department chairs and program directors in Winter Term 2019. The survey had two purposes: to discover how familiar academic departments and faculty were with the list of HIPS, and to gather more detailed information on which HIPS were being used in courses or in experiences offered outside of classroom. The survey acknowledged that programs may have been engaged in HIPS without having knowledge of the AAC&U list, or the terminology of 'high-impact practices'.

## 10    Findings

Findings of the three methods used to examine participation in HIPS are reported below. The first are findings from the analysis of the 2013 NSSE, followed by HIPS enrollment and graduation (course mapping), and the survey of program directors and department chairs.

### 10.1    *NSSE Results*
The 2013 NSSE was sent to survey was sent to 2,234 first-year students and 7,834 seniors enrolled in Spring Term 2013. The response rate from first-year students was 235, or 11% (170 fully-completed surveys and 65 partially completed) and from seniors, 1,074, or 14% (854 completed and 220 partially completed. Results published by NSSE showed that, at Portland State, 57% of first-year students indicated that they were participating or planning to participate in one HIP, compared to 46% of first-year students at all institutions covered by the

survey. For Portland State seniors, 68% had participated or planned to participate in one HIP, compared to 60% for seniors at all other NSSE institutions. Community-based learning was the category most frequently selected by first-year students at Portland State; seniors selected community-based learning and capstone most frequently.

One interesting finding suggested that Portland State's first-year students may not have been familiar with the term 'learning community,' and thus may not have been aware that their UNST courses represented this category. This resulted in an under-reporting of participation in this HIP: only 14% indicated that they were enrolled in or had completed a learning community experience, while 31% indicated that they did not plan to participate. A comparison of survey results with actual enrollment revealed that 90% of first-year students had participated in the learning communities of FRINQ or University Honors. Also, only 69% indicated that they planned to participate in a capstone course, which is a graduation requirement for all undergraduates.

The results for seniors reflected the large number of transfer students at Portland State, most of whom do not enroll in either FRINQ or SINQ, which are designed as learning communities: 62% of them reported that they did not plan to participate in a learning community before graduating. They did report higher levels of participation in courses with a community-based learning component (75% of most or some courses), and capstone courses (90% planned or completed), which corresponds to the types of courses available or required in the last two years of an undergraduate program of study.

Using the NSSE data, IR conducted t-tests for "Done or in progress" responses by first-year students and seniors and their actual enrollment in courses coded as HIPS in the course mapping process. In Tables 11.5 and 11.6, HIPS participation is reported in the aggregate. Not surprisingly, the results showed differences in reported and actual performance, most notably for first-time students, as evidenced from the NSSE findings. For this analysis, the number of students reported in each table represents the number of survey respondents who answered the HIPS question.

TABLE 11.5    Freshman NSSE responses and enrollment in HIPS (N = 179)

| Sample | n | Mean | SD | df | p |
| --- | --- | --- | --- | --- | --- |
| Indicated HIPS participation in NSSE | 179 | 0.31 | 0.53 | 178 | <0.001 |
| Actual HIPS participation | 179 | 2.72 | 0.81 | | |

HIGH-IMPACT PRACTICES, DEGREE COMPLETION 219

TABLE 11.6   Senior NSSE responses and enrollment in HIPS (N = 912)

| Sample | n | Mean | SD | df | p |
|---|---|---|---|---|---|
| Indicated HIPS participation in NSSE | 912 | 1.29 | 1.02 | 911 | <0.001 |
| Actual HIPS participation | 912 | 2.45 | 0.76 | | |

## 10.2   *Course Mapping*

Enrollment records in the university's student information system were examined by IR to determine which courses assigned to the HIPS in the mapping phase of the study had been completed by students who entered as new undergraduates (freshman and transfer students) in Fall Term 2012 (N = 4,442). The data covered Fall Term 2012 to Summer Term 2018 to determine whether or not these students had graduated within six years: both students continuing and those dropping out before graduation were included. By summer 2018, 2,508 of these students had graduated (56%).

Student characteristics, such as full-time/part-time status, entering status as a freshman or transfer student, race/ethnicity, legal sex, cumulative GPA, and completion or non-completion of a degree within six years, were included in the analysis. A regression analysis was used to determine the relationship between these characteristics and HIPS enrollment, and between HIPS enrollment and degree completion.

Results of the regression analysis are reported in Figure 11.3. In examining the odds ratios for HIPS, student characteristics and degree completion, two HIPS were shown to have a strong, positive relationship to graduation within six years: Common Intellectual Experiences and Internships. It should be noted, however, that students tend to complete internships closer to graduation, so these results may favor students who persist to the degree. Writing Intensive Courses, Diversity/Global Learning, and Service Learning/Community-Based Learning also showed some relationship, although not as strong. As might be expected, being a transfer student was positively related to graduation within six years because most transfer students finish in less time, having completed one or more years at another institution. First-term GPA, a measure of academic success, had some relationship to graduation, but underrepresented minority status (African-American, Hispanic/Latinx, and Native American, combined) and legal sex (male or female) showed no or very low relationships.

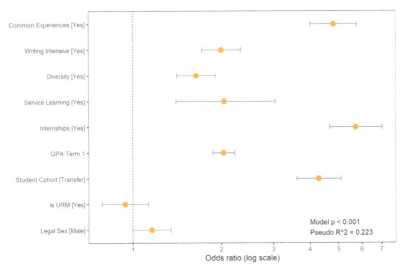

FIGURE 11.3  Course mapping: Participation in HIPS by students graduating in six years or fewer

## 11  Survey of Programs

The AQC and IR sent surveys to 56 program directors and departments chairs in the spring of 2019, using a web-based survey tool. Of these, 32 surveys were returned, for a 57% response rate. Survey recipients were responsible for coordinating as many as five individual degree programs within their academic areas. The survey began with the AAC&U list of HIPS and their definitions, and then asked recipients to provide the following information:
- Which of their majors or programs of study included HIPS;
- Where were HIPS offered in the curriculum (individual courses, major requirements, or in experiences outside the classroom); and
- Whether not the term 'high-impact practices' was used in communication with students, or among faculty when discussing the curriculum.

The survey was intended to collect detailed information so that courses could be mapped more accurately to HIPS in the future, and also to encourage more discussion among faculty regarding the relationship between academic quality and teaching and learning practices. Responses provided rich information about how HIPS are used in many of the university's degree programs. A follow-up survey was planned for winter 2020 to collect information from those who had not responded in spring. Table 11.7 shows which HIPS survey respondents reported most frequently as offered across courses, generally, in major requirements, or outside the classroom. For individual courses, Writing Intensive Courses, Service Learning/Community-Based Learning, and Collaborative Assignments and Projects were cited most often, while for major requirements,

HIGH-IMPACT PRACTICES, DEGREE COMPLETION

which include a selection of courses within and outside the department, Diversity/Global Learning, and Collaborative Assignments and Projects were the most frequently mentioned. HIPS offered outside the classroom were primarily Internships and Undergraduate Research, but Collaborative Assignments and Projects, which likely included capstone or community-based learning experiences, were also mentioned frequently.

TABLE 11.7    Program and department survey: HIPS in the curriculum

Individual courses:
   57% Writing-Intensive Courses
   54% Service Learning/Community-Based Learning
   50% Collaborative Assignments and Projects
   43% Capstone Courses and Projects
   40% Diversity/Global Learning
Major requirements:
   61% Diversity/Global Learning
   54% Collaborative Assignments and Projects
   36% Writing-Intensive Courses
Outside the classroom:
   68% Internships
   54% Undergraduate Research
   43% Collaborative Assignment and Projects

When asked if the term 'high-impact practices' was used to describe these courses or experiences, 82% of respondents said no; only 18% used the term when talking with other faculty members. The term was not used with students, on syllabi, or in promotional materials. However, respondents were familiar with the practices and were able to report that they were included in the curriculum, which suggests that they are actively applied and that students experience them to some degree outside of general education.

## 12    Discussion

The questions posed by the AQC and IR in this study were:
1.    Does enrollment in courses that include HIPS have an effect on degree completion at Portland State?
2.    How does student self-reported participation in HIPS correspond to actual enrollment in classes that include HIPS?

In answer to the first question, two HIPS were shown to have a strong relationship to degree completion within six years (Internships and Common Intellectual Experiences), while three others (Writing-Intensive Courses, Service Learning, Community-Based Learning, and Diversity/Global Learning) showed a somewhat weaker relationship. This is similar to Johnson and Stage (2018), where it was found that 8 of 10 HIPS had no significant relationship to graduation rates. No relationship was found between HIPS participation and graduating in six years for underrepresented minority students, and only a weak relationship for students by legal sex (Male/Female).

Next, comparison of students' responses to the 2013 NSSE and their enrollment in HIPS at Portland State showed that self-reported participation did not necessarily match actual enrollment, primarily for first-year students. It appeared that freshman students were not familiar with the 'learning community', or that a capstone course was required for graduation. These results suggest that, for Portland State, examining enrollment records, rather than self-reports from surveys, would provide a better understanding of the relationship between HIPS and degree completion. However, the survey results could be useful in developing effective communication with students about the teaching and learning practices they experience.

Prior research on the NSSE indicated that traditionally underserved students appear to benefit most from participation in HIPS. This is an important question when examining factors leading to persistence and graduation for underserved, minority populations. While no relationship was shown between HIPS enrollment and graduation for underrepresented minority students, further disaggregation of the data may show differences by individual category, or within the categories, themselves: for example, there may be differences by income levels or GPA within any one race or ethnic category.

By far the most complicated and difficult piece of the analysis was mapping courses to HIPS. Without knowing whether or not HIPS are used in the classroom, it is difficult to say whether or not HIPS are having an effect. Also, course descriptions may include language that overlaps multiple HIPS, so attempting to categorize courses as one or another, or to identify whether or not individual HIPS have more impact than others, may be a complicated task. Additional research should be conducted, once courses are more clearly mapped to HIPS, on whether or not combinations of certain HIPS, or at different points in a student's undergraduate career, have a relationship to degree completion.

Another approach proposed by the AQC may be to take the results of the faculty survey and sample a few of the courses or programs that were mentioned as including HIPS. The survey showed that while they may not use the terms to communicate to students or in conversations among themselves, faculty do embrace the practices in their courses and programs and can identify where they occur in the curriculum. An initial approach for further research would be for the AQC to work with the program coordinators and faculty who responded to the survey, perhaps through interviews or focus groups, to gather more detailed information. A deeper analysis of the practices used in these courses, gathered through interviews, syllabi review, or examination of assignments could provide a framework for conversations among faculty about effective teaching and learning practices, as well as further research on factors contributing to student success.

The project incorporated research questions and techniques from previous studies, and involved multiple data sources and methods, both quantitative and qualitative. While some of the findings were inconclusive or needed additional investigation, the project provided the foundation for further research at Portland State, as well as other institutions that are interested in examining the impact of HIPS on student success. Finally, a key outcome of the research was the collaboration that developed between the AQC and IR in addressing questions of quality and teaching and learning effectiveness. The work reflects the model of faculty/IR collaboration in examining these questions that Hutchings and Schulman (1999) envisioned when they wrote:

> If we reconceived 'institutional research' to be about such questions, in the service of its faculties, led by faculty members, then the scholarship of teaching would not be some newly conceived arena of work, or a new route to tenure, but a characteristic of the institution that took learning seriously. (p. 15)

### References

Hutchings, P., & Schulman, L. S. (1999). The scholarship of teaching: New elaborations, new developments. *Change: The Magazine of Higher Learning, 31*(5), 10–15.

Johnson, S. R., & Stage, F. K. (2018). Academic Engagement and student success: Do high-impact practices mean higher graduation rates? *Journal of Higher Education, 89*(5), 735–781.

Kinzie, J., Gonyea R., Shoup, R., & Kuh, G. D. (2008). Promoting persistence and success of underrepresented students: Lessons for teaching and learning. *New Directions for Teaching and Learning, 115*, 21–38.

Kuh, G. D. (2008). *High-impact practices: What are they, who has access to them, and why they matter.* Association of American Colleges and Universities.

Pascarella, E. T., & Blaich, C. (2013). Lessons from the Wabash National Study of liberal arts education. *Change: The Magazine of Higher Learning, 45*(2), 6–15.

CHAPTER 12

# The Productivity of Leading Global Universities: Empirical Insights and Implications for Higher Education

*Jiale Yang, Chuanyi Wang, Lu Liu, Gwilym Croucher, Kenneth Moore and Hamish Coates*

## Abstract

The global significance of higher education prompts interest in the costs of and returns on education and research. This drives interest in higher education productivity. There is particular value in studying the productivity of leading global universities given their distinctive characteristics and contributions. To this end, this chapter analyzes the productivity of a sample of such universities to tease out implications for higher education. The results reveal that higher education systems set boundaries and play an important role in explaining performance, leading universities appear to pursue different productivity growth strategies, and a more positive story for research than education productivity. This signals the need to reach outside the higher education system to develop regionally or globally. This requires globally rather than nationally focused governance and leadership. It requires further development of education productivity.

## Keywords

productivity – higher education – world-class universities – policy and strategy

## 1 Introduction

The growing global significance of higher education prompts much greater interest in the costs and returns of education and research. This amplifies interest in higher education productivity, which stimulates substantial debate. Yet there is surprisingly little conceptual, technical or practical research into the productivity of core academic activities, with important works just starting

© KONINKLIJKE BRILL NV, LEIDEN, 2020 | DOI: 10.1163/9789004436558_013

THE PRODUCTIVITY OF LEADING GLOBAL UNIVERSITIES                    225

to emerge (e.g. Agasisti, Egorov, & Leshukov, 2018; Hoxby & Stange, 2019). Much work in this area has been funded for political or commercial purposes and commonly misapplies general productivity models to higher education, hindering effective analysis and development of methods relevant to the role of universities (Witte, 2017). As argued in the pioneering work of Massy (1996, 2003), building better scientific foundations for the study of higher education productivity carries potential to improve policy and practice.

Higher education productivity is inherently challenging to grasp, through recent research has done much to clarify definitions, techniques and the need for broader analysis. The basic idea is straightforward, being the ratio of outputs to inputs, taking account of quality, usually examining change or time, and ideally considering multiple outputs and multiple inputs. Undertaking meaningful productivity analysis becomes more complex, however, when it comes to defining indicators, models, source data, and to reporting results in meaningful ways. To clarify and navigate such complexity, the current research builds on and advances work conducted over the last decade across a range of universities and countries (Coates, 2010; Sullivan, Mackie, Massy, & Archer, 2012; Coates, 2017; Moore, Coates, & Croucher, 2018; Moore, Croucher & Coates, 2019). This work has affirmed the need for scholarly or scientific (rather than commercial or confidential) work that clarifies productivity in ways relevant not just to economists but to a much broader array of higher education stakeholders. Stakeholders invariably bring vested interests to already complex and controversial analyses, and these play an important role in making sense of findings and implications.

This chapter focuses on what we refer to as 'leading global universities'. Of course, all higher education institutions manifest leadership in many and varying ways. But there are a small number which have a mission to operate academically, socially and economically on a global scale. These are prominent, elite and established institutions, typically with explicit purposes and funds to advance the frontiers of higher education and associated communities. The term 'flagship' could be used to describe these institutions, though this is a United States term with distinctive historical and contextual significance. Since the turn of the century, and particularly since the development of world university rankings around 2003–2004, these institutions have also been called 'world-class universities' (Salmi, 2009). The 'leading global universities' analyzed in this chapter align most closely with these. Salmi and Altbach (2020) characterize these as

> top universities [which] operate at the cutting edge of intellectual and scientific development, as recognized by the global rankings ... a

small but very important part of any nation's higher education system. These universities produce most of the research, are heavily involved in advanced education at the master's and doctoral levels, and are the primary links between a country's science establishment and the global academic community.

There is particular value in studying the productivity of such leading global universities. As the definitional remarks convey, these universities make direct contributions through their own research, education and public engagement. They also make indirect contributions, by reifying government policy aspirations, often by working with governments and other actors to co-create significant policies, by signalling behaviours and intentions to other lower-tier universities, and sometimes by breeding spinoff institutions (Zhong, Coates, & Shi, 2019). While always prominent, the role of leading universities has been strengthened following the late 1990s global massification of higher education, and particularly since the post-2003 advent of the 'world-class era'. They are charged with making contributions which reverberate globally and advance academic and social frontiers.

Studying the productivity of leading global universities raises wide-ranging questions. For instance, what is the value of cross-system comparison? Technically, is it feasible to research beyond international rankings and take account of broader inputs and outcomes? Are leading global universities indeed performing globally, or bounded by national contexts? Do leading universities converge in ways that influence productivity? How do contextual and institutional factors shape the development and productivity? Wide-ranging questions like these necessarily touch on theories and contexts regarding new institutionalism (Meyer et al., 2007; Powell & DiMaggio, 1991), governance and leadership (Austin & Jones, 2015), institutional isomorphism (Croucher & Woelert, 2016; Stensaker & Norgard, 2001), institutional logics perspective (Thornton et al., 2012), as well as productivity itself (Coates, 2017a). This chapter draws from these wide-ranging perspectives to frame and interpret the empirical analyses.

Most specifically, this chapter seeks to advance understanding of how leading universities have behaved, played, performed and contributed. The aim of the research is to analyze the productivity of a sample of leading global universities and tease out strategic implications for higher education. This aim is divided into two research questions: First, what has been the productivity of leading global universities during the 'world-class era'? Second, what implications can be distilled for higher education from analyzing the productivity of leading global universities? This chapter presents responses to these questions

THE PRODUCTIVITY OF LEADING GLOBAL UNIVERSITIES

using empirical results and policy analysis. The findings highlight implications for contemporary planning and future development.

## 2 The Analytical Approach

To help frame this chapter's empirical analysis of higher education productivity, this section clarifies the approach to sampling countries and universities, specifying productivity indicators and models, collecting and modelling data, and generating and validating the interpretations.

Several criteria were used to select the countries. A relatively small number of countries was sought to make data collection and analysis feasible. At the same time an effort was made to select a regionally diverse suite of countries to test generalizability. The countries needed to have internationally oriented higher education systems (e.g. Williams & Leahy, 2019). The countries needed to have and report necessary data. For the current analysis a decision was made to focus on Australia, China, Japan, United Kingdom and United States. It would be feasible to extend the selection of countries in subsequent generalizations of this study, but current sample was sufficiently diverse and sized to respond to the target questions. There would particular value in building out the country and university sample with more European universities.

The chapter focuses on the productivity of leading universities within these countries. As noted, these universities are most relevant to analyze as they have been the main focus of the world-class university competition, are the most internationally exposed, are internationally comparable, are most strategically similar, and are often the most prominent in the respective national higher education systems. Table 12.1 lists the 42 universities sampled. These universities were selected based on performance across multiple global rankings (notably, the ARWU (Shanghai Ranking, 2018) and World University Rankings (THE, 2018), in-country research classifications (e.g. Australia's 'Group of Eight', China's 'C9', Japan's 'Imperial Universities') consultation with experts within each country, and data availability. It was relatively easy to determine the university list for all but the United Kingdom and United States, where it was necessary to sample ten universities from a list initially double the size. In both of these countries universities were selected which had consistently the highest rankings.

Productivity is a complex concept, which can be modelled in many ways. A plethora of approaches has emerged in recent decades, providing insight into models of potential relevance to higher education. Moore, Croucher and

TABLE 12.1    List of sampled countries and universities

| Australia | China | Japan | United Kingdom | United States |
|---|---|---|---|---|
| Australian National University | Fudan University | Hokkaido University | Imperial College London | Columbia University |
| Monash University | Nanjing University | Kyoto University | King's College London | Cornell University |
| University of Adelaide | Peking University | Kyushu University | London School of Economics | Harvard University |
| University of Melbourne | Shanghai Jiaotong University | Nagoya University | University College London | Massachusetts Institute of Technology |
| University of New South Wales | Tsinghua University | Osaka University | University of Bristol | Princeton University |
| University of Queensland | Xian Jiaotong University | Tohoku University | University of Cambridge | Stanford University |
| University of Sydney | Zhejiang University | University of Tokyo | University of Edinburgh | University of California-Berkeley |
| University of Western Australia | | | University of Manchester | University of California-Los Angeles |
| | | | University of Oxford | University of Chicago |
| | | | University of Warwick | Yale University |

Coates (2019) provide an overview of important work. Table 12.2 illustrates the different approaches and indicators which have been investigated by researchers. This highlights the kinds of indicators which may be relevant and reveals the diversity of potential approaches that could be adopted.

Taking this methodological context into consideration, and constraints around data availability and comparability, Table 12.3 lists the indicators and data selected for the current study. In the field of higher education, expenses and labour are two pivotal input elements that can be measured by total annual operational expenditure and institutional staff respectively. Outputs include both education outcomes and research outcomes. The former are measured

TABLE 12.2    Potential indicators for modelling productivity of higher education

*Calculation technique — columns 1–13: Linear programming; columns 14–16: Econometrics; columns 17–20: Indexing.*

| Parameter | Indicator | Linear programming | | | | | | | | | | | | | Econometrics | | | Indexing | | | |
|---|---|---|---|---|---|---|---|---|---|---|---|---|---|---|---|---|---|---|---|---|---|
| | | Yaohua et al. (2018) | Olariu & Brad (2017) | Tran et al. (2017) | Wolszczak-Derlacz (2017) | Moradi-Motlagh et al. (2016) | Arjomandi et al. (2015) | Avilez-Sacoto (2014) | Nazarco & Saparauskas (2013) | Klimpp & Zelewski (2008) | Worthington & Lee (2008) | Johnes (2006) | Carrington et al. (2005) | Abbot & Doucouliogos (2003) | Sales-Velasco (2018) | Titus & Eagan (2016) | Agasisti & Johnes (2015) | Izadi et al. (2002) | Coates (2017b) | Miles et al. (2018) | Moore et al. (2018) |
| "Education outputs" | Student load | | | | | X | | | X | | | | X | X | | | | | X | X | |
| | Student enrolment | X | X | X | X | | | | X | | | | | | | | | | | X | |
| | Student achievements | | | | | | | | X | | | | | | | | | | | X | |
| | Degree completions | | | X | X | | X | | | | X | X | X | | | X | X | | | X | |
| | Adjusted credit hours | | | | | | | | | | | | | | | | | | | X | X |
| | Exceeded or passed credits | | | | | | | | | | | | | | X | | | | | | |
| | Graduate employment | | | | | | | X | X | | | | | | | | | | | X | |
| | Revenue from government | | X | | X | | | | | | | | | | | | | | | | |
| | Revenue from student fees | | | | X | | | | | | | | | | | | | | | | |
| "Research outputs" | Publications | X | | | X | X | X | | X | | X | | X | | | | | | | X | X |
| | Citations | X | | | | | | | | | | | | | | | | | | X | |
| | Institutional rankings | | | | | | | | | X | | | | | | | | | | | |
| | Research degrees awarded | | | | | | | | | | | | | | | | | | | X | X |
| | Patents | | | | | | | | | | | | | | | | | | | X | |
| | Research income | X | | X | | | | | | | X | X | X | X | | | | X | | X | X |
| Micellaneous | Reputation | X | | | | | | | | | | | | | | | | | | | |

by student load and degree completions at undergraduate and postgraduate levels. The latter primarily takes quantity and quality of scholarly publications into consideration. In line with Sullivan, Mackie, Massy and Sinha (2012) student load is considered as an output because they represent the scale of education operations and service delivery for an institution.

TABLE 12.3    Parameters, indicators and data selected for this research

| Parameter | Indicator | Variable | Data |
| --- | --- | --- | --- |
| Input | Expenses | $X_1$ | Total annual operational expenditure |
| | Labour | $L_1$ | Academic staff count FTE[a] |
| | | $L_2$ | Non-academic staff count FTE |
| Output | Undergraduate student load | $E_1$ | Number of FTE undergraduate students |
| | Postgraduate student load | $E_2$ | Number of FTE postgraduate students |
| | Undergraduate completions | $E_3$ | Number of undergraduate degrees awarded |
| | Postgraduate completions | $E_4$ | Number of postgraduate degrees awarded |
| | Publications | $R_1$ | Total scholarly journal articles |
| | Top publications | $R_2$ | Articles in the top-25 citation percentile |

a  Full time equivalent

This study adopted two models to embrace complexities associated with analyzing productivity and to triangulate the results. The first model, based on a Törnqvist Index (TI), extended work initiated in the United States (Massy, Sullivan & Mackie, 2013) and then replicated and extended across ten countries in Asia (Coates, 2017a). The second, based on Data Envelopment Analysis (DEA), deployed modelling like prior studies within the field of higher education (Johnes, 2006). The value of employing two models is that it helps move beyond the assumptions and constraints of any single model, helps generate different statistics which provide alternative insights into university productivity, and helps cross-validate results and interpretations.

The Törnqvist Index (TI) techniques estimate productivity change by dividing a composite output change index and a composite input change index. The composite change indexes are systematic aggregations of the rates of change of the data elements listed in Table 12.3. Analysis is performed on each institution in the dataset, as well as on aggregated totals for each country. Country-level analysis illustrates strategic trends and patterns playing out across each nation's leading universities. The TI model explores education and research dynamics both separately and jointly, deploying a single model with different weighting schemes. In one weighting scheme, research and education outputs are weighted equally. The other two schemes serve to emphasize education outputs and research outputs. The TI uses two different models to generate estimates of total factor productivity and single factor productivity. The total factor productivity change estimates relate total expenditures to education and research outputs, while the single factor productivity estimates reflect only labour productivity by relating staff numbers to education and research outputs. The TI method produces change indexes for each institution that are normalized based on initial conditions at the beginning of the period examined. That is, each institution's productivity change is measured relative only to its own base level of productivity. TI productivity change indices represent percentage increases or decreases from initial conditions without explicitly identifying institutions initial productivity levels. Thus, only rates of change can be compared across institutions.

Data Envelopment Analysis (DEA) estimates the optimal (not average) function of the productivity of decision-making units using multiple inputs and outputs. Given the available expenses and labor inputs, efficient units are registered as those producing the maximum amount of research/education outputs. With the intention to identify the primary drivers of productivity change, research outputs and education outputs are put into the model respectively using the same weighting scheme as for the TI modelling. The slack based measure of the super efficiency DEA model (Guo et al., 2017; Wang et al., 2017; Tran et al., 2019) and the fixed Malmquist index (Raei et al., 2017; Eva et al., 2017; Visbal-Cadavid et al., 2017) were used in sequential fashion to measure static and dynamic productivity of the universities. First, the slack based measure of the super efficiency DEA model was used to estimate the static productivity of the leading global universities in 2015. Second, the fixed Malmquist index was applied to study productivity change from 2007 to 2015, using 2007 as the base year.

Data collection and validation took place over several months. Data was collected from large-scale databases, from national systems, and from university webpages (Australian Government Department of Education, 2018; Chinese Ministry of Education, 2018; Higher Education Statistics Agency, 2018; National Center of Education Statistics, 2018; Scopus, 2018). It was feasible to procure consistent data for the years 2007 to 2015. This is an important timeframe, for it starts just a few years after the launch of the 'world-class era' in the early years of the new century and moves through until reasonably recently. The data was cleaned and validated. Financial figures for each country were adjusted for currency inflation using each countries' respective CPI data and a fixed value for money with a base year of 2007.

The econometric modelling was conducted by two different teams working in a parallel manner. The teams worked independently at first, then compared initial results, refined the models, rechecked data, and then re-ran the models. The need for such iteration and replication was to ensure the integrity of the data, design the most informative productivity models, and enhance the veracity of results. The modelling was run for research, for education, and for research/education, and run at the university and country level. Results were compiled for the aggregate level for each of the five countries and for individual universities.

Policy analysis is methodologically diverse in nature, and the approach taken in this study was no exception. The interpretative framing stemmed from initial review of institutional practice, government policy and scholarly research contexts, as signaled in the introduction. This framing was used to design the productivity models and derivative empirical research. Results from this empirical analysis to a certain extent need to stand alone, as they could give rise to varying and even inconsistent interpretations. To provide greater meaning to the results and help frame them with respect to the motivating contexts and contemporary circumstances, there remains value in drawing out what appear to be the main trends and implications. This interpretative work was initially conducted by the researchers which led to the creation of various plausible hypotheses. These hypotheses were then tested through consultation with experts through at scholarly meetings in Australia, China, France, the Netherlands, Russia, Singapore and the United States. The refined conclusions are reported in this chapter.

Several limitations and assumptions shape this research. For instance, there are inherent limitations around data, particularly regarding education outcomes, and it is necessary to assume that institutional accreditation and the characteristics of leading universities underpin quality. Given the opacity of university budgets it is not possible to distinguish how funding is distributed between education and research. It is necessary to make a number of assumptions about the treatment of data and how it should be matched temporally given the lagging nature of many of the indicators. DEA modelling estimates relative not absolute productivity and changing the sample may change the productivity calculations. Many complexities arise given the formative nature

THE PRODUCTIVITY OF LEADING GLOBAL UNIVERSITIES

of this work, and while this chapter is empirical rather than technical in character it does help provoke important forces shaping this work.

## 3 Empirical Insights into the Productivity of Leading Universities

This section responds to the first research question. Specifically, it presents empirical results which convey insights into the productivity of leading global universities during their concerted push to prominence during the 'world-class era'.

Table 12.4 presents descriptive statistics for the nine selected indicators for the start year of 2007 and the end year of 2015. As with all results that follow, this data is for the sampled leading universities only and not all higher education institutions in the country. This summary already reveals substantial patterns in the data. For instance, the annual expenditure of China has risen substantially from 2007 to 2015, as has the count of top publications. Australia shows growth with regards postgraduate students and graduations, as well as with publications. The United Kingdom and United States publications have grown, with increase in postgraduate education, though without marked growth in inputs. Japan appears reasonably flat across most of the indicators.

Figure 12.1 graphs total factor productivity change statistics for the five countries, modelled using TI. Working from the 2007 base year, numbers above 1.0 signal productivity increase whereas numbers below 1.0 reflect productivity decrease. The leading Australian universities have shown consistent growth, irrespective of assumptions made about distribution of inputs between education and research, potentially reflecting substantial structural reforms to stimulate greater outcomes from existing infrastructure and faculty. There is evident productivity decline in the case of China until around 2011, likely reflecting steep investment in new infrastructure and faculty to bring funding levels into general alignment with those of the other countries, though there is growth since 2011 and increasing differentiation between education and research (Zhong, Lu, Coates, & Kuh, 2019). The leading Japanese universities exhibit slow and consistent productivity decline. Productivity statistics for the United Kingdom and the United States have remained stable, with modest decline since 2013–2014. The research-weighed estimates higher than the education-weighted estimates in all countries except Japan.

Figure 12.2 presents single factor productivity estimates combined for the sampled world-class universities in each of the five countries. These estimates

TABLE 12.4    Descriptive statistics for selected indicators

| Indicator | Australia | | China | | Japan | | UK | | USA | |
|---|---|---|---|---|---|---|---|---|---|---|
| | 2007 | 2015 | 2007 | 2015 | 2007 | 2015 | 2007 | 2015 | 2007 | 2015 |
| Annual expenditure ($X_1$) | 7.1 | 9.5 | 16.4 | 41.8 | 851.6 | 1,028.50 | 5.1 | 7.1 | 18.3 | 24.8 |
| Academic staff ($L_1$) | 19,429 | 22,786 | 18,760 | 20,780 | 18,340 | 20,079 | 29,045 | 40,520 | 23,403 | 24,427 |
| Non-academic staff ($L_2$) | 22,664 | 27,398 | 19,745 | 23,406 | 15,989 | 17,609 | 33,539 | 37,670 | 88,520 | 1,03,391 |
| Undergrad FTE ($E_1$) | 1,61,701 | 1,90,854 | 1,15,944 | 1,12,104 | 83,645 | 87,200 | 1,31,384 | 1,45,163 | 1,03,385 | 1,14,532 |
| Undergrad degrees ($E_2$) | 44,133 | 49,935 | 27,840 | 24,865 | 19,374 | 19,334 | 32,405 | 37,000 | 27,387 | 29,966 |
| Postgrad FTE ($E_3$) | 50,155 | 89,097 | 95,526 | 1,37,434 | 57,967 | 59,296 | 58,139 | 77,926 | 86,443 | 95,170 |
| Postgrad degrees ($E_4$) | 28,324 | 42,936 | 26,480 | 34,296 | 20,214 | 18,784 | 27,065 | 43,770 | 31,488 | 38,010 |
| Publications ($R_1$) | 21,279 | 42,899 | 31,687 | 58,384 | 30,797 | 34,548 | 35,117 | 58,008 | 52,184 | 77,446 |
| Top Publications ($R_2$) | 9,018 | 19,054 | 6,814 | 18,723 | 9,481 | 10,186 | 15,903 | 27,732 | 25,041 | 36,660 |

# THE PRODUCTIVITY OF LEADING GLOBAL UNIVERSITIES

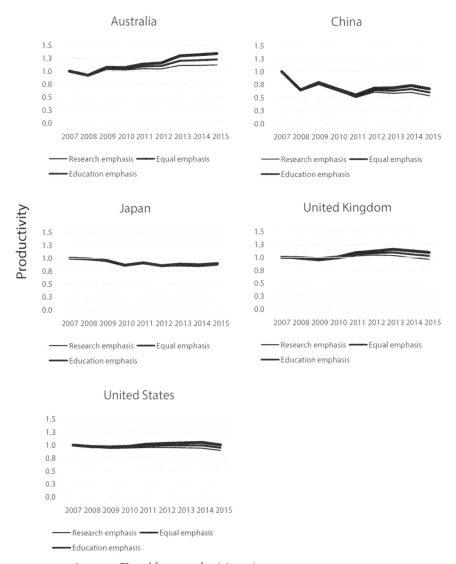

FIGURE 12.1   Aggregate TI total factor productivity estimates

take just labour rather than labour and expenses as the input. The total factor productivity situation for Japan is like that for single factor productivity. For the other countries' combined institutional samples, the single factor productivity estimates are generally larger than the total factor productivity estimates, signalling the impact of non-labour expenses and highlighting the stability of staffing numbers in the period sampled. As well, there is greater differentiation between education and research estimates. Both the United Kingdom and United States, academically mature systems before the massification, show

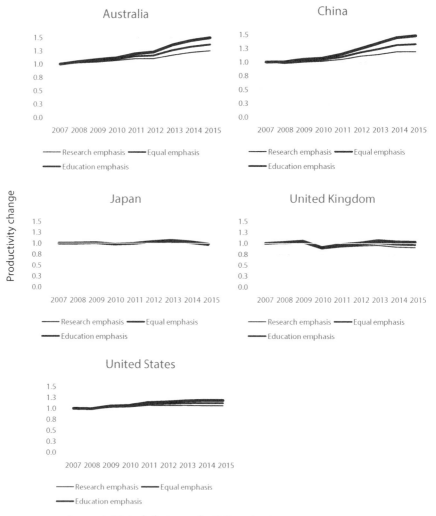

FIGURE 12.2    Aggregate TI single factor productivity estimates

positive and broadly stable productivity change. Overall, it could be observed that there are two different Anglospheric stories (Australia compared with the United Kingdom and the United States), and two different East Asian stories (China compared with Japan).

Statistics for individual universities can be reviewed, moving beyond these national aggregates of the sample universities. Figure 12.3 presents education and research productivity change estimates sorted by each university's total factor productivity rank, with linear lines of best fit included to facilitate interpretation. The figure reveals that productivity growth has come through research rather than education, and that certain universities with relatively high research productivity show low education productivity.

# THE PRODUCTIVITY OF LEADING GLOBAL UNIVERSITIES 237

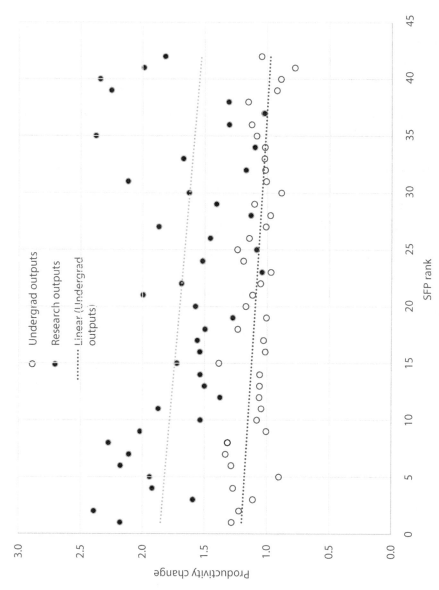

FIGURE 12.3   Education and research productivity change estimates sorted by total factor productivity rank

TABLE 12.5 University TI education, research, TFP and SFP estimates

| University | Country | Research | Education | TFP | SFP |
|---|---|---|---|---|---|
| Nanjing University | China | 2.4 | 1.3 | 0.8 | 1.7 |
| Monash University | Australia | 2.4 | 1.3 | 1.3 | 1.6 |
| University of Western Australia | Australia | 2.2 | 1.4 | 1.4 | 1.5 |
| Zhejiang University | China | 1.7 | 1.2 | 0.8 | 1.4 |
| Fudan University | China | 2.3 | 1.1 | 0.7 | 1.4 |
| Xian Jiaotong University | China | 2.3 | 1.0 | 0.6 | 1.4 |
| The University of Warwick | UK | 2.0 | 1.1 | 1.2 | 1.4 |
| University of Queensland | Australia | 2.1 | 1.4 | 1.2 | 1.4 |
| University of Melbourne | Australia | 1.9 | 1.3 | 1.2 | 1.4 |
| Australian National University | Australia | 1.6 | 1.4 | 1.3 | 1.3 |
| University of Adelaide | Australia | 2.3 | 1.3 | 1.2 | 1.3 |
| Shanghai jiaotong university | China | 2.0 | 1.1 | 0.6 | 1.3 |
| The University of Manchester | UK | 1.5 | 1.1 | 1.1 | 1.3 |
| University of Sydney | Australia | 1.9 | 1.2 | 1.1 | 1.3 |
| Cornell University | USA | 1.4 | 1.1 | 1.1 | 1.3 |
| University of New South Wales | Australia | 2.2 | 1.3 | 1.2 | 1.3 |
| King's College London | UK | 1.9 | 1.4 | 1.3 | 1.3 |
| Kyushu university | Japan | 1.3 | 1.0 | 1.0 | 1.3 |
| University of Bristol | UK | 1.5 | 1.2 | 1.0 | 1.3 |
| Columbia University | USA | 1.5 | 1.3 | 0.9 | 1.2 |
| Tsinghua University | China | 1.8 | 1.3 | 0.2 | 1.2 |
| London School of Economics | UK | 2.0 | 1.2 | 1.0 | 1.2 |
| Peking University | China | 2.1 | 1.3 | 0.9 | 1.2 |
| University of Chicago | USA | 1.5 | 1.1 | 1.0 | 1.2 |
| University of California-Berkeley | USA | 1.3 | 1.1 | 0.8 | 1.1 |
| Imperial College London | UK | 1.5 | 1.3 | 1.1 | 1.1 |
| University College London | UK | 1.7 | 1.8 | 1.1 | 1.1 |
| Harvard University | USA | 1.5 | 1.1 | 1.0 | 1.1 |
| Yale University | USA | 1.6 | 1.1 | 1.0 | 1.1 |
| Princeton University | USA | 1.4 | 1.1 | 0.9 | 1.1 |
| Massachusetts Institute of Technology | USA | 1.5 | 1.1 | 1.1 | 1.1 |

(*cont.*)

THE PRODUCTIVITY OF LEADING GLOBAL UNIVERSITIES                    239

TABLE 12.5    University TI education, research, TFP and SFP estimates (cont.)

| University | Country | Research | Education | TFP | SFP |
|---|---|---|---|---|---|
| Stanford University | USA | 1.7 | 1.0 | 1.0 | 1.1 |
| The University of Edinburgh | UK | 1.6 | 1.3 | 1.0 | 1.0 |
| University of Tokyo | Japan | 1.1 | 1.0 | 0.9 | 1.0 |
| University of Oxford | UK | 1.9 | 1.1 | 0.9 | 1.0 |
| Hokkaido University | Japan | 1.0 | 0.9 | 1.0 | 1.0 |
| University of Cambridge | UK | 1.6 | 0.9 | 0.9 | 1.0 |
| University of California-Los Angeles | USA | 1.3 | 1.1 | 0.7 | 1.0 |
| Nagoya University | Japan | 1.2 | 1.0 | 0.8 | 0.9 |
| Osaka University | Japan | 1.1 | 1.1 | 1.0 | 0.9 |
| Kyoto University | Japan | 1.1 | 1.0 | 0.8 | 0.9 |
| Tohoku University | Japan | 1.0 | 1.0 | 0.8 | 0.8 |

Table 12.5 lists the sampled universities, showing university name, country, composite research productivity estimate, composite education productivity estimate, and total factor productivity (TFP) and single factor productivity (SFP) estimates. The light grey shading flags universities that manifest stable productivity estimates over the period, and the darker grey shading universities in which productivity has been below 1.0. The total factor productivity list appears to distinguish between universities which have leveraged infrastructure to generate greater outputs (Australia, United Kingdom), systems which are well-established (United States and United Kingdom), and systems which have been investing either in infrastructure (China) or in expensive labour (Japan). The single factor productivity list appears to tell a story of rising systems (Australia, China) compared with stable systems (United Kingdom, United States) and a declining system (Japan).

Though the methods are different, the DEA analyses revealed essentially similar results and trends compared with TI. Figure 12.4 reports results aggregated for the selected universities within each country. Australia shows strong productivity growth from 2007 to 2015 across both education and research functions. China manifests salient productivity increase, especially in relation to research. Productivity in the United Kingdom and the United States

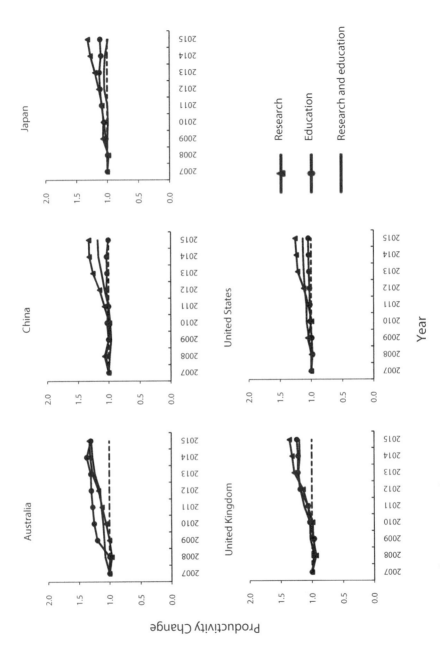

FIGURE 12.4  Aggregate DEA estimates

THE PRODUCTIVITY OF LEADING GLOBAL UNIVERSITIES

rise steadily, and the former tends to be more efficient since 2012. Productivity is stable and even declining in Japan, though with slight increases for research.

Table 12.6 presents individual university DEA productivity estimates for education and research. The shading is the same as for Figure 12.4. This alternative DEA analytical technique affirms several features of the TI analysis, such as the increase of Australian and Chinese universities, the stability of United Kingdom and United States universities, and the decline of Japanese universities. It also affirms disparities between research and education, for instance with relation to the University of Manchester, Nagoya University and the Shanghai Jiaotong University. For each of these universities research productivity has improved while education has remained stable. Conversely, education productivity has improved more than research productivity at the University of Cambridge and the University of Queensland.

Figure 12.5 shows DEA results for each university in Australia and Japan (for parsimony) across the nine years being studied. Certain universities display growth (e.g. University of Western Australia, Kyushu University, and Cornell University), whereas the growth of other universities is inconsistent (e.g. Australian National University, Nagoya University), and there are certain outlying universities (e.g. University of Adelaide). While beyond the scope of this chapter, these estimates reveal important trajectories which can be contextualized with further institutional information to identify productivity correlates and facilitators.

These productivity analyzes reveal important insights into the performance of leading universities for around a decade following the launch of the world-class university period. For instance, higher education systems appear to play a more important role. There are interesting differences between countries, which could be explored by further analysis. Education and research have played out differently, most particularly revealing research productivity growth and education productivity stability. Each university, as well, appears to have its own productivity story which, as with higher education systems, could be unpacked with further analysis. Insights such as these help to tease out interesting characteristics of higher education policy and practice at global, national and institutional levels.

TABLE 12.6    University DEA total, education and research estimates

| University | Total | Research | Education |
|---|---|---|---|
| University of Western Australia | 1.6 | 1.2 | 1.1 |
| Cornell University | 1.5 | 0.9 | 1.0 |
| King's College London | 1.4 | 1.6 | 1.0 |
| Australian National University | 1.4 | 1.2 | 1.2 |
| University of Queensland | 1.4 | 1.7 | 2.6 |
| Kyushu university | 1.4 | 1.5 | 1.2 |
| University of Melbourne | 1.4 | 1.0 | 1.1 |
| University of Cambridge | 1.4 | 1.2 | 2.4 |
| University of Edinburgh | 1.3 | 1.6 | 1.1 |
| Zhejiang University | 1.3 | 0.5 | 0.8 |
| Shanghai jiaotong university | 1.3 | 2.2 | 1.2 |
| Fudan University | 1.3 | 1.0 | 0.9 |
| University of Manchester | 1.3 | 1.5 | 0.9 |
| University of Oxford | 1.3 | 1.2 | 0.9 |
| Nanjing University | 1.2 | 1.5 | 1.1 |
| Harvard University | 1.2 | 0.9 | 1.1 |
| Monash University | 1.2 | 1.1 | 1.1 |
| University of Chicago | 1.2 | 1.1 | 0.9 |
| University of Sydney | 1.2 | 1.0 | 0.9 |
| Nagoya University | 1.2 | 1.4 | 0.9 |
| University of Warwick | 1.1 | 1.6 | 1.7 |
| Peking University | 1.1 | 1.5 | 1.0 |
| University College London | 1.1 | 0.8 | 0.8 |
| Yale University | 1.1 | 1.6 | 1.2 |
| University of New South Wales | 1.1 | 2.1 | 1.2 |
| Massachusetts Institute of Technology | 1.1 | 1.4 | 1.0 |
| Xian Jiaotong University | 1.1 | 1.5 | 1.2 |
| University of California-Los Angeles | 1.1 | 2.2 | 1.0 |
| Columbia University | 1.1 | 0.8 | 0.9 |
| Stanford University | 1.1 | 1.4 | 1.1 |
| Imperial College London | 1.1 | 1.7 | 1.3 |
| University of Tokyo | 1.0 | 1.4 | 1.4 |
| University of Adelaide | 1.0 | 1.4 | 1.2 |
| London School of Economics | 1.0 | 1.6 | 1.2 |

*(cont.)*

THE PRODUCTIVITY OF LEADING GLOBAL UNIVERSITIES                    243

TABLE 12.6     University DEA total, education and research estimates (*cont.*)

| University | Total | Research | Education |
|---|---|---|---|
| Princeton University | 1.0 | 1.0 | 1.1 |
| University of California-Berkeley | 1.0 | 1.1 | 1.0 |
| University of Bristol | 1.0 | 0.8 | 1.0 |
| Hokkaido University | 0.9 | 1.7 | 1.1 |
| Tsinghua University | 0.9 | 1.1 | 0.8 |
| Kyoto University | 0.8 | 1.0 | 1.0 |
| Tohoku University | 0.8 | 1.2 | 1.1 |
| Osaka University | 0.7 | 1.0 | 1.0 |

## 4     Characteristics of Contemporary Higher Education

What are the implications for higher education from analyzing the productivity of leading universities? To respond substantively to this question, this section evaluates the empirical results in greater depth, linking them with relevant research, to provide deeper insights into the characteristics of contemporary higher education. As noted, these interpretations have been validated through consultations in Australia, China, France, the Netherlands, Russia, Singapore and the United States. The section first touches on systems, then institutions, then academic functions. This evaluation sets foundations for the last section, which analyzes implications and future developments.

The results suggest that higher education systems set boundaries and play an important role in explaining performance. The results reveal evident orderings among the countries and among the leading universities within the countries. Leading universities within similar systems manifest similar growth patterns and constraints. Broadly, the pre-existing leaders (Japan, United Kingdom and United States) manifest flat or reducing productivity gain whereas Australia and China appear to have benefited most from the world-class university environment. From one perspective, this is to be expected. Universities obviously exist within systemic and usually national or provincial contexts that furnish all kinds of histories, accreditations, resources and missions on universities. Yet from another perspective, the finding is inconsistent with the idea of a 'world-class university' which by definition seeks to go beyond systemic contexts and contribute globally. After two decades of growth, this raises the question as to whether 'world-class universities' in fact plateau as

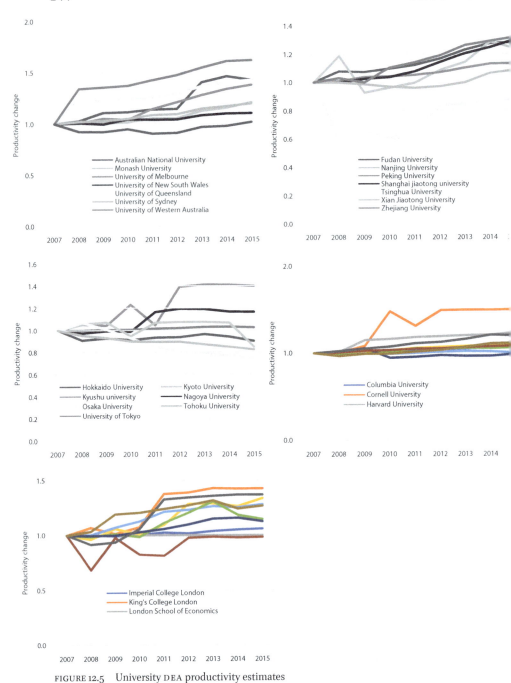

FIGURE 12.5    University DEA productivity estimates

'national class universities' bounded by similar national externalities which in turn shape isomorphic behaviour? (e.g. Croucher & Woelert, 2016). It may also be that leading universities are looking sideways towards competitors rather than outwards beyond national frontiers? The productivity modelling gives merit to these interpretations, raising further questions about the characteristics and potential for genuinely global universities. What must universities and perhaps even systems do to go beyond existing constraints? Does a new phase of 'global' beckon, moving universities beyond 'world' or even 'system' constraints?

Analysis of the university-level results reveals that leading universities appear to pursue different productivity growth strategies. There are six basic ways in which inputs and outputs can relate to increase, sustain or decrease productivity growth. Certain universities appear to have pursued growth via increasing outputs without marked augmentation of inputs (e.g. University of Western Australia, University of Warwick and Australian National University). Other universities have increased both outputs and inputs, with relatively greater increase in outputs (e.g. Tsinghua University, Shanghai Jiaotong University and Fudan University). Still other universities have increased outputs marginally while decreasing inputs (e.g. Kyushu university, Hokkaido University and Harvard University). Similar permutations can be observed about evident productivity decline, though presumably such movement was not the result of strategic intent. These patterns are interesting in themselves, revealing the ways in which leading universities have responded to operating contexts in recent decades. They also convey the need for additional analysis that gives greater insights into distinctive institutional portraits. This carries immediate need for more nuanced university-to-university benchmarking, perhaps drawing on more elaborate and diversifying information resources such as U-Multirank (Van Vught & Ziegele, 2012), but also taking into account financial information. It also affirms the value of benchmarking management strategies or processes, not just university performance.

Looking within universities, the results convey a more positive story for research than education productivity. Results for the sampled leading universities within each of the selected countries show potential upper and lower bounds on measured productivity, and the upper bound is consistently defined by emphasizing research output indicators. It may be tempting to infer that research productivity is thus increasing more quickly than education productivity. This may be the case. Without further information on resource allocation to the two functions, however, this cannot be confirmed. The results only show that joint productivity change is portrayed more positively with increased emphasis on research outputs. Information about direct education and research expenditure, however, would be needed to generate accurate estimates for separate education and research productivity. The results do convey changes in institutional operations, strategy and priorities in favour of producing and reporting research.

## 5 Broader Implications for Planning and Development

This chapter has contributed insights into the productivity of leading global universities during the 'world-class era'. It adapted two refined productivity models, selected a sample of countries and leading universities, collected and modelled data, and synthesized results. The results show that systems play a substantial role in fueling or bounding productivity growth that countries have prospered differently during this period, that universities have adopted different strategies to respond to external circumstances, and that the fortunes of education and research may have played out differently. These high-level results convey interesting insights, have implications for understanding the nature of what it means to be 'world-class', and provide insights into institutional strategy.

Revealing contemporary circumstances and tracing these empirically to a few years after the start of the world-class era is informative. What do the results and interpretation convey, however, for the next phase of higher education? Of course, it is impossible to know, and forecasting is inherently fraught with uncertainty and variability. The productivity modelling and interpretations do sustain selected modest implications. Three implications are noted here, in relation to systems, t institutions, and t academic functions.

First, the era of the world-class university may be yielding declining returns, particularly for leading universities in major university systems. This is indeed signalled in turns towards new policy options such as China's Double World Class University policy (Zhong, Lu, Coates, & Kuh, 2019) and Australia's focus on leveraging provincial universities to spread higher education services away from elite invariably urban concentrations (Commonwealth of Australia, 2019). Such development is also signalled in regional initiatives in Europe and Asia.

Second, it suggests that while universities have fostered governors and leaders seemingly adept at exploiting national opportunities, there is further value to be procured from reaching outside the system to develop truly global universities. Certain systems and universities have built acumen in earning foreign student fee income (Croucher et al., 2016), but there is much more to globalization than this. Might a world-class university be one which is accredited globally, secures funds globally, conducts research globally, locates staff and students globally, and contributes globally? The world-class era spawned several institutions with growth in such directions (e.g. NYU, Minerva, Monash University), though none yet which are truly global in the same way as major companies in other sectors such as banking, health or transport.

Third, interpretation of the productivity modelling hints that the world-class era may have helped construct 'world-class research' but not necessarily, and

THE PRODUCTIVITY OF LEADING GLOBAL UNIVERSITIES 247

possibly at the expense of, 'world class education'. Future growth, therefore, is almost certain to derive from unleashing similar change in this core academic function. This does appear to be happening, with the recent development of globally contributing and billion-dollar scale education service firms, parallel-ing the emergence of bibliometric firms. As the indicators and data in the pro-ductivity models bring out, however, there remains little objective information about learning or vocational outcomes which would be important in bringing such change about.

This chapter makes empirical, technical and substantive contributions to the research on leading global universities, on productivity, and on higher edu-cation. It suffers from necessary breadth and limitations with the model and data. For instance, there would particular value in building out the country and university sample with more European universities. But by taking account of financial considerations and looking at leading universities across five coun-tries, it reveals new insights into system, university and academic dynamics. It goes well beyond analysis of rankings, which typically say little if anything about resources hence important inputs and constraints. As such, it advances the frontiers for researching the higher education performance in the last two decades, and for considering future directions for growth.

### Acknowledgement

The authors are grateful to the experts who provided advice on the selection of universities and models and indicators, and the selection of universities.

### References

Agasisti, T., Egorov, A., Zinchenko, D., & Leshukov, O. (2018). *Universities' efficiency and regional economic short-run growth: Empirical evidence from Russia.* Higher School of Economics.

Austin, I., & Jones, G. A. (2015). *Governance of higher education: Global perspectives, theories, and practices.* Taylor and Francis.

Australian Government Department of Education. (2018). *Higher education statistics.* Retrieved from https://www.education.gov.au/higher-education-o

Chinese Ministry of Education. (2018). *Compilation of basic statistics of universities under the Ministry of Education.* Retrieved from http://www.moe.gov.cn/

Coates, H. (2010). *Measuring and monitoring productivity in Australian higher educa-tion.* Invited paper delivered at the second meeting of the National Academy of

Science project Measuring Higher Education Productivity: Conceptual Framework and Data Needs, Washington DC.

Coates, H. (Ed.). (2017a). *Productivity in higher education: Research insights for universities and governments in Asia.* Asian Productivity Organisation.

Coates, H. (2017b). *The market for learning: Leading transparent higher education.* Springer.

Commonwealth of Australia. (2019). *National regional, rural and remote tertiary education strategy final report.*

Croucher, G., & Woelert, P. (2016). Institutional isomorphism and the creation of the unified national system of higher education in Australia: An empirical analysis. *Higher Education, 71*(4), 439–453.

Eva, M., Gómez-Sancho, J. M., & Perez-Esparrells, C. (2017). Comparing university performance by legal status: A Malmquist-type index approach for the case of the Spanish higher education system. *Tertiary Education and Management, 23*(3), 206–221.

Guo, I. L., Lee, H. S., & Lee, D. (2017). An integrated model for slack-based measure of super-efficiency in additive DEA. *Omega, 67,* 160–167.

Higher Education Statistics Agency (HESA). (2018). *Open data and official statistics.* Retrieved from https://www.hesa.ac.uk/data-and-analysis

Hoxby, C. M., & Stange, K. (Eds.). (2019). *Productivity in higher education.* University of Chicago Press.

Johnes, J. (2006). Data envelopment analysis and its application to the measurement of efficiency in higher education. *Economics of Education Review, 25,* 273–288.

Massy, W. F. (1996). Value responsibility budgeting. In W. F. Massy (Ed.), *Resource allocation in higher education.* University of Michigan Press.

Massy, W. F. (2003). *Honoring the trust : Quality and cost containment in higher education.* Publishing Company.

Massy, W. F., Sullivan, T. A., & Mackie, C. (2013). Improving measurement of productivity in higher education. *Change: The Magazine of Higher Learning, 45*(1), 15–23.

Meyer, J. W., Ramirez, F. O., Frank, D. J., & Schofer, E. (2007). Higher education as an institution. In P. J. Gumport (Ed.), *Sociology of higher education: Contributions and their contexts* (pp. 187–221). Johns Hopkins University Press.

Moore, K., Coates, H., & Croucher, G. (2018). Investigating applications of university productivity measurement models using Australian data. *Studies in Higher Education, 44*(12), 2148–2162.

Moore, K., Croucher, G., & Coates, H. (2019). Productivity and policy in higher education. *Australian Economic Review, 52*(2), 236–246.

National Center of Education Statistics. (2018). *Integrated postsecondary education data system.* Retrieved from https://nces.ed.gov/ipeds/datacenter/Default.aspx

Powell, W. W., & DiMaggio, P. J. (Eds.). (1991). *The new institutionalism in organisational analysis.* University of Chicago Press.

THE PRODUCTIVITY OF LEADING GLOBAL UNIVERSITIES 249

Raei, B., Yousefi, M., Rahmani, K., Afshari, S., & Ameri, H. (2017). Patterns of productivity changes in hospitals by using Malmquist–DEA index: A panel data analysis (2011–2016). *Australasian Medical Journal, 10*(10), 856–864.

Salmi, J. (2009). *The challenge of establishing world class universities.* The World Bank.

Salmi, J., & Altbach, P. G. (2020). World-class universities. In J. C. Shin & P. Teixeira (Eds.), *Encyclopedia of international higher education systems and institutions.* Springer Netherlands.

Scopus. (2018). *SciVal.* Retrieved from https://scival.com/

Shanghai Ranking. (2018). *2018 academic ranking of world universities.* Retrieved from http://www.shanghairanking.com

Stensaker, B., & Norgard, J. D. (2001). Innovation and isomorphism: A case-study of university identity struggle 1969–1999. *Higher Education, 42*(4), 473–492.

Sullivan, T. A., Mackie, C., Massy, W. F., & Sinha, E. (2012). *Improving measurement of productivity in higher education.* National Academies Press. https://doi.org/10.17226/13417

Thornton, P. H., Ocasio, W., & Lounsbury, M. (2012). *The institutional logics perspective: A new approach to culture, structure, and process.* Oxford University Press.

Times Higher Education (THE). (2018). *2018 world university rankings.* Retrieved from http://www.timeshighereducation.com

Tran, T. H., Mao, Y., Nathanail, P., Siebers, P. O., & Robinson, D. (2019). Integrating slacks-based measure of efficiency and super-efficiency in data envelopment analysis. *Omega, 85*, 156–165.

Van Vught, F. A., & Ziegele, F. (Eds.). (2012). *Multidimensional ranking: The design and development of U-Multirank.* Springer Science & Business Media.

Visbal-Cadavid, D., Martínez-Gómez, M., & Guijarro, F. (2017). Assessing the efficiency of public universities through DEA. A case study. *Sustainability, 9*(8), 1416.

Wang, C. N., Hsu, H. P., Wang, Y. H., & Pham, T. T. H. (2017). Performance assessment for electronic manufacturing service providers using two-stage super-efficiency SBM model. *Applied Economics, 49*(20), 1963–1980.

Williams, R., & Leahy, A. (2019). *U21 ranking of national higher education systems 2019.* Retrieved from https://universitas21.com/sites/default/files/2019-04/Full%20Report%20and%20Cover.pdf

Witte, K. D., & López-Torres, L. (2017). Efficiency in education: A review of literature and a way forward. *Journal of the Operational Research Society, 68*(4), 339–363.

Zhong, Z., Coates, H., & Jinghuan, S. (Eds.). (2019). *Innovations in Asian higher education.* Routledge.

Zhong, Z., Liu, L., Coates, H., & Kuh, G. (2019). What the US (and rest of the world) should know about higher education in China. *Change: The Magazine of Higher Learning, 51*(3), 8–20.

CHAPTER 13

# Third Mission at Austrian Universities of Applied Sciences and the Translational Role of Hybrid Middle Managers

*Martina Gaisch and Daniela Nömeyer*

## Abstract

This chapter looks at third mission activities as an integral part of universities of applied sciences (UAS) in Austria and sheds light on the perceived role of these institutions of higher learning as to their responsibilities for regional engagement, innovation and knowledge transfer in their local areas. We seek to identify key institutional players and departments that promote third mission amongst Austrian UAS. By means of a desktop research and website enquiry, we explore how the 21 Austrian UAS present themselves online with regard to third-stream activities. In addition, expert interviews with 'hybrid middle managers' devoted to third mission provide information on their specific task portfolio and views of institutional transfer centers that deal exclusively with services and transfer to the community. Finally, parallels are drawn between the German UAS sector where transfer centers are broadly established at the sectoral level and the Austrian higher education landscape where three regionally dispersed knowledge transfer centers were established to start-up finance projects along the lines of knowledge and technology transfer.

## Keywords

third mission – knowledge transfer – transfer center – regional engagement – University of Applied Sciences – middle managers – Austria

## 1 Introduction

As an umbrella term that "refers to a wide variety of principles and strategies for economic and social development" (Jongbloed et al., 2008, p. 313), third mission (TM) gives a name to those activities that beside teaching and research

© KONINKLIJKE BRILL NV, LEIDEN, 2020 | DOI: 10.1163/9789004436558_014

THIRD MISSION AT AUSTRIAN UAS 251

have – especially in the context of applied institutions of higher learning – become the third pillar of higher education institutions (HEIs). In the 1980s, there was a substantial increase of studies that dealt with the role and impact of universities on society, pointing to the growing need of TM activities (Etzkowitz, 1998). Consequently, the entrepreneurial university model entered the academic debate and with it, TM has gradually become a major component of the European higher education discourse. Today, no university, be it applied or research-oriented can afford to ignore activities along the lines of technology transfer, innovation and social and regional engagement (Gaisch et al., 2019b).

It is for this reason that this chapter looks at third-stream activities at the Austrian sector of universities of applied sciences, as compared to the more systemic and systematic TM approach adopted in the German higher education landscape.

More recently, Trencher et al. (2014a, 2014b) introduced a further function, which they refer to as the fourth mission of higher education and theorize as 'co-creation for sustainability'. They argue that the entrepreneurial model has evolved to a transformative one where a multi-stakeholder platform is "engaged with society in a continual and mutual process of creation and transformation" (Trencher et al., 2014a, p. 158).

This integration of sustainable development values has led to societal transformations with the aim to materialize sustainable development in a specific location, region and societal subsector (Trencher et al., 2014a). In this sense, they have adopted a further lens to the third-stream debate, which can be included in a broader conception of TM.

While TM has traditionally been considered as a one-way knowledge transfer from the knowledge supplier (HEIs) to the knowledge user (industry and society) (also see Mitton et al., 2007), this one-directional perspective has gradually changed towards a more symbiotic and multi-directional way of looking at knowledge exchange (Davey, 2017). In this vein, critical voices have been raised questioning the TM approach that adopts an economic and technological lens with an exclusive eye on the exploitation of research findings for industrial innovation (Pinheiro et al., 2015; Cai and Liu 2015). It was argued that an increasingly diversified HE system also serves the purpose of the TM mission mandate according to which HEIs may cooperate with non-university institutions for the sake of a societal contribution. Such regional engagement may then be along the lines of teaching, learning, applied, fundamental research activities, or social responsibility (Gaisch et al., 2019a).

Consequently, discussions regarding TM have also become more diversified as to what to incorporate into the definitional scope, ranging from cultural, social, political and economic elements (Roessler et al., 2015; Gaisch et al.,

2019b). This was further reinforced by evidence that successful knowledge exchange needs genuine interaction among researchers, decision makers, and other stakeholders (Lavis et al., 2003). Hence, a broader TM definition has emerged that focuses on socio-economic development of the region as well as on economic innovation. Such a perspective goes beyond the traditional unilateral perspective and embraces emerging bilateral relations.

Such dynamic cooperation processes together with a broad variety of TM mandates require not only an explicit and international institutional articulation and strategic outlook but also persons that can proficiently engage in third-stream activities. Depending on the specific interest and orientation, TM activities can foreground either economic gains (Entrepreneurial University, Triple Helix, Mode 2) or non-economic purposes (Engaged University, Regional Innovation Systems, Sustainable University).[1] What proves to be particularly challenging in this regard is to identify the right persons for these diverse and multifaceted tasks, be they transfer managers, innovation scouts or other middle managers. They represent a distinct occupational group with a gate-keeping role and a broad base of knowledge and expertise. This new type of university employee, frequently referred to as middle managers, has not yet been well established, their job profile is not uniformly defined and still very heterogeneous (Gmelch & Miskin, 2011; Floyd, 2016). It is for these reasons that the hybrid role of middle managers is examined in more detail in the next section.

## 2     A Brief Definition of Middle Managers

While middle managers were traditionally associated with persons in charge of curriculum development, their roles have gradually expanded in line with the requirements of entrepreneurial universities (Floyd, 2016). Emerging market-orientated perspectives encompass an ever-increasing portfolio of tasks – from income generation, TM activities and quality assurance, alongside the more traditional roles of program leaders, head of departments, curriculum managers and cross-college managers with pedagogical responsibilities (Briggs, 2005). Research places the hybrid role of middle managers on a 'strategic continuum' characterized by two extremes. On one end of the continuum, the middle manager is regarded in line with his or her operational or administrative role, a conduit through which strategy is translated into action and is inevitably short-term (Briggs, 2001). On the other end of the continuum, the middle manager is associated with a much more strategic function that aims at developing cross-institutional support for institutional change or long-term improvements (Leader, 2004), and actively participate in shaping and defining direction (Briggs, 2001).

Unsurprisingly, then, there is a wide variety of tasks that manager academics were found to perform, ranging from department governance, program management, human resource management, budget and resource management, external communication and office management (Nyguen, 2013). An Austrian study (Ehrenstorfer et al., 2015) that looked at the duties of manager academics found that they were challenged by manifold and multi-faceted requirements in their daily professional lives.

The brokerage function of middle managers is considered to be one that mediates conflict between senior managers and practitioners, bridges gaps in provision and resources, and engages in underground work to get things done (Gleeson & Shain, 1999; Beresford & Michels, 2014). Despite their creative, entrepreneurial and brokering abilities, it was stated that middle managers mostly remain invisible, unrecognized, and essentially defensive in nature (Beresford & Michels, 2014) and hence are hardly recognized as key agents of change.

On a more positive note, other studies point to the significant role that middle managers can take in specific fields. For one, it was identified by Nonaka and Takeuchi (1995) that they may act as crucial integrators and synthesizers, especially in the field of knowledge creation and in corporate settings. They were also found to endorse, refine and shepherd entrepreneurial opportunities, and identify and acquire the resources needed to deploy them (Kuratko et al., 2005). In addition, their ability to lobby and influence their institutional leaders was foregrounded as a major asset (Nelles & Vorley, 2010). In sum, it can be argued that in view of their intermediary function, middle managers have the potential to act as 'creative nodes' (Bilton, 2006) in cross-functional team constellations. As such, they can proactively engage in connections but also step out of rigid boundaries in line with institutional requirements and opportunities. In this context, de Boer et al. (2010) point to the ability of middle managers to make use of their powerful 'sandwich' position for promoting their own interests and agendas. Here, it needs to be outlined that this contribution predominantly looks at middle managers that assume their role with TM type activities. Other types of middle managers concerned with e.g. student support, libraries/information resources, health and wellness are not taken into account in this descriptive account.

Over the past years, both the role of middle managers and TM agendas have become more important, which is why a number of countries have not only established transfer/service centers to encourage third-stream activities, they have also taken on numerous change agents that assume the translational role of hybrid middle managers. In the following, a particular focus is placed on the German UAS sector and on how TM is promoted by the excellence initiative launched by the German Federal and State Government in 2016.

Given that Austria takes a less systemic and systematic approach towards TM activities it tends to have more similarities with the more 'market-driven' strategies pursued in the UK and US with less government control or direct policy influence. In view of its geographic, linguistic and cultural proximity, it may be interesting to look at Germany and given its success, it may even serve as a useful frame of reference.


## 3    Transfer Centers at the German UAS Sector

In the German UAS sector, the first transfer centers were established in the early 1980s with the aim to act as modernizers for applied research and foster cooperation and closer ties with industry partners (Angerer, 2002). While at the beginning the focus was mainly placed on technology transfer, contract management, and licensing, concerns arose that there was also a need to fulfil the legal mandate for further training on a larger scale. This resulted in the establishment of the first technical academy for further education in 1988 (Angerer, 2002,). Since then, there has been a constant rise of cross-university transfer centers (Liening et al., 2019) that not only encourage transfer between science and industry but also foster entrepreneurial thinking and sustainable action (Roessler et al., 2015). Through curricular and extra-curricular teaching, a variety of educational offerings and other activities have been subsumed under the term entrepreneurial education (Liening et al., 2019).

It is argued that by linking science (training, research and development) and industry, HEIs will in future not only contribute to the creation of jobs and growth but will also, in particular, support the digital restructuring of Germany as an industrial location (Knoll, 2019). The direct exchange of knowledge and mutual interaction form the core of research-oriented cooperation with all relevant groups from the business world. Depending on the task, these may include not only companies but also associations, foundations, clubs, local authorities or ministries as well as business development agencies. The stronger orientation of the German science system towards social and sustainability issues has led to a politically desired expansion of the economic linkages between science and industry (Hachmeister et al., 2016).

This desire was translated into the excellence initiative launched by the German Federal and State Government in 2016 with the aim to promote research-based transfer of ideas, knowledge and technology. Of 48 participating HEIs, 35

UAS take part in 29 state-funded projects. Applications can only be submitted by those HEIs that have developed both a transfer strategy and a sustainability concept for their institution of higher learning. A further funding condition is that the sustainability initiatives remain effective after five years. It is therefore not surprising that these control mechanisms and incentive systems have led to a more systematic collection of sustainable TM activities (Nölting & Pape, 2017) in line with the establishment of numerous transfer and service centers and the creation of innovative and new task areas.

In view of this broad and diverse range of TM activities, new professional and occupational profiles came into existence, from transfer managers to transfer and innovation scouts. Next to technology transfer there has been a more recent discourse that has sparked the TM debate, evolving around issues such as knowledge and idea transfer. While knowledge transfer can be understood as knowledge generated at university that is passed on to society, idea transfer can be seen as ideas that are taken up by the society, used, and further developed in a university setting. In this regard, the actual meaning of TM is more accurately reflected as third mission bundled services through mutual interactions. Until recently, it appeared that current trends from society that flow into HEIs were not sufficiently taken into account. This, so it seems, has changed over the last two years in the German UAS sector (Roessler, 2015).

Undoubtedly, this shift of attention has also left its traces on the professional portfolio that persons working at transfer or service centers need to possess. While so-called transfer scouts were traditionally persons with administrative backgrounds, their operational field has become more and more diverse, requiring an increasingly scientific perspective.

## 4    Transfer Centers at the Austrian UAS Sector

While the German sector of universities of applied sciences was already established in 1971, Austria only started with a binary system 25 years ago. Hence, the Austrian UAS sector is relatively young compared to the one of Germany, which may help explain why the two countries have substantial differences with regard to the implementation of transfer centers and the existence of comprehensive transfer and sustainability strategies. Another reason why Germany is significantly ahead of Austria in this area lies in the fact that Austria does not have a state initiative like the one of "Innovative Hochschule". This federal and state initiative targets TM topics such as transfer and innovation with generous financial support and is particularly aimed at small and medium-sized universities and universities of applied sciences.

In Austria, numerous university actors involved in TM are active in one or more fields of action and thus move in a space of intersection of their 'traditional' professional field (mainly research and/or teaching) and societal expectations, trends and influences (Ehrenstorfer et al., 2015). The success of this interplay and thus of third-stream activities is often dependent on the commitment of individuals, since transfer services are neither institutionalized nor publicly financed in Austria and thus predominantly built on the intrinsic motivation of the acting persons.

Both sides – i.e. the higher education institution and the civil society – speak a different language, come from different specialist worlds, possibly think in different time frames and are likely to apply different standards of success to transfer services (Nölting et al., 2018, p. 38). This is why, next to scientific and professional expertise, a good personal network has proven to be a vital ingredient of the occupational portfolio of proficient transfer agents, also in Austria (Meißner, 2001; Henke, 2019). In this sense, transfer is directly influenced by the various actors who, in addition to knowledge, also transport their own personal attitudes, views and values.

The success of TM activities at universities of applied sciences are facilitated or obstructed by aspects of both internal and external organization and culture, as well as the interaction between these internal and external contexts. In a previous study on TM of the Austrian UAS sector (Gaisch et al., 2019b) a number of factors were identified. For one, it was found that the understanding and mindset for all forms of cooperation with industry and society was highly prevalent amongst academics due to the sector-specific application orientation of research and teaching. In addition, the institutional encouragement for transfer and TM activities was perceived as very strong. The overall picture changes, however, when it comes to the availability of resources: almost all Austrian UAS reported that there was a substantial lack of resources, both material and immaterial. Here, it may be interesting to look at external framework conditions, notably at the background of the German context. In contrast to the Excellence Initiative in Germany, funding or financial incentives for TM initiatives at the Austrian UAS sector are lacking.

A specific characteristic of the Austrian HEI landscape is so-called knowledge transfer centers (WTZ). Set up as a project and financed by the National Foundation for Research, Technology and Innovation, they are currently running until the end of December 2021. The aim of these "Knowledge Transfer Centers for Universities and Universities of Applied Sciences" is to further strengthen knowledge and technology transfer and cooperation between universities and universities of applied sciences and subsequently with companies. In total, there are three knowledge transfer centers in place, which are

THIRD MISSION AT AUSTRIAN UAS

structured according to regions (East, South, West). The funding board consists of experts from four Austrian ministries and representatives from the Austrian National Bank. Funds are provided in the form of non-repayable grants. Both research universities and universities of applied sciences are free to become involved in one of these geographically dispersed centers. About half of the Austrian universities of applied sciences (11 out of 21) and almost all universities (20 out of 22) are currently participating in one of these projects. In this context, one interviewed expert positively highlighted that due to this cross-sectional project scheme the "glass wall between research universities and UAS is gradually being dismantled".

The knowledge transfer centers see themselves as mediators of know-how and knowledge between university research, science, economy and society. They focus on the goal of optimally bringing together research results, new findings, technologies, inventions and expertise not only within the participating Universities of Applied Sciences and universities, but also of making them accessible to the economy, society and politics. Participating universities can benefit from the exchange and network activities with other HEIs and can develop their competitiveness in research and knowledge transfer. Funding is available in the area of personnel and costs of material, which allows for some reduction of the overall research expenditure. The basic idea behind this initiative is that universities position themselves as innovation leaders and that industry and society benefit more easily from the generated knowledge.

In contrast to Germany, where the Excellence Initiative has promoted and facilitated the establishment of transfer centers at German HEIs, the Austrian system does not provide for such funding structures. Another difference is that WTZ do not have any strict and binding requirements with regard to the sustainability of the funded projects. Finally, there is a substantial difference regarding the funding amount. While Germany supports projects with about 55 million euros a year,[2] Austria only provides a funding sum of 1.1 million euros a year.[3] Even though Germany is ten times larger than Austria in terms of population, the subsidy is almost 50 times higher in Germany than in Austria.

## 5    Research Questions

This contribution looks at TM activities at the Austrian UAS sector with the aim to situate them in the respective institutional context. It is further attempted to compare them with the German system and draw some broader conclusions.

Research questions are:

1. What is the development status of Austrian knowledge transfer or service centers?
2. Which UAS staff are most responsible for promoting TM activities?
3. What is the scope or operational practices among such staff?
4. How do departments and administrative units work with and depend on each other to promote TM activities?

## 6 Research Methodology

To get in-depth insight into third-stream activities of the Austrian UAS sector, a multifaceted research approach was adopted. It involved an extensive literature review, an online questionnaire (15 informants), a systematic investigation of all 21 UAS websites and telephone interviews with identified TM experts that were made explicit at the institutional websites (6 informants). Overall, 42 well selected persons (2 at each of the 21 UAS) were contacted. These informants were either heads of transfer centers, research coordinators or had job descriptions that were in line with TM activities.

Of the 21 persons surveyed (15 online and 6 telephone interviews), 7 had a professional background in Research & Development (33%), 8 in Teaching (38%) and 6 in Administration (29%). Due to the highly differentiated internal structures of the individual UAS, a systematic and consistent TM distribution was not possible. The Austrian UAS sector has no clear guidelines as to where third-stream activities are located. It is therefore the responsibility of each institution to entrust specific departments or persons with these agendas. For one, an online questionnaire was developed and sent to all 21 Austrian UAS with the invitation to participate in this sectoral survey. Through a literature review and an in-depth analysis of previous TM surveys,[4] 15 groups of questions with specific criteria generally addressed in TM discourse were identified. They were grouped into the broad categories of terminological, attitudinal, economic, educational, social, environmental, regional and stakeholder questions.

As the aim was to interview those informants that are most heavily involved in TM activities of the respective institution of higher learning, 42 previously defined persons were encouraged to take part in this survey.

In total, 15 of these experts completed the questionnaire, which corresponds to a sectoral response rate of 71.4%. The remaining UAS did not participate for reasons of workload, timing and institutional frameworks with regard to disclosure policy. In this online questionnaire, the informants were asked about

THIRD MISSION AT AUSTRIAN UAS

their roles, their scope of responsibilities and assessment of future developments concerning TM. To get a thorough understanding of their occupational fields, their functional background and interfaces with other departments, a semi-structured format was used with a number of open questions that allowed for more nuanced responses.

In parallel, a systematic investigation of all 21 UAS websites was performed to explore how the sector represents itself with regard to TM activities. Further, it was sought to identify how many institutions have transfer or similar service centers installed and if and how they are made explicit via the university website. This analysis was conducted in December 2019 and filtered by the following keywords: 'transfer', 'transfer office', 'transfer center', 'knowledge transfer', 'exchange', 'third mission' and 'societal engagement'. If publicly available, further UAS documents such as strategy, guideline, vision, and mission of the respective institutions were searched for these keywords.

The institutions that made both their transfer centers and the relevant contact persons explicit on the website were contacted via phone. In sum, six additional persons were interviewed and asked about further details. The guided interview questions were semi-structured to invite open responses on their job profiles, the task portfolio of the specific transfer center and the major TM agendas. The interviews were carried out between December 2019 and January 2020, lasted between 20 and 45 minutes and were audio recorded. The data was analyzed by means of thematic analysis (Clarke & Brown, 2006) using an open coding technique. It is described as "a method for identifying, analysing and reporting patterns (themes) within data" (Braun & Clarke, 2006, p. 79) and was found to be a good tool of analysis due to its great flexibility.

## 7  Findings

In the following, the key findings are outlined in more detail. Question 1 sought to examine if the Austrian UAS sector had well-established transfer or services center devoted to third-stream activities and if not, if there was any intention to do so. The respondents were given a definition of TM and asked whether they were doing activities corresponding to this definition.

### 7.1  *Transfer or Service Center for Third-Stream Activities*
Based upon the responses of the first question in the questionnaire as to whether a transfer center for third-stream activities is already in operation or likely to be installed in the near future, it was stated by 87% of the interviewed persons that no institutional transfer center was in place at their institution

that dedicates itself to TM alone. It was indicated by two respondents that their HEIS incorporated third-stream activities in already existing transfer centers, namely a teaching and learning center and a program development and knowledge generation center. A recent inquiry at the relevant ministry revealed that an excellence initiative similar to the one in Germany was not planned in the medium term. This may explain the reluctance of the majority of Austrian UAS to establish service centers exclusively devoted to third-stream activities. More importantly than transfer centers, so it was stated, are funding schemes that allow for more initiatives along the lines of knowledge and technology transfer.

The systemic website analysis revealed that only 4 out of 21 Austrian UAS established (and made explicit) their own department for knowledge transfer. Such service centers are either referred to as 'transfer office' or 'transfer center'. In other words, 19% of Austrian UAS have set up a department that is exclusively responsible for transfer services. If one takes into account that not every UAS participated in the online survey, this figure (81% do not have a transfer office according to the website analysis) corresponds to the figure of 87%.

It was found that the focus of these service centers varies greatly, which is hardly surprising in view of the lack of a common understanding of transfer. For example, one UAS describes its transfer center as a 'digital transfer center' where research findings are made available for industry partners. Another one focuses purely on start-ups and consulting for spin-offs and start-up companies. Yet another UAS has set up a separate transfer center for each degree program, from which research findings are transferred. The fourth transfer center focuses on the transfer of research and knowledge and is thus probably closest to what German transfer centers do. The analysis of Austrian UAS thus shows a highly diverse picture of transfer activities.

Yet, it is interesting to note that almost all Austrian UAS have mentioned 'transfer', 'knowledge transfer' or 'exchange with society' in one way or another on their homepage. Almost half of Austrian UAS (10 out of 21) have included 'transfer' or 'knowledge transfer' in their strategy or guidelines.

Question 2 sought to examine the group of persons at Austrian UAS that engages in TM activities as well as their functional background. In the following, a synthesis is provided of the findings of the questionnaire, the website investigation and the expert interviews.

### 7.2 Institutional Key Players of Third Mission Engagement

In response to being asked where TM activities are most likely to be assigned, participants stated that they are mainly to be found in Research and Development (71.4%), followed by the management (57.1%) and diversity management (50%). Marketing, academia and quality management were also considered to have a crucial impact on TM engagement. What stood out was the low significance attached to internationalization departments, as shown in Figure 13.1.

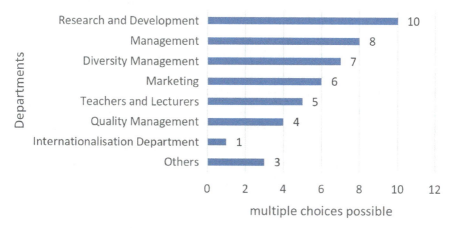

FIGURE 13.1   Departments where TM activities are most likely to be found

Question 3 looked at the key persons involved in TM activities and sought to explore if their scope of operational practices corresponds to those assigned to middle managers.

## 7.3   *Middle Managers and the Third Mission Mandate*

In the following, answers of persons who had been specifically assigned for transfer as support for researchers and those who assume this role in addition to other tasks in administration, research and/or teaching are provided. Asked about essential competencies that third-stream agents might possess, they provided the following ranked responses. Ranked highest was sound communicative skills as well as good social skills together with an excellent diplomatic instinct. This presupposes a generalistic mindset, a good general and profound institutional knowledge. It was found essential to also have expertise and experience in research. For one, it was argued that the research community is more likely to accept and cooperate with persons that have also scientific or scholarly backgrounds. In this regard, informant 3 stated "I act as an interface, I need to be at home in multiple worlds – in academia and research as well as in the practitioner's world". Informant 1 added "You have to be credible as a scientist, otherwise you lack valuable standing in this community".

Another highly ranked criterion was that transfer scouts need to be the academic cadre that is capable of bridging the gap between administrative, teaching and research staff. Moreover, it was identified that they needed to possess the translational capacity to not only link and involve all the stakeholders with a meaningful narrative, but also be able to dynamically change perspectives and frames of reference and consider alternative points of view. This also requires a broad professional network that spans across multiple levels of institutions and organizations to integrate dispersed information from various sources.

The biggest challenge identified by the informants was related to the lack of resources. More precisely, it was stated that there was too little time for systematic transfer activities, research proposals and maintenance of differing networks. In this regard, informant 2 states that "transfer is a complex matter" that involves an ever-increasing administrative burden, fundamentally at odds with the high expectations that are placed on these middle managers. Informant 2 also points to the big 'translation effort': "One must translate scientific knowledge at a level that is high and scientific, but still needs to be understood".

To further professionalize the area of science management, more financial resources and a more systematic support for knowledge transfer were considered vital. Here, the occupational role of knowledge managers was outlined. To strengthen their professional function, it was seen as vital to also raise their symbolic capital and provide them with more organizational power and financial means. A further lever to improve their standing was seen in closer cooperation with diverse federal contact points and funding bodies. In this connection, informant 1 outlines the following: "One must create a feeling of indispensability. The better you do the work, the more invisible your activity becomes. You only stand out when something does not work out".

Finally, we address the fourth research question, exploring which types of interfaces and dependencies exist among different departments.

All informants agreed that in view of their gate-opening function they acted as an interface between a number of departments. Given that the majority of the interviewees were researchers and/or teachers themselves (15 out of 21), they could draw from this occupational background in terms of status, credibility and network. It was stated that, in order to be accepted by the research community, it was vital to 'be one of them'.

Apart from R&D where most of TM agendas were said to be located, overlaps were mainly mentioned with the departments of Finance, Accounting, or Controlling, followed by Marketing, the International Office and Diversity Management. De facto, however, points of contact were outlined with all departments, depending on the type and content of the respective TM projects. In this vein, it became obvious that the respondents tended to consider TM as a cross-sectional matter that required a collective institutional effort; this, so it was stated, would also need more functional diversity to change perspectives and understand each other's standpoints more clearly. While research cooperation and

THIRD MISSION AT AUSTRIAN UAS

knowledge transfer were seen as an integral part of R&D, outreach activities were regarded to be partly a responsibility of diversity management and partly a topic on the marketing and PR agenda.

It came to the fore that specific transfer centers were considered essential in their role as 'one stop shops' that bundle and coordinate all third-stream activities and integrate multiple, often conflicting tasks. In doing so, they enable a broad range of internal and external stakeholders to connect through one single point.

## 8    Conclusion

In view of the broad range of identified third-stream activities that are performed outside academic environments, it was not surprising that TM tasks are taken on by a variety of different departments and key players. This may partly explain why 87% of the participating UAS in Austria stated that they did not have a transfer center in place or no intention to incorporate one. Not only is the Austrian UAS sector much younger than the German one, third stream activities were also found to be less structured and less politically controlled. Thus, it is a little surprising that in view of the lack of state support initiative such as the one of the German "Innovative Hochschule" there are also no comprehensive transfer or service strategies in the investigated sector. Although the sector may invest independently from state support and did so in four cases by setting up transfer centers, it became obvious that the motivation for such proactive initiatives was rather limited. The same applies to sustainability management of the UAS sector, which is strongly encouraged by the above-mentioned excellence initiative in Germany.

As to TM activities, it was generally identified that Austrian UAS place a major focus on their territorial embeddedness and their regional engagement, yet to a differing degree. In view of the widespread range of third-stream activities and widening access policies it was not considered practical by the majority of Austrian informants to install one center but rather distribute the tasks to as many institutional stakeholders as possible. At the same time, it became obvious that those UAS that had a kind of transfer center in place saw major advantages in bundling the required expertise and in the coordination of third-stream activities in a one-stop shop.

On a more critical note and despite the wish to do so, it was stated by the majority of UAS that it was difficult to distribute TM tasks among several departments and actors. Here, it was perceived as essential to clearly define and communicate the roles and tasks of the persons involved in third-stream activities. At a number of Austrian UAS without transfer centers, the role of research coordinators has gradually been enriched by more and more transfer agendas.

Due to the lack of resources, both financially and in terms of personnel, it came to the fore that many transfer activities were only 'co-managed' and done on the side. This, so it was stated, does not allow for the explicit value and visibility that such outreach and transfer action deserve. One reason for this was found in the set of priorities. At Austrian UAS teaching and research are still granted a higher priority than third-mission activities. In addition, it came to the fore that TM was frequently incorporated into other activities and not seen independently. In view of the highly diversified sector, it was not possible to provide evidence whether one model or strategic approach works better or gives better results than another one.

In other words, the Austrian path to transfer services is paved with customized solutions and individual commitment of a number of dedicated agents. It was found that TM and transfer are neither institutionalized nor systematically or systemically structured. Rather, it appeared that many, if not most, activities are based on the intrinsic motivation of individual actors. This is why some UAS are strongly involved in TM or transfer services and some are less involved, mostly because they are smaller and find it harder to raise the required resources. A similarly varied picture can be observed when looking at the departments where TM activities are bundled. Although mostly agree that R&D is the 'place to be' for third-stream activities, there were eight other departments mentioned that take on these agendas.

A clearer picture emerges when looking at how Austrian UAS make their transfer centers visible on their websites. Here, the vast majority of transfer activities was located in the R&D section, with a clear focus on applied research and close ties to the industry and a lesser emphasis on societal engagement.

Overall, it can be said that TM at the Austrian UAS sector is perceived as a multifaceted cross-sectional matter that needs to be addressed by numerous entities and stakeholders. Thereby, the translational role of hybrid middle managers was identified as a crucial ingredient in successful third-stream activities. It was stated that although it may be beneficial to have a scientific background in terms of credibility and standing in the relevant community, it might not be enough to be a good researcher. What was identified as even more important was the translational capacity to not only involve all relevant stakeholders with a meaningful narrative, but also be able to dynamically change perspectives and frames of references and consider alternative points of view.

## 9 Discussion

When looking at third-stream activities in UK higher education, it becomes apparent that more organic, market-driven approaches tend to focus on metrics around commercialization that are based on pure economic criteria (Lockett et al., 2015). Historically, in less state controlled models (such as the US and the UK) TM has focused on the management of industrial research contracts. Post 1985, however, universities were given the opportunity to prove that they could commercialize the technology themselves, creating an incentive for universities to become more interested in their intellectual property (IP) and mirroring the introduction of the Bayh–Dole Act (1980) in the USA (Lockett et al., 2015). The Labour government provided some financial incentive for UK universities to engage more fully in knowledge transfer and third-stream activities. This stimulated a wave of activity throughout the sector and the number of transfer offices increased substantially and became a norm at the UK higher education sector (Lockett et al., 2013).

Arguably, this expansion was not only driven by government funding but also by higher education institutions themselves that started to invest more of their own money into TM. In this regard, state funding triggered the awareness that substantial returns could be made from the commercialization of IP (Lockett et al., 2015).

Although the German initiative also encourages transfer strategies with an eye on commercialization, the funding criteria go beyond pure economic considerations. It appears that a more centralized approach can better control initiatives along the lines of sustainability, local impact and societal contribution. In Germany, both incentives and control mechanisms have resulted in a systemic and systematic collection of sustainable third-stream activities (Berthold et al., 2010).

When focusing on different contexts, it becomes even more apparent that universities are complex organizations that operate in dynamic social contexts, whose values and rules are subject to constant change. At the same time, HEIs must act within the national and institutional frameworks of their (often limited) possibilities and resources and are subject to rational decisions within their scope of activities.

For third mission and knowledge transfer in Austria, this means that – even if a high level of intrinsic motivation can be assumed for many actors within the Austrian UAS sector – they will only 'invest' in new activities if their institution or its individual actors benefit from them. This can be a gain in reputation, enhanced viability, a unique selling proposition or even a higher allocation of resources.

Overall, it can be stated that no predominant model of transfer or third mission can be discerned at the Austrian UAS sector. What stands out is that it tends to be more market-driven, which is further underlined by the lack of governmental guidelines and control mechanisms. Although a first state-structured initiative can be found in the establishment of transfer centers, there are no binding regulations on the part of the government. Both participation and cooperation between HEIs are on a voluntary basis.

Based on the German funding model "Innovative Hochschule", a substantial increase in the number of higher education transfer offices can be observed in the German higher education landscape. It can be assumed that this would not have happened without state funding and the previously described framework conditions. Due to comparable structures of the higher education systems, it may be expected that such an initiative brings similar beneficial results in Austria.

### Notes

1. For a systematic description of the distinguishing characteristics of these concepts, their overlaps, blurred boundaries and differing orientations, see Gaisch et al. (2019b)
2. See https://www.bmbf.de/upload_filestore/pub/Innovative_Hochschule.pdf
3. See https://www.aws.at/foerderungen/wissenstransferzentren/
4. Previous studies on third mission were:
   a. Henke, J., Pasternack, P., & Schmidt, S. (2015). *Viele Stimmen, kein Kanon. Konzept und Kommunikation der Third Mission von Hochschulen.* HoF-Arbeitsbericht 2015. Institut für Hochschulforschung an der Martin-Luther-Universität, Halle-Wittenberg.
   b. Hachmeister, C. D., Duong, S., & Roessler, I. (2015). *Hemmnisse und Fördermaßnahmen für Forschung und Third Mission an Fachhochschulen.* Centrum für Hochschulentwicklung GmbH.
   c. Koschatzky, K., Hufnagl, M., Kroll, H., Daimer, S., & Schulze, N. (2011). *Relevanz regionaler Aktivitäten für Hochschulen und das Wissenschaftssystem (No. R3/2011).* Working papers firms and region.

### References

Angerer, R. (2002). *Zum Praxisbezug der wirtschaftswissenschaftlichen FH-Studiengänge: Vergl.* Studie, diplom.de.

Beresford, R., & Michels, N. (2014). Embedding change through the entrepreneurial role of middle managers in the UK further education sector. *Research in Post-Compulsory Education, 19*(2), 147–164. doi:10.1080/13596748.2014.897505

Berthold, C., Meyer-Guckel, V., & Rohe, W. (Eds.). (2010). *Mission Gesellschaft. Engagement und Selbstverständnis der Hochschulen. Ziele, Konzepte, internationale Praxis.* Stifterverband.

Bilton, C. (2006). *Management and creativity: From creative industries to creative management.* Wiley-Blackwell.

Briggs, A. (2001). Academic managers in further education: Reflections on leadership. *Research in Post-Compulsory Education, 6*(2), 223–236.

Briggs, A. (2005). Middle managers in English further education colleges: Understanding and modelling the role. *Educational Management and Administration, 33*(1), 27–50.

Braun, V., & Clarke, V. (2006). Using thematic analysis in psychology. *Qualitative Research in Psychology. 3*, 77–101.

Cai, Y., & Liu, C. (2015). The roles of universities in fostering knowledge-intensive clusters in Chinese regional innovation systems. *Science and Public Policy, 42*(1), 15–29. doi:10.1093/ scipol/scu018

Davey, T. (2017). Converting university knowledge into value: How conceptual frameworks contribute to the understanding of the third mission role of European universities. *International Journal of Technology Transfer and Commercialisation, 15*(1), 65–96.

De Boer, H., Goedegebuure, L., & Meek, V. L. (2010). The changing nature of academic middle management: A Framework for analysis. In V. L. Meek, L. Goedegebuure, R. Santiago, & T. Carvalho (Eds.), *The changing dynamics of higher education middle management* (pp. 229–241). Springer.

Ehrenstorfer, B., Sterrer, S., Preymann, S., Aichinger, R., & Gaisch, M. (2015). Multitasking talents? Roles and competencies of middle-level manager-academics at two Austrian Higher Education Institutions. In R. M. O. Pritchard, M. Klumpp, & U. Teichler (Ed.), *Diversity and excellence in higher education* (pp. 173–200). Sense. doi: https://doi.org/10.1007/978-94-6300-172-4

Etzkowitz, H. (1998). The norms of entrepreneurial science: Cognitive effects of the new university–industry linkages. *Research Policy, 27*, 823–833.

Floyd, A. (2016). Supporting academic middle managers in higher education: Do we care? *Higher Education Policy, 29*(2), 167–183.

Gaisch, M., Noemeyer, D., & Aichinger, R. (2019b). Third mission activities at Austrian universities of applied sciences: Results from an expert survey. *Publications, 7*(3), 57.

Gaisch, M., Preymann, S., & Aichinger, R. (2019a). Diversity management at the tertiary level: An attempt to extend existing paradigms. *Journal of Applied Research in Higher Education, 12*(2), 137–150. doi: https://doi.org/10.1108/JARHE-03-2018-0048

Gleeson, D., & Shain, F. (1999). Managing ambiguity: Between markets and managerialism – A case study of 'middle managers in further education. *The Sociological Review, 47*(3), 461–490.

Gmelch, W. H., & Miskin, V. D. (2011). *Department chair leadership skills*. Atwood Publications.

Hachmeister, C. D., Henke, J., Roessler, I., & Schmid, S. (2016). Die Vermessung der Third Mission. Wege zu einer erweiterten Darstellung von Lehre und Forschung. *Die Hochschule: Journal für Wissenschaft und Bildung, 25*(1), 7–13.

Henke, J. (2019). Third Mission als Organisationsherausforderung. *Perspektiven der Professionssoziologie, 66*, 70.

Jongbloed, B., Enders, J., & Salerno, C. (2008). Higher education and its communities: Interconnections, interdependencies and a research agenda. *Higher Education, 56*(3), 303–324.

Knoll, T. (2019). Technologie-und Wissenstransfer als gesellschaftliche Aufgabe. In *Wissenschaft auf Messen präsentieren* (pp. 5–6). Springer Gabler.

Kuratko, D. F., Ireland, R. D., Covin, J. G., & Hornsby, J. S. (2005). A model of middle-level managers' entrepreneurial behavior. *Entrepreneurship Theory and Practice, 29*(6), 699–716.

Lavis, J., Ross, S., McLeod, C., & Gildiner, A. (2003). Measuring the impact of health research. *Journal of Health Services Research and Policy, 8*, 165–170.

Leader, G. (2004). Further education middle managers: Their contribution to the strategic decision-making process. *Educational Management Administration and Leadership, 32*(1), 67–79.

Liening, A., Geiger, J. M., Haarhaus, T., & Kriedel, R. (2019). Entrepreneurship Education und Industrie 4.0 aus hochschuldidaktischer Perspektive. *Hochschullehre & Industrie 4.0: Herausforderungen-Lösungen-Perspektiven, 41*.

Lockett, A., Wright, M., & Wild, A. (2013). The co-evolution of third stream activities in UK higher education. *Business History, 55*(2), 236–258.

Lockett, A., Wright, M., & Wild, A. (2015). The institutionalization of third stream activities in UK higher education: The role of discourse and metrics. *British Journal of Management, 26*(1), 78–92.

Meißner, D. (2001). *Wissens-und Technologietransfer in nationalen Innovationssystemen* (Dissertation). Dresden.

Mitton, C., Adair, C. E., McKenzie, E., Patten, S. B., & Perry, B. W. (2007). Knowledge transfer and exchange: Review and synthesis of the literature. *The Milbank Quarterly, 85*(4), 729–768.

Nelles, J., & Vorley, T. (2010). From policy to practice: Engaging and embedding the third mission in contemporary universities. *International Journal of Sociology and Social Policy, 30*(7–8), 341–353.

Nguyen, T. L. H. (2013). Middle-level academic management: A case study on the roles of the heads of department at a Vietnamese university. *Tertiary Education and Management, 19*(1), 1–15.

Nölting, B., Dembski, N., Kräusche, K., Lehmann, K., Molitor, H., Pape, J., Pfriem, A., Reimann, J., Skroblin, J.-H., & Walk, H. (2018). *Transfer für nachhaltige Entwicklung an Hochschulen. BMBF-Projekt „Nachhaltigkeit an Hochschulen: entwickeln – vernetzen – berichten (HOCHN)*. Eberswalde, 38 pp.

Nölting, B., & Pape, J. (2017). Third-Mission und Transfer als Impuls für nachhaltige Hochschulen. In *Innovation in der Nachhaltigkeitsforschung* (pp. 265–280). Springer Spektrum.

Nonaka, I., & Takeuchi, H. (1995). *The knowledge-creating company*. Oxford: Oxford University Press.

Pinheiro, R., Langa, P. V., & Pausits, A. (2015). One and two equals three? The third mission of higher education institutions. *European Journal of Higher Education, 5*(3), 233–249.

Roessler, I. (2015). Third Mission. Die ergänzende Mission neben Lehre und Forschung. *wissenschaftsmanagement, 2*(2015), 46–47.

Roessler, I., Duong, S., & Hachmeister, C. D. (2015). *Welche Missionen haben Hochschulen? Third Mission als Leistung der Fachhochschulen für die und mit der Gesellschaft*. Centrum für Hochschulentwicklung.

Trencher, G., Bai, X., Evans, J., McCormick, K., & Yarime, M. (2014b). University partnerships for co-designing and co-producing urban sustainability. *Global Environmental Change, 28*, 153–165.

Trencher, G., Yarime, M., McCormick, K. B., Doll, C. N., & Kraines, S. B. (2014a). Beyond the third mission: Exploring the emerging university function of co-creation for sustainability. *Science and Public Policy, 41*(2), 151–179.

CHAPTER 14

# Lessons Learned and Future Directions

*Bruno Broucker, Victor M. H. Borden, Clare Milsom and Ton Kallenberg*

### Abstract

The evolving societal, political and economic landscape has led to increased demands on higher education institutions to make their contribution and benefit to society more visible, and in many cases with fewer public resources. European and national policy developments call for the university to embrace a transformation process and to be more proactive in strengthening our critical stance and role as a knowledge institution and champion for truth, evidence and science. This book has offered a comprehensive review of the higher education sector's responsibilities for the traditional university tri-partite mission: teaching and learning; research and scholarship; and public service and engagement. Three parts can be identified in the book. The first part discusses higher education's students and staff; the second part discusses higher education systems; the third part focuses on higher education impact.

### Keywords

higher education policy – higher education impact – students and staff – higher education systems

### 1 Taking Stock

The chapters of this volume review and analyze issues related to the responsibilities of higher education institutions internationally. Although not exhaustive, as no single volume can be, the chapters offer a comprehensive review of the higher education sector's responsibilities for the traditional university tri-partite mission: teaching and learning; research and scholarship; and public service and engagement. Noting that the higher education sector is surrounded by inter-related global trends, including the spread of neoliberalism, new public administration, marketization, and commodification, the chapters

© KONINKLIJKE BRILL NV, LEIDEN, 2020 | DOI: 10.1163/9789004436558_015

## LESSONS LEARNED AND FUTURE DIRECTIONS

of this volume bring into sharp relief the ongoing conflict between the private and public benefits of higher education.

Though not made explicit in the structure of the book, three large parts can be distinguished that glue the different chapters together. We highlight those parts, their main conclusions and trends in the remaining of this concluding chapter.

## 2 Higher Education's Students and Staff

The first part of the book encompasses the first five chapters. A first element in this is the message Wafa Singh (Chapter 1) draws our attention to: because higher education has increasingly become more international, and practices across the globe have been benchmarked, compared, sometimes copied and adapted, it cannot be denied that Higher Education Systems still need customization. Despite the progress Indian Higher Education has made, the call for contextualization within an international Higher Education market remains high. This implies that responsible policies recognize their own limitations, identify the boundaries of policies, and more importantly are able to distinguish to which extent a Higher Education System can move in the same direction as other countries, and where it cannot. In this respect, internationalization does not mean 'blindly going with the wind', but rather navigating national policy in such a way that internationalization contributes to enhancement of higher education policy. A comparable message is produced by Mark Engberg and Lisa Davidson, emphasizing the discomfort students can experience when studying abroad. Internationalization for students in this respect is not only an enormous enriching opportunity, but can also signify a huge challenge, on many different fronts. Successful and responsible internationalization policy therefore does not end with creating possibilities for mobility. On the contrary, responsible policy for students and staff only start at that moment. The third chapter calls upon another element of responsibility, i.e. the responsibility education in general has regarding detecting, guiding and mobilizing talent to the right educational system. Despite all efforts that higher education institutions have taken in the past to lower the negative consequences of the impact of socio-economic status on attracting and delivering graduates, the problems and challenges remain high. Responsibility in this respect means continuing and intensifying policy efforts in this domain as well.

While the first three chapters had a closer look on students and the responsibility of higher education towards students, responsible higher education should also pay attention to staff. Chapters 4 and 5 both highlight the increasing complexity of higher education, both in respect of policy and organizational governance. With the diversification of staff roles in both the academic and non-academic domains, the boundaries between researchers, third space professionals, middle managers, policy makers and politicians in the determination of higher education policy has become more blurred. The arena has become more complex, and responsibilities and tasks of internal stakeholders in this respect have diversified.

Responsibility of higher education towards staff and students is not self-evident. Despite increased accessibility to higher education, increasing mobility, and international collaboration, higher education has become a more complex arena – wherein students and staff on a daily basis have to find their way. An important question is how higher education will evolve in the next years. For that reason it is no wonder that the theme of the subsequent EAIR-forum will be on sustainability of higher education.

## 3    Higher Education Systems

Chapters 6 through 10 focus on higher education systems, their policies and reforms. Chapters 6 and 8 discuss traditional managerial reforms. While Pausits discusses mergers within the higher education sector, Friedrich discusses agentification within the sector. It is interesting that, despite reforms that have taken place across the globe within the higher education sector, the initiatives for modernization remain relevant to discuss, and are still very active. Responsibility of higher education in this respect means constantly adapting and trying to improve organizational configurations for the benefit of higher education and society. Yet, is also means increasing our knowledge of the impact of those reforms. A responsible higher education system should therefore question its position in and responsibility for society, and how organizational development in fact positively contributes to that goal. As researchers, policymakers and practitioners it should be recognized that organizational (re)configurations should remain a means to an end, and knowledge in this respect still needs to grow.

Webbstock, Gebru and Shenderova discuss ongoing reforms from the perspectives of their country and how higher education systems try to modernize or improve national tertiary education. The Ethiopian case for instance makes explicit the potential of higher education in the country and the enormous growth the sector has seen through the last decade. However, growth does not automatically imply a significant increase in quality of performance. Creating access in this respect does still not mean that the sector is where it should be

LESSONS LEARNED AND FUTURE DIRECTIONS

or would like to be. The same conclusion can be made for the Russian-Finnish case and the the South African higher education system.

While countries are still reforming their higher education sectors, we are behind in investigating what those changes will bring for higher education in general. This is not only important for some countries to know, but also for other countries looking for inspiration. Sustainable and responsible higher education systems imply that the sectoral reforms look further than acute problems, and look beyond while asking themselves what kind of higher education society we will need for the future. While those questions are being asked by South African and Ethiopian systems, they might have been forgotten by European systems that have limited their scope to ameliorating current flaws with their systems instead of exploring the structural inequities of current systems in relation to fundamental goals of expanding access and improving outcomes equitably. The implications for increased responsibility are in this respect quite high.

## 4     Higher Education Impact

Implicitly the element of higher education impact has been mentioned in the previous sections. Higher education aims to have an impact. On students' lives, on staff's professional experience, on society in general. Ketchenson's chapter tries to combine several of those elements, by indicating how her institution's Academic Quality Committee should or could collaborate with institutional research to further improve quality of teaching and learning effectiveness. Indeed, responsibility in this respect means increasing quality to generate beneficial effects. Yang et al. message regarding impact in this is quite clear: the value of higher education might be gained by reaching more outside the system to innovate to become truly global universities. They emphasis the courage needed by academic leaders to strive for 'world class' research and possibly 'world class education'. In the Introduction to the book the Covid-19 epidemic is mentioned. The message developed by Yang et al. make their claim quite significant, and maybe even scarily accurate. The last chapter discusses the concept of third mission, a term that – despite its conceptual unclarity – definitely emphasizes the responsibility of higher education to society, be it the direct economic and social environment, or the global social challenges with which the world is confronted. Though the authors highlight the role of Austrian institutions in terms of regional engagement, innovation and knowledge transfer in local areas, the lessons learned are relevant to societies across the globe.

## 5 What's Next? From Responsibility to Sustainability

The topic of the EAIR-Forum 2020 that would have followed the Leiden forum from which these chapters were generated, would have been on sustainability, as this is increasingly a part of responsibility. Due to the Covid-19 outbreak postponement of the conference to probably 2021 was the logic consequence of it. If the conference will take place in 2021, it is likely that it will address the critical role of higher education professionals in preparing their organizations for the future, be they senior leaders, policy makers, academics, researchers or practitioners. The evolving societal, political and economic landscape has led to increased demands on higher education institutions to make their contribution and benefit to society more visible, and in many cases with fewer public resources. European and national policy developments call for the university to embrace a transformation process and to be more proactive in strengthening our critical stance and role as a knowledge institution and champion for truth, evidence and science. There is a new emphasis on the need for higher education institutions to listen, learn and engage on issues of common concern; to cooperate and cohere with the European Higher Education Area; to welcome the UNESCO Global Convention on the Recognition of Higher Education Qualifications; and to contribute to the implementation of the United Nations Sustainable Development Goals. Our greatest challenge in recent years is to maintain the most cherished aspects of our core values, while simultaneously responding to the threats and opportunities of an ever-changing world. Students, concerned for their future, have become powerful activists, focusing our attention on the climate change crisis, global inequalities and health. Our young people rightfully demand that higher education institutions evolve to play an integral role in the development of the future global economy, society and the environment (EAIR, 2020).

Fundamental questions in this respect include:
- How crucial is higher education to a sustainable future?
- What are the responsibilities of higher education institutions and professionals for developing sustainable governance, management and educational practices?
- What is the role of higher education in preparing professionals to live and work sustainably?
- How do we develop the social foundations, character and morals of the next generation professionals?
- How can higher education equip learners with the attributes and values that will empower them to take action for a more sustainable future?

- Are we doing enough to prepare our students as socially minded, engaged citizens who seek solutions to global challenges?
- How do we evolve as professionals and as organizations to sustain the future of higher education in an ever-changing world?

The Higher Education sector is constantly on the move, and this is quite appropriate, as society is on the move as well and not always in positive directions. At the time of writing this chapter, one in five of the world's population was on lockdown (including all of the volume editors) to mitigate the spread of the Covid-19 virus. The questions above and the current circumstances increase the necessity for higher education policymakers, practitioners and researchers to work together, and to think together about what Higher Education should and can do, but also what it *cannot* do. Thinking about responsibility also implies thinking about the boundaries of responsibility. But in all this, there is one certainty: it is all stakeholders' responsibility to think and question permanently what higher education should do, as it is to the benefit of all of us.

Printed in the United States
By Bookmasters